646.406

Childrenswear Design

Second Edition

Childrenswear Design

HILDE JAFFE

Professor

Fashion Design—Apparel

Fashion Institute of Technology

ROSA ROSA

Assistant Professor

Fashion Design—Apparel

Fashion Institute of Technology

FAIRCHILD PUBLICATIONS
New York

Illustrated by *Rosemary Torre*

Associate Professor

Illustration Department

Fashion Institute of Technology

Designed by *Delgado Design Inc.*

F.I.T.
COLLECTION

Copyright © 1990 by Fairchild Publications
A Division of Capital Cities Media, Inc.

First Edition © 1972 by Fairchild Publications
A Division of Capital Cities Media, Inc.

Second Printing 1979

Standard Book Number: 87005-706-5

Library of Congress Catalog Card Number: 89-81423

Printed in the United States of America

Preface
to the first edition

Designing childrenswear requires a certain amount of background knowledge and various technical skills along with the intangible but essential innate creative talent that the aspiring designer must have. The purpose of this book is to provide the special information needed by the childrenswear designer to function effectively on a professional level.

Part 1 of the text explores the various areas that form the framework by which childrenswear design is limited. Limitations imposed by size ranges, textile performance and production methods are analyzed. A rudimentary outline of the physical and mental growth of children is presented with emphasis on children's clothing requirements at each developmental stage. Since understanding the needs and the growth of children is most important for the designer, I hope that the relatively sketchy information presented here will serve as motivation for continued interest and further study in this area. The brief look into the history of children's apparel manufacturing should help the designer see her work in the context of a continuously evolving industry that has emerged from the small, individually owned shop into "big business." Finally, I have attempted to show the new designer where inspiration can be found for the fresh, saleable ideas that must appear in every collection to impress the buyers and make the season a financial success.

Since wearable, well-proportioned children's apparel is dependent on the designers ability to express her ideas in fabrics, emphasis throughout Part 2 has been placed on creative patternmaking. Although patterns can be made both by draping and drafting, the usual practice in the childrenswear industry is to work with the flat patternmaking method. I have found that both methods can be used to advantage. New foundation patterns can be draped much more quickly and accurately on the dress form rather than by drafting them from measurements. Also, by draping directly in fabric, it is easier to develop new shapes and silhouettes. On the other hand, once a foundation pattern has been perfected, it is much more efficient to work out variations by flat patternmaking.

Step-by-step instructions are given for each method as it is used to solve individual cutting problems. It is important to note that the problems selected are only those typical of childrenswear. This is not a comprehensive patternmaking book, and the methods used may, at times, seem somewhat unorthodox to the traditional pattern-maker of women's wear.

In Part 3, the special problems encountered by designers in particular areas of childrenswear are explored. Since the problems inherent in designing children's dresses are covered in the section devoted to basic patternmaking, there was no need to treat this specialty separately. This, of course, does not deny its importance in the childrenswear industry.

Although the book is primarily intended as a guide to young designers, the garment measurements in the Appendix should also be useful to patternmakers and graders.

It is expected that the reader has had some previous experience in sketching, sewing, draping and patternmaking before specializing in childrenswear design. For the F.I.T. students who use this text, this will not present any problem, since they do not usually enroll in childrenswear classes before the fourth semester. By this time they have acquired an excellent background in the basic skills of design. Others with some previous elementary training should also be able to use this book to learn the professional know-how of childrenswear design.

Although both men and women are successfully designing childrenswear today, the majority of our students are women. Therefore, for the sake of expedience, I shall refer to the designer as "she" throughout the book. I do hope that all the men will forgive me.

The need for a text in childrenswear design has been evident since the introduction of Childrenswear as a course of study at the Fashion Institute of Technology. Nothing on a professional level had been published in this area. Childrenswear designers were trained on the job, and the quality of the training depended on the manufacturer who was willing to hire the novice. At F.I.T. every effort has been made to establish a curriculum that is grounded on the best experience in industry. This text is in line with this practice.

Where my own personal experience was deficient, other designers readily cooperated to supply the necessary expertise. Particular thanks are due to Barbara Palmer, of Pandora, for her help with the section on sweaters; Estelle Halpern, of Divettes, for her help with swimsuit design; and Annette Feldman, of Immerman Corp., who not only assisted with sleepwear, but contributed a willing ear and friendly counsel throughout.

I would also like to express my appreciation to the experts who are not designers, but who read special chapters and let me benefit from their invaluable experience. Thanks are due to Walter Lilie, for years a production man in the Industry, who read the chapter on production methods, and David Singer, Instructor in Textile Technology at F.I.T., who was particularly helpful with the chapter on fabrics.

To the many enthusiastic students who readily cooperated with the testing of the material in this book, I am deeply indebted. Jo Bidner, who tested the patternmaking without classroom instruction, and Miriam Freilich, who read several chapters, were particularly helpful in providing the student's point of view.

Not only was the material tested in my own classes, but also in the classes of my colleagues at F.I.T., Selma Rosen and Rosa Rosa. They were both unfailingly generous with constructive suggestions. Rosa Rosa, the designer for Tidykins, teaches at F.I.T. in the evening and was most helpful since her concurrent roles as designer and teacher enable her to see problems from both points of view. But most of all, appreciation is due to Selma Rosen, who read and tested just about every chapter of the book, and whose astute criticism and constant encouragement were priceless.

Hilde Jaffee

August 1971

Preface
to the second edition

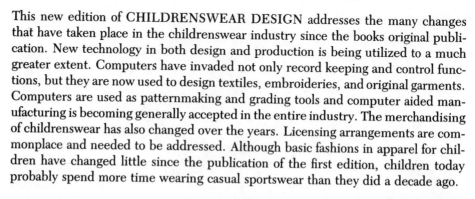

This new edition of CHILDRENSWEAR DESIGN addresses the many changes that have taken place in the childrenswear industry since the books original publication. New technology in both design and production is being utilized to a much greater extent. Computers have invaded not only record keeping and control functions, but they are now used to design textiles, embroideries, and original garments. Computers are used as patternmaking and grading tools and computer aided manufacturing is becoming generally accepted in the entire industry. The merchandising of childrenswear has also changed over the years. Licensing arrangements are commonplace and needed to be addressed. Although basic fashions in apparel for children have changed little since the publication of the first edition, children today probably spend more time wearing casual sportswear than they did a decade ago.

Instructions for several new patterns have been inserted. The raglan sleeve, kimono and cap sleeves have been added to the sleeves section. Instructions for hoods, linings, and various pockets have been included in the Outerwear chapter. The section on trimmings for childrenswear has been greatly expanded, and a new chapter on professional samplemaking methods has also been added.

We gratefully acknowledge the generous response of all the wonderful people in the childrenswear industry who shared with us their expertise. Special thanks are due to Ruth Scharf Incorporated, Ed Newman, formerly of Dan River and now on F.I.T. faculty, Diane Specht of Earnshaws, Alan Burgess of Health Tex, David Finkelstein of AGH Trimsource, Larry Moskowitz of Division Embroidery, and Paul Levine of Hirsch International Corporation.

Joe Miranda, our editor, deserves our special gratitude for his patience, good humor, and guidance as we worked on this second edition. But most of all, we want to thank our students who continue to be our constant inspiration.

Hilde Jaffe

Rosa Rosa

December 1989

Contents

PART 1

BACKGROUND INFORMATION

1
Size Ranges

Most aspiring childrenswear designers have a mental image of the child they are planning to dress. It is usually a bright and charming youngster of uncertain age, with the dimples of a baby, and the unselfconscious grace of the four-year-old, and enough baby fat to give the body a delicious roundness. Of course, there are any number of delightful children who fit this picture. It is important, however, to become aware of what children really look like before attempting to clothe them. The infant is vastly different in appearance from the pre-schooler, and the youngster in kindergarten will go through many changes in physical development before he becomes a teenager.

It then follows that a design which might be perfect for a two-year-old toddler will appear ridiculous on a ten-year-old schoolgirl. In addition, since garments for children should be functional, it becomes apparent as we acquaint ourselves with children at different stages of development that the same outfit does not suit children of all ages. Later, we will explore at greater length the development of children, and how their clothing satisfies some of their essential needs at various stages of growth. For the present, however, let us limit ourselves to the specific problems that the designer and manufacturer face in providing clothes to fit children as they grow from birth to adolescence.

To solve the problems of fit and merchandising as children grow and proportions change, manufacturers have divided clothing for children into several *size ranges*. Each size range consists of a group of sizes for children of similar body proportions and with similar developmental needs. When children outgrow one size range, they proceed to the next one. Sizes, by tradition, have been related to the age of the child. There are however great variations in body build and development so that it rarely follows that a five-year-old wears a size 5. Children vary greatly in height and

3

weight at any given age because of heredity, nutritional habits, and environmental influences. Both merchants and manufacturers now tend to view the numbers in each size range merely as symbols and use height and weight ranges on the hang tag of each garment as a better guide for the consumer.

Let us now examine each size range and determine the distinguishing characteristics of each.

■ Infants or Babies

The garments in this range are for the baby from birth to the time when he begins to walk alone, at about one year. In infancy the childs head is large in proportion to the rest of his body. It is approximately one fourth of his entire body length. The infant grows at a rapid rate during his first year. Although the average newborn weighs about 7½ pounds and is 20 inches tall, he almost triples his weight and his body length increases over one third by the time he is a year old. Because of this swift development, sizes for garments change quickly, and the dress or sweater which seemed much too large for the baby is often outgrown before it is tried on again.

The sizes in this range are: 3 months, 6 months, 9 months, 12 months, and 18 months; or Small, Medium, Large, and Extra Large. In preparing models for this size range, the designer usually works in a size 12 months, the sample size, because it is typical of this range.

■ Toddlers

The Toddler size range fits the child after he has learned to walk, until he is about three years old. During this period, general growth is not as spectacular as during infancy, but the arms and legs develop considerably. The legs become straight, and strong enough to support the body weight easily, and the arms become comparatively longer. The head of the child grows slowly in relation to the rest of his body, and the toddler does not seem quite as top-heavy as the infant.

The stance of the young child is different from the posture of the adult. The spine seems to curve in, producing what is called a swayback, and the stomach almost always protrudes. This baby stance sometimes continues into adolescence, but more often it disappears during the early school years. Clothing for this size range must still be designed with adequate fullness to accommodate diapers, for toilet training is usually not complete until the child is two and a half to three years old. At that point they usually move on to the next size range.

Toddlers sizes are: 1T, 2T, 3T, and 4T. The "T", which stands for toddler is used to avoid confusion; size 3 and size 4 appear again in the next size range. Sample size is 2T.

■ Children

This is the size range in which most designers love to work. Here, children are encountered who are still charmingly unselfconscious, but old enough to be fashionable. These are the youngsters of preschool age, from about three to six years. Their physical growth continues at a gradual, steady pace during this period. The average five-year-old child weighs 42.8 pounds and is 43.6 inches tall. His body is beginning to assume adult proportions and his legs grow rapidly; his trunk develops more slowly; and the size of his head changes very little. There is as yet no indication of a waistline, and the baby stance is still strong.

Sizes are: 3, 4, 5, 6, and 6x. Size 6x is larger than size 6 and of similar proportion. It has been a transitional size, filling the gap for some children before they fit into size 7 of the next size range where proportions gradually change. Some manufacturers have eliminated size 6x and have adjusted the body measurements for sizes 5, 6, and 7 so that they reflect the actual growth patterns and gradual changes in proportion of the child. (See Appendix, page 287.)

Until this stage, both boys' and girls' wear are manufactured in the same size ranges, often by the same manufacturer. There is one exception. In the Children's size range, Boys' sizes are 3 to 7. There is no size 6x for boys. For the school-age child, however, size ranges and manufacturing techniques diverge. Boys' wear assumes the same styling and production methods as men's wear and, therefore, steps out of our present discussion. From school age on, we shall limit our studies to clothing for girls.

■ Girls

This size range is for the grade-schooler, usually the child from seven to ten years old. Growth continues at a gradual pace, but there is now a difference in the general appearance of the child; much of the baby fat decreases and is replaced by muscle tissue. For many girls, this is an awkward age, the stage between baby appeal and the eventual blossoming of young feminine proportions. There is a definite slimming and lengthening of the torso and limbs, but as yet none of the curves of adolescence.

Sizes are: 7, 8, 10, 12, and 14. Size 14 is often eliminated by manufacturers because changes in dietary habits have made the chubby, shapeless ten- or eleven-year-old almost nonexistent, and by the time the girl is twelve years old, she usually prefers to wear clothes from the Pre-teen or Young Junior size range. Some of the large mail-order houses, on the other hand, have requested manufacturers to size some garments from size 7 through 16. Such a long, continuous range is particularly appropriate for standard items, such as shirts and jeans that are fashion-right for all ages. Product standards, developed by the United States Department of Commerce, have supported this practice. Taking into consideration the proportional growth of the school-age girl, as determined by a survey conducted by the Department of Agriculture, standard body measurements have been developed for sizes 7 to 16. (See Appendix, page 288.) When the size range is 7–12, the sample size is size 8; for 7–14 or 16, the sample size is size 10.

There is a limited market for a 7–14 Chubby size range. The large mass retailers usually carry a small group of these garments. These garments are cut decidedly fuller for the girl who is overweight for her height. In designing for the chubby customer it is important to carefully proportion design details to achieve a slenderizing effect, but it is even more important to remember that the chubby girl will want the same fashion items that all the other girls are wearing.

■ Pre-teens or Young Juniors

At early adolescence, girls experience a spurt of growth. The torso becomes elongated and a natural waistline becomes apparent. Gradual breast and hip development begins, and although many children have only outgrown size 10 in the Girls' size range at this time, size 12 or 14 does not fit the newly emerging figure. The child in question will more likely fit into a size 6 or 8 of the Pre-teen range. This size range has been developed to fit the girl at the intermediate stage between late childhood and before the time that they become an adult.

The sizes are: 6, 8, 10, 12, and 14. Sample sizes vary. Some dress manufacturers use size 8; others prefer size 10. Sportswear manufacturers usually use size 12 as their sample size.

■ Juniors

At about the time when the adolescent girl enters high school, her figure has developed to almost adult maturity and she has outgrown-Sub-teen sizes. Now she has a definite waistline; high rounded breasts; and slim shapely hips. Junior sizes fit the teenager in late adolescence.

The sizes are: 3, 5, 7, 9, 11, and 13. Samples sizes vary, but size 7 seems to be the most popular. This range is not usually considered a part of the childrenswear industry. Nevertheless, occasionally childrenswear manufacturers produce a Junior line.

2
Child Development and Clothing for Children

Children develop in many ways. Aside from the obvious physical growth, intellectual, emotional, and social development occurs. What are some of the needs of children as they gradually grow to adulthood, and what is the role of clothing in their lives? For example, it is widely believed that clothing affects the social behavior of children—the assumption being that the boy who is dressed like a gentleman will behave like one; or, on the other hand, that the child who is unkempt and goes to school in torn dungarees and dirty sneakers is a potential candidate for juvenile delinquency. Others believe that children acquire a sense of security by being dressed in the same kind of clothing as the other children in their group. Obviously, when we see a group of girls going to school, all wearing similar outfits, this appears to be true. But how important is this really to the child? If it is a real need, when does it begin to manifest itself, and at what age does it cease to be important? The designer is vitally concerned with these and other questions, but so far there has been very little research in this area.

This is rather surprising since children in our civilization wear some kind of body covering from birth on through the entire span of their lives. Child psychology, although it has made tremendous progress in recent years, has rarely concerned itself with the effect of clothing on the development of the child, and very little verified evidence has been established. Whereas some studies have been done concerning teenagers and their clothing, the years from infancy to adolescence have been almost totally neglected. Nevertheless, by observation and the use of the limited data available, it is possible to arrive at some conclusion concering the early function of clothing as we outline the development of the child from infancy, to the age of the toddler, on to the preschool years, through school age and adolescence.

■ Infancy

At birth, children are completely helpless and dependent on the adults who surround them for survival. They sleep most of the time, except when they are hungry or otherwise uncomfortable. Within their limited sphere of perception, hunger and the discomfort caused by wetness, cold, excessive warmth, or the weight of heavy or restrictive coverings become extremely acute suffering if not soon alleviated by those who care for them. Their skin is very tender and chafes easily. They are extremly sensitive to changes in temperature, because their adjustment mechanism in this area is as yet underdeveloped. Their sense of touch, however, functions almost perfectly from birth; they withdraw from sources of irritation or become restless and cry.

In view of the needs of infants, their clothing should be lightweight, soft, warm, and washable. Synthetic fibers, although very practical in terms of washability and care, should be carefully tested for comfort. When selected for use in outerwear, there is usually no problem, but for garments that touch the skin of infants, nylon and polyesters should be blended with cotton for increased absorbency. Since infants grow at a very rapid rate, garments made of stretch fabrics will fit for a longer period of

time. These garments also permit more freedom of movement, a factor that has been generally acknowledged to be advantageous for optimum development of the child. The bulk of the ever-present diaper must be considered for the infant, and easy accessibility for quick changes is essential. Disposable diapers or plastic diaper pants, which are used with cloth diapers should be carefully designed so that all edges touching the baby's skin are soft and non-irritating.

Babies learn about their world by looking at, touching, smelling, tasting, and manipulating the objects they can see and reach. Since part of this learning process is exploring themselves and the clothes they wear, it is an essential safety factor that all small decorative details and buttons be either eliminated entirely or securely fastened to infants' garments.

At this stage, children are not aware of the design of clothing as long as it is not a source of discomfort. Therefore, styling features are planned to appeal to the purchaser of the garment rather than the wearer. There are primarily two classifications of purchasers for infants' wear: the mother and the grandmother. Mother is attracted by the functional and practical attributes of the design. She is especially concerned with the ease of maintenance: washability and no-iron features are of primary importance. On the other hand, grandmothers and other doting relatives look for the luxury touches, such as exquisite embroidery, delicate colors, ruffles, laces, and painstaking hand finishing.

■ Toddlers

During the period of beginning mobility, when babies learn to walk, they are generally referred to as toddlers. Their world is expanding as they begin to know and recognize more of the people and objects around them. It is a period of exploration and experiment. As they move about, toddlers want to handle everything they see. They begin to speak and respond to others. In their first attempts to feed themselves, they are often clumsy, and invariably mealtime is followed by a general cleanup of baby and the entire feeding area. Nevertheless, their muscular control develops and soon they are ready for toilet training, a process which is usually accomplished by the time children are three years old.

Toddlers' interest in clothes seems to be confined to taking them off, which they do whenever they have the opportunity. Evidently they are happiest in as few garments as possible, and the ability to remove their clothing represents an enormous accomplishment.

Clothes for toddlers should be comfortable and protective. Overalls, protecting the knees against falls, and knitted shirts seem to be the most popular garments for boys as well as girls. This is the time for training pants and they should be large enough so that children can pull them on and off easily and quickly by themselves. Since children at this stage dislike restrictive and heavy clothing, it is particularly important that out-

erwear be designed of lightweight, warm fabrics. Washable, quilted jackets and snowsuits are a perfect answer to this problem, for they are warm,
waterproof, and almost weightless.

Now girls' wear begins to differ somewhat from boys' wear; girls will
wear dresses and little boys wear pants and shirts for parties and special
occasions. Sometimes, the difference between girls' and boys' wear is
merely a choice of color, pink being reserved for girls, while other colors
are used for both sexes.

■ The Preschool Years

From three to six years, children mature rapidly. Although physical
growth does not proceed at the same rate as earlier, the childrens' bodies
change markedly in their proportions. The legs become longer and
stronger. Children lose some of their baby fat, and, in general, become
more graceful and adept in their movements. They learn to run, skip, and
climb. They ride tricycles and throw balls. They eat with reasonable table
manners and communicate verbally. They gradually learn to play with
other children and value each others' companionship.

Preschool children become aware of their clothes as they realize that
an attractive outfit will bring attention and approval from adults. New
garments are particularly important, for adults will notice and pay com-
pliments. To children, clothing appears to be an extension of the concept

of self. Therefore, it would seem that when boys are dressed in little suits and girls are dressed in dresses, they identify as future men and women, and they grow up feeling more comfortable with their role. This may or may not be desirable. Some parents may prefer to minimize sexual differences by dressing boys and girls in similar clothing, hoping that in this way they will foster the optimum development of the child as a human being without the limitations imposed by sex roles.

At some time during this period, children begin to try out various adult roles in play and daydreams. Dr. Joyce Brothers alludes to this when she writes:

> Clothing for the four to seven year-old can appeal to his active fantasy life. Through playful dressing up, the growing child tries on the many possible and sometimes impossible roles he one day hopes to fulfill—Daddy, Mommy, Superwoman, Superman, doctor, lawyer, Indian chief. Children at this age adopt a favorite shirt—often with a screen print of a well-loved comic character—and wear it ad infinitum.[1]

Children at this age are generally eager to dress themselves, and by the time they are four to five years old manage to do so quite efficiently as long as the clothing is easy to handle and has no complicated fastenings. Arnold Gesell and his colleagues observed children at the Yale Clinic of Child Development and arrived at the following developmental sequence for dressing:

15 months: [1] Cooperates in dressing by extending arm or leg.
18 months: [1] Can take off mittens, hat, and sox.
[2] Can unzip zippers.
[3] Tries to put on shoes.
24 months: [1] Can remove shoes if laces are untied.
[2] Helps in getting dressed—finds large armholes and thrusts his arms into them.
[3] Helps pull up or push down panties.
[4] Washes hands and dries them, but does neither very well.
36 months: [1] Greater interest and ability in undressing. May need some assistance with shirts and sweaters.
[2] Is able to unbutton all front and side buttons by pushing buttons through buttonholes.
[3] In dressing, does not know front from back. Apt to put pants on backwards; has difficulty in turning sox to get heels in back. Puts shoes on, but may put them on wrong feet.
[4] Intent on lacing shoes, but usually laces them incorrectly.
[5] Washes and dries hands.
[6] Brushes teeth with supervision.

[1]Brothes, Joyce. "How Clothes Form A Child's Self Image," *Earnshaw's*, November 1979, pp. 48–49.

48 months: [1] Is able to dress and undress himself with little assistance.
[2] Distinguishes between front and back of clothes and puts them on correctly.
[3] Washes and dries hands and face.
[4] Brushes his teeth.

60 months: [1] Undresses and dresses with care.
[2] May be able to tie shoelaces. [usually at six years][2]

Aside from the obvious benefits to mothers and nursery-school teachers, it is generally conceded that children who are encouraged and manage to successfully dress themselves at an early age will also act independently in other situations. Large armholes, back and front either alike or very easy to tell apart, front opening, and fasteners easy to manipulate are factors that make learning to dress an easier task for the child.

Children from three to six are very much aware of color. They prefer bright primary colors, and red seems to be the favorite. Texture is also important to young children. They love the feel of fur and smooth, soft fabrics. On the other hand, they often refuse to wear scratchy textures, such as some woolens and crisp organdy. The preschooler has not yet acquired the willingness to suffer for beauty or appearance.

In considering the desire to conform in dress to other children, most authors agree with Mary Ryan Shaw when she states: "Unlike the older child, the preschool child is usually not interested in whether or not his clothing conforms to the type that other children are wearing. He doesn't yet belong, or wish to belong, to a peer group and so is not interested in factors which make him conform to the group."[3]

To test the above supposition, 60 children from four to twelve years old were asked a series of questions weighing their desire to conform in dress against various factors that are generally deemed to be more important for the preschool age group. There were 20 children four to six years old, 20 children seven to nine, and 20 children ten to twelve. The wish to conform was tested against the desire to wear a favorite color, a new garment, mother's preference and general comfort. In the total evaluation, 31 percent of the four to six group gave replies indicating the desire to conform: and only 20 percent of the early adolescents answered in favor of conforming. We must remember that the alternative factors were valid, and that the actual wish to conform is probably much more evident when there is no opposing pressure. As a result of this study, we may conclude that preschoolers prefer to be dressed in the same styles as their friends. The desire to conform in dress begins in kindergarten and reaches its height in the early elementary grades, before it seems to decline in adolescence.

[2]Gesell, Arnold. *The First Five Years of Life—A Guide to the Study of the Preschool Child.* New York: Harper & Row Publishers, 1940, p. 248.

[3]Ryan, Mary Shaw. *Clothing, A Study in Human Behavior.* New York: Holt, Rinehart & Winston, 1966, p. 216.

For the designer of childrenswear, there must be a totally different approach to designing for preschoolers as compared to younger children. In contrast to toddlers, children from three to six are individuals who are aware of clothing and have quickly developed some very definite preferences and opinions. Unfortunately, young children are rarely present when clothing is purchased. Subsequently, they will often irritate mother by refusing to wear a garment for no apparent reason. A little investigation usually reveals the cause of the refusal. Perhaps a scratchy seam, uncomfortable fit, or the fact that they do not like the color could be responsible. Situations such as these could be avoided if children were taken along for the purchase and permitted to try on the garment. Discomfort and poor fit, especially, could be identified before buying. Most preschool children do not enjoy shopping and trying on clothes, but if a shopping afternoon could be made short and pleasant, many purchasing mistakes would be avoided.

In summary, then, we must consider that preschoolers like bright colors, interesting textures, basic comfort, clothing that is easy to get into and out of, and clothing that is similar to what other children are wearing. On occasion, preschoolers like the old familiar garment for its sense of security, but almost all of them like new clothes because they bring admiration and attention.

■ Middle Childhood

When the child enters school, his world expands. Parents, who were until now the only major influence on the child, begin to share their position of authority with teachers and other children. In order to adjust to this expanded environment, children will attempt to modify their behavior so that they will gain approval from parents, teachers, and peers—not necessarily in that order, much to the dismay of some parents. There is usually very little conflict between the demands of parents and teachers. Both are pleased with intellectual progress, good social manners, and neat appearance.

The demands of the peer group, however, are often more complex, and children must try to fit in and gain acceptance. This acceptance is usually based on the skills and desirable characteristics a newcomer brings to the group, and lacking these, he may be quickly rejected. Rejection or disapproval of peers at this age can have a continued effect on the self-image of the child, often lasting into adolescence and adulthood.

In order to be accepted, most youngsters will strive to be as good as, but not too much better than, the other children in the group. This applies to school, sports, and play skills. Vigorous active play is universally enjoyed by the school-age child. These children practice for hours to throw a ball competently, skip rope, skate, swim, and dive. When economically feasible, this natural desire is supplemented by professional lessons, for modern parents want their children to become competent in all sorts of sports and social activities. Appropriate equipment and sports clothing are necessary items for middle-class children's wardrobes, and swimsuits, skating skirts, ski suits, and tennis dresses find a ready market.

As has been previously mentioned, it becomes most important to conform in appearance to other children at this age. The desire to conform has nothing to do with adult standards of beauty. Some children have been known to wish they had braces on their teeth just because everyone else was wearing them. When an already insecure child is not dressed like other children, the results can be devastating, as demonstrated by the following case history:

> Priscilla was about fourteen when the climax of her difficulties was reached. From year to year she had become more stubborn and withdrawn. In school she sat with an air of complete detachment. Although of superior intelligence, her work was inadequate and often incomplete. She had few friends and participated in no social activity. Often she would give no reply to questions and would sit biting her nails and stare truculently at people.
>
> Priscilla was a graceful and attractive child who, had she been dressed in becoming clothes, might have been unusually charming. She had a small, sensitive face, but usually she had a hard and hostile expression. She seemed completely inaccessible and nobody really understood her.
>
> Priscilla's parents were essentially well-meaning, but completely lacked understanding. The father was a minister, the mother a former schoolteacher. Both parents were educated and conscientious in their approach to life. They were sensitive, had high standards of duties and obligations, considered good manners and proper behavior important, and devoted themselves unselfishly to the upbringing of their two children, in whom they tried to instill their principles.
>
> In spite of all these virtues, these parents were damaging their daughter. Priscilla was a timid and fearful little girl who craved warmth and closeness which she never obtained, since both parents were rather distant. When, at two years of age, Priscilla had a little brother who, different from the family pattern, was a gay and jolly baby, delighting his parents and everyone else with his cuteness, Priscilla felt utterly rejected and withdrew into a shell.
>
> There is no doubt that her mother gave her much reason to feel that the brother was preferred. For one thing, the mother lacked understanding to such a degree that, following her moral principles, she demanded that the defeated little daughter enjoy the baby as much as she did, and later share things with him and not be jealous.
>
> The unhappiness in which Priscilla lived, feeling rejected and also condemned for her jealousy, was increased by her unhappy school experiences. Priscilla went to school feeling that all the other children were happy and loved. Her feeling of isolation was increased as she became aware of the awkwardness of her clothing. Her mother believed in practical, homemade dresses. Neither parent believed in vanities. Thus Priscilla always wore too large, bulky dresses which the other children sometimes ridiculed.
>
> Sullenness and a negative, stubborn antagonism toward the whole world became the mask beneath which Priscilla hid her hurt feelings. Her work was poor, although her intelligence was high. She had no friends. Her parents felt completely bewildered and outraged at their daughter's behavior. They tried everything they could think of—they admonished, scolded, punished, but to no avail. At twelve, Priscilla was fairly embittered, withdrawn, lonely and unhappy.[4]

[4]Mussen, Paul Henry, John Janeway Conger, and Jerome Kagan. *Child Development and Personality*. New York: Harper & Row Publishers, 1956, p. 394.

Dr. Joyce Brothers writes:

> School-age children who are insecure about their physical appearance will often shrink in the classroom to avoid answering questions because they don't want to call attention to themselves. They also avoid participating in "action games" for fear of being teased or laughed at, and spend many recesses alone.
>
> Attractive, appropriate clothing can go a long way in helping a young child feel more confident about his body. Unlike the preschooler who craves attention, the school-age child does not want to draw attention to his appearance at the expense of acceptance. His greatest fear is being labeled "different."[5]

Psychoanalytic writers often refer to middle childhood as the Latency Period. It is a time when children withdraw from the heterosexual play of preschool age to spend their time almost exclusively with companions of their own sex. Research has revealed that this phenomenon occurs only in highly civilized cultures. In more primitive societies, heterosexual behavior increases continuously during middle childhood. The fact that children of this age group prefer friends of their own sex may erroneously give the impression that boys are not interested in girls or that girls are not interested in boys, whereas, in fact, below the surface there is much concern and speculation about the opposite sex.

Girls of school age find expression for this concern in their identification with their mothers or, as is frequently the case, with a glamourous TV or movie star. Sometimes, the model is a favorite teacher or an older sister. In any case, the tomboy often begins to hide her aggressiveness when she realizes that to be feminine is considered more attractive by those persons whose approval she seeks. Baseball, mechanics, and science are then left to the boys; to be replaced by an interest in clothes, cooking, music, and art.

Clothes should look like those worn by the identification model. This explains the preference of schoolgirls for miniature versions of "Junior" styling. Childrenswear design features, such as suspender skirts, smocked dresses, and puffed sleeves, if they are not currently used in adult fashion, are vehemently rejected by the schoolgirl as being too babyish. On the other hand, sheer pantyhose and shoes with heels a little too high, worn with a grown-up dress, are the nine- and ten-year-old girl's idea of a really "together" outfit.

It is up to the designer to create clothing for the schoolgirl with just the right touch of sophistication to satisfy the need of the child to feel feminine and attractive. At the same time, the designer should remember that the schoolgirl is still a growing child, and that her clothing should be comfortable and practical for play as well as school activities.

■ Adolescence

Adolescence is often a period of disorganization and stress. There are rapid spurts of growth and development on physical, emotional, and intellectual levels. High demands are made on youth by our society. The emphasis

---

[5]Brothers, op. cit., p. 111

on academic excellence creates tremendous pressures on many young people. Vital decisions have to be made. There is the necessity of career choice as adult responsibilities loom ahead. Rapid changes in body structures are disturbing and bring about the need for sexual adjustment. Adult values are often contradictory, and teenagers must come to terms with them, eventually forging their own code of ethics. Mussen, Conger, and Kagan write: ". . . the adolescent in our culture is vitally concerned with assessing his liabilities and assets, trying on various roles to see which fit him most comfortably.[6]" In this way, by trial and error, adolescents will eventually develop their adult identities, but until this goal is realized there is usually much frustration and strain.

Competitive activities are encouraged. Many adolescents are expected to perform at least as well as, but possibly better than, their peers. This emphasis on excellence becomes more and more pronounced as teenagers

---

[6]Mussen, Conger, and Kagan, op. cit., p. 507.

become aware that the prizes of prestigious schools, recognition from teachers and peers, and general popularity are the result of outstanding performance.

The concept of being a leader becomes, for the most part a desirable goal. For the designer, this means that many girls are now willing and eager to stand out among others as the best dressed. However, it must not be assumed that a girl is willing to be radically different in the choice of her apparel; in most cases, she merely wants to stand out to the extent of having chosen the most recent and attractive version of the accepted fashion of the current season.

Many adolescents, especially girls, are more concerned about their physical appearance than their intellectual or social characteristics. The majority, even pretty ones, wish they could change themselves so that they could measure up more closely to the stereotyped ideal of their group. In the effort to camouflage shortcomings and enhance physical assets, clothes play an important role. Dressed in the current fashion of the peer group, the adolescent can favorably revise her self-image. Fashion gives the teenager a sense of belonging to the group. She has accepted the standard of dress, which gives reassurance that she may anticipate recognition and approval from those who count.

Those who count at this time are usually not the parents. Unlike younger children, teenagers love to go shopping, but a shopping trip with mother can prove to be a disaster. Mother has her conviction of what is appropriate and good-looking for a young girl, but daughter has her own ideas of what is right and attractive for her way of life. Often these are legitimate differences, reflecting the difference of taste between the older generation and the young people of today. But on the other hand, some adolescents use the shopping decision as a means of asserting their independence and will oppose mother no matter what her preferences may be. As a result, many parents let their teenagers do their own shopping without any supervision. Surprisingly, most of the young people are quite knowledgeable in their choices, and quickly learn to appreciate quality and value as well as style. Special magazines keep teenagers informed about the latest fashions and ideas for young people. Many department and specialty stores have charge accounts for teenagers, and are finding the operation profitable. Departments catering to the young set are swinging with lively decor and rock music.

To successfully design for the adolescent girl, one must understand her need to stand apart from the older generation, so that she may develop her own identity. Therefore, her clothes must be different, reflecting the taste of her own age group. Her self-confidence is bolstered by approval from her friends. She needs the companionship of boys to convince herself that she is sexually attractive, and she expects her clothing to enhance her appearance. She expects much, and she shops endlessly until she gets what she wants. She is an important customer and her expenditures are formidable. For the designer, it is a constantly exciting challenge to keep up with young fads and fancies within the framework of fashion.

3 The Industry

■ Historical Beginnings

The manufacture of childrenswear began somewhat later than the manufacture of ladies' garments toward the end of the Industrial Revolution. Until the later half of the nineteenth century all garments were either made in the home or by professional dressmakers who created fashions to order for the individual customer. Unless mother was a talented seamstress, children's garments were either pretty clumsy or relatively expensive. As late as Spring 1897, only three pages were devoted to little girls' wear in the entire Sears Roebuck catalogue.[1] There were some infants' dresses and cloaks, and an assortment of jackets for children up to twelve years old. These garments did not seem to present too much of a fitting problem. Evidently, dresses and playclothes for children did not have much mail-order business potential, or they were not available in sufficient volume.

Aprons were popularly used to safeguard the precious dresses against spills and other usual mishaps of active children. There were party aprons and school aprons, tailored aprons and aprons lavishly embroidered or trimmed with lace. Aprons were fairly easy to sew, and it developed that aprons were among the first garments to be manufactured in volume outside the home. Louis Borgenicht, an immigrant from Galicia (in Central Europe) who settled in New York City and tells his story in *The Happiest Man*, was one of the first to enter the children's apron manufacturing business in the 1880's.[2] At first, his wife did the actual sewing, and he

[1]*1897 Sears Roebuck Catalogue*, pp. 277, 278, 283.

[2]Borgenicht, Louis, as told to Harold Friedman. *The Happiest Man*. New York: G.P. Putnam's Sons, 1942.

peddled the finished garments from door to door. He found that the early aprons had one serious problem. It was difficult to fit them on the various children of his customers. He then measured children of different ages and arrived at a set of corresponding sizes. The often-unwilling subjects received a custom-made apron as a reward for standing still long enough to supply the vital statistics.

Louis Borgenicht decided to expand into the production of dresses. Recalling this period, he writes:

> From my study of the market, I knew that only three men were making children's dresses in 1890. One was an East Side tailor, near me, who made only to order, while the other two turned out an expensive product with which I had no desire at all to compete. I wanted to make "popular price" stuff—wash dresses, silks, and woolens. It was my goal to produce dresses that the great mass of the people could afford, dresses that would—from the business angle—sell equally well to both large and small, city and country stores.[3]

Borgenicht made up his first line with his wife's help, and since there was no competition, he was an immediate success. The customers at this time were the early New York merchants along with many retail customers who constantly came to the store-front factory to buy. Soon, aprons were abandoned altogether, because of the pressure from stores to make dresses. Borgenicht now provided employment for other immigrants, many of whom were relatives, recent arrivals from his own region in Central Europe.

Wholesale manufacturing was on its way. By the beginning of the twentieth century, there was a thriving childrenswear industry, mostly located in lower Manhattan. Competitors were other immigrants from Eastern or Central Europe, some of whom had learned the rudiments of the business in the employ of Borgenicht. These were the years of the sweatshop. Labor was plentiful and cheap in New York, as wave after wave of immigrants arrived, all looking for employment. The men, having learned their trade in the old country, were skilled tailors, or readily trained as cutters, and the women, mostly expert seamstresses manned the sewing machines.

After 1920, there was an impressive change in manufacturing. Competition was keen, and we see some of the characteristic pressures of the garment business developing as Borgenicht writes:

> In the old days there had been one fall and one spring line of samples made up, with minor improvements and changes now and then between times. Year in and year out children's dresses had retained approximately the same characteristics. After 1920, however, when the need for volume made novelty and style prerequisites overnight, the public—exerting its influence through the store buyers—became the capricious dictator of our field. Not that we objected to this. It was simply not what we were accustomed to.
>
> We had to forget our old schedule of two sample lines a year. We had to put out five, six, and sometimes seven. The days when buyers came in and bought for the entire season were over. Instead they bought for two weeks. . . . Gone also were the days when we could buy our own raw goods six months in advance. Someone might bring out a pattern that would take the market by storm and we would be left with a loft full of worthless stock.[4]

---

[3]Ibid., p. 230.
[4]Ibid., p. 336.

It was at this time that the old production methods, where each garment was completed by one skilled worker, were replaced by modern section work. Training of workers was simplified as each operator needed to develop only the skill necessary to complete one unit of work, such as setting collars, sewing the side seams, or making buttonholes. This speeded up production tremendously and provided a much more economical use of the available labor.

As the industry expanded and buyers became increasingly selective, the role of the designer became more and more important. Parents and children, even in small towns and rural areas across the country, were exposed to improved communications media, and the current fashion message found its way into almost every home. In the 1930's, movies had a tremendous impact on the childrenswear market. Every little girl wanted to look like Shirley Temple, and stage-struck mothers encouraged tap-dancing and singing lessons for their offspring in the hope of duplicating the glamorous moppet. Shirley Temple dresses, produced by Rosenau of Philadelphia, were a fantastic success and contributed to making this firm the largest producer of childrenswear in the world, a position that it maintained for many years.

■ Present-Day Set-Up

There have been many changes in the childrenswear industry over the years. As the industry expanded and grew more sophisticated, manufacturers gradually shifted their headquarters uptown, and the majority are now located in mid-Manhattan at the southern end of the garment center. The buildings located at 112 and 130 West 34th Street are almost exclusively utilized for showroom and office space by chlidrenswear manufacturers. Other "childrenswear buildings" are located at Broadway and at Eighth Avenue near 36th Street. Having the industry so concentrated enables the buyer to shop the childrenswear market without wasting too much time traveling from one manufacturer to the other. Space in the mid-town area, however, is expensive. Many manufacturers use this prime location for showroom and office space only. Others also locate design-room, patternmaking, grading, and the shipping departments here. The firms that use independent contractors for their sewing operation may also locate their cutting departments in mid-Manhattan.

Manufacturers who own their own plants concentrate all their production in one place. Plants for New York-based firms are located in many areas. Pennsylvania and southern New England have had childrenswear plants for many years. The southern states, North and South Carolina, Georgia, and Alabama have also provided desirable locations for childrenswear factories. These modern plants, many in rural and suburban settings, with large parking lots for employees, are spacious and airy—a far cry from the early sweatshop.

Many sewing plants are independently owned. The owners contract work from several noncompetitive manufacturers, or they might have an

A Burlington House plant in Reidsville, North Carolina. This modern-day plant in a rural setting is spacious and airy with large parking lots for employees. (Courtesy of Burlington Industries, Inc.)

arrangement to work for one manufacturer exclusively. Working for a number of manufacturers assures the contractor of steady work for his employees.

More recently, there has been a shift toward off-shore production of childrenswear. American manufacturers work with contractors or their own factories overseas. Markedly cheaper labor costs have lured the apparel producer to the Far East, Latin America, and the Caribbean in order to produce better priced merchandise in a highly competitive market.

■ Seasonal Lines

The garment industry is a seasonal business. In childrenswear, as in other areas of the industry, the designer has to produce several lines a year. Opening dates for each line depend on the type of firm. The following analysis can serve only as a rough guide because buyers tend to change delivery dates to meet current marketing needs. Some of these changes may affect the entire industry, while others are limited to certain manufacturers. Most manufacturers are willing to change the timing of their lines to meet the needs of their customers.

Mail-order houses and large chain stores, such as Sears and J.C. Penney, will want to see a line two to three months before department and specialty stores are ready to place orders. Merchandise for catalogues must also be ready early. Catalogues are now a big business at all price levels.

Department stores and specialty shops as well as large volume chains do a thriving catalogue business as a greater number of working mothers learn to appreciate the convenience of making their shopping selections at home. The buyers for department and specialty stores prefer to work more closely to the delivery dates for each season because business and fashion trends can be more easily and accurately assessed on a short-term basis.

The major lines in the childrenswear industry are fall or back to school, holiday, spring, and summer. Designers are busy on a year-round basis. When one collection or line is finished, the next one must be started.

By far the largest and most important line for most manufactuers is the fall line. This must be ready to show to buyers by March 1st. Most designers begin to work on this collection in December and work through the winter creating the sportswear, outerwear, and dress wear for back to school and early fall holidays. This is the season for tailored fall dresses and separates, as well as jackets and coats for school wear. Fabrics used are mostly washable wool blends, corduroy, and cottons. The warm climate of early fall and the generally mild temperatures of the southern part of the country require a good proportion of lightweight clothing in this collection. Even though infants and toddlers do not go back to school, fall lines are designed for their size ranges to coincide with the rest of the industry. Dress manufacturers usually include a small group of understated party dresses for early fall social occasions.

During the summer months, the designer is busy with the velveteens and sheer fabrics of the holiday line. After the catalogue orders for Christmas and holiday have been placed, by about August 15th, the main holiday collection, including early spring and cruise wear, must be ready. Buyers now place orders for in-store holiday selling, and this collection includes items appropriate for gift-giving. This is usually a smaller collection with a relatively short selling season. Orders are placed in August; merchandise is delivered in November; and if it is not sold by Christmas, it is marked down in January. Although the season is short, this is often the line with which the designer has most fun. Here is the chance to create those imaginative designs for special party occasions. Many manufactuers are willing to experiment with more expensive fabrics at this time, for this is the season when customer price-resistance is somewhat relaxed. Children's apparel is a popular gift item, and the major emphasis has temporarily shifted from utility and value to fantasy and fashion.

In September, work is begun on designing the spring line. The first showing of this collection usually takes place in early November, and buyers place orders for January delivery. There must be fresh merchandise in the stores after the post-holiday clearance sales. These orders are usually small, but they give the manufactuer an indication of which numbers are going to sell. There is usually much discarding and filling in until the spring collection is in its final form for the January showing. During the first two weeks of January, buyers place substantial orders for February/March delivery. Spring merchandise is distinguished by light, bright colors. Wool blends are used for coats and suits. Many lines include ensembles, dresses with jackets or coats. For southern climate, most manufacturers include some sleeveless cottons in their lines. There should be a good balance of tailored and dressy styles.

The summer line is designed in January and shown to buyers in late February for after-Easter delivery to the stores. For dress manufacturers, this is a very small line, and outer wear producers do not have any summer collections at all. On the other hand, this is the most important season for manufacturers of sports and swimwear. After all, what do children wear during summer vacation? Many dress manufacturers shift to playsuits and separates at this time in order to maintain a volume of business.

■ Various Specialties

In a discussion of childrenswear manufacturing and manufacturers, we must understand that the field is so vast that it would be impractical for any one company to produce all the items necessary for a child's wardrobe. Therefore, the industry is divided into many specialties. Some manufacturers produce garments only for a certain age group, such as infant's wear. Others produce a certain type of garment for various age groups. For example, a dress manufacturer may produce dresses in the 3-to-6x and the 7-to-14 size ranges. Another may be so specialized as to produce only Sub-teen sportswear. The present trend toward mergers in the industry tends to result in large conglomerate firms with many divisions, manufacturing a variety of different specialties. When this is the case, however, different designers are usually employed to design each particular line.

Following is an outline of the many specialties in the childrenswear industry:

A. Infants' wear
  - Layettes—shirts, wrappers, gowns, buntings, etc.
  - Stretch coveralls
  - Diaper pants
  - Dresses and suits
  - Outerwear—pram suits, snow suits
  - Knitwear—sweaters and cardigans, booties and hats
  - Separates—diaper sets, crawlers, cotton knit polo shirts

(Although some infants' wear manufacturers produce most of the above items, others specialize only in a limited type of merchandise.)

B. Toddler wear for boys and girls
  - Brother and sister sets—shorts, skirts, overalls, shirts, etc.

C. Sportswear
  - Slacks and shorts
  - Skirts and jumpers
  - Blouses and shirts

- Jackets and vests
- Sweaters
- Swimsuits

D. Dresses
- Tailored and party dresses
- Ensembles
- Jumpers and blouses

E. Sleepwear and lingerie
- Robes
- Pajamas and nightgowns
- Slips and petticoats
- Shirts and panties
- Hosiery

F. Outerwear
- Coats
- Jackets and parkas
- Ski and snow suits

■ The Manufacturing Process

To understand the organization of the industry as it affects the designer, it might be useful to trace the manufacture of a child's garment from its original idea to the finished product.

Before the designer begins to work on a line, she usually selects the fabrics to be used for her collection. At this time, many designers visit the fiber and textile showrooms to get an overview of color and fabric trends for the season ahead. The fiber houses present elaborate productions focusing on color, fabrics, and fashion trends. It is important for designers to have a broad overall concept of fashion direction before work is begun on the specifically focused collection at hand. Although designers may order fabrics for their samples in the showrooms of the textile firms, most designers prefer to work with fabric salespeople as the collection develops.

As salespeople from the various textile houses come to see her, she picks the fabrics and textures that appeal to her and orders a sample cut of each. The sample cut consists of three to six yards of fabric, depending on the size range and type of garment for which it is intended. Sometimes the fabric suggests an idea to the designer. At other times, the designer sketches the idea first and then finds suitable fabric. In any case, once the sketch is made and the fabric selected, the first sample has to be cut.

In contrast to the usual practice in other areas of the garment industry, most designers of childrenswear make their own first patterns and cut their own samples. In recent years, however, the practice of having an assistant cut the first sample has been adopted by some of the larger manufacturers. This permits the designer to devote herself exclusively to the creative aspect of her work, and in most cases results in more efficient

utilization of her talents. Other designers still prefer to cut their own samples, evolving changes as they go along. To them, draping and cutting are part of the creative process.

Once the first garment is cut, the samplemaker takes over. She is an expert seamstress, and following the designer's sketch, she sews the sample. In some sample rooms, there are finishers who do hand finishing, such as sewing hems and attaching buttons. Other sample rooms are equipped with special machines for these operations, and the sample is finished to look like the stock garment. A professional presser is employed for the final pressing and the sample is complete. Throughout this process, the designer keeps a close watch as the sample takes shape, making changes or corrections as needed.

Before being presented to the executives of the firm for approval, the sample is "draped" on a hanger. This process involves pinning up and stuffing with tissue paper or pinning over a cardboard frame so that the garment is displayed to best advantage. This effort to create ultimate hanger appeal is very important, since childrenswear is not shown on live models as is the practice in the adult areas of the garment business.

When the first sample has been completed, it is presented for adoption by the firm at what is usually scheduled as a weekly staff meeting. Among the executives who usually have to approve a first sample are the sales manager, the production manager, the piece-goods buyer, and the owner of the firm, if he or she does not function in any of the already mentioned capacities. All of them usually have to agree that they like the sample's styling. At this time, the designer must point out the new trends in fashion and other sales features that have been incorporated in the design. Production and sales people are usually not as alert to new directions as designers. The sales manager should keep in mind what appeal the garment will have in the various regions of the country. What will sell in New England in mid-winter might have no market value in Florida or Texas at the same time of the year. He considers the sample in terms of value. Will it sell at the market price it must get, in view of particular fabric and labor costs?

These manufacturing costs are analyzed in detail by the production manager. To help in the analysis, the designer completes a cost sheet for every sample. The garment is figured with cost of fabric, cost of trimming and notions, and the cost of labor carefully considered. Before the actual wholesale price is arrived at, a percentage is added to cover general overhead expenses and to provide for profit. If the garment does not figure into the usual price range of the particular manufacturer, it may be discarded or changed so that it will conform, in price, to the rest of the line. The piece-goods buyer will be consulted to determine if lower priced fabrics might be available for possible substitution. Perhaps the designer can simplify or reduce the amount of trimming. If the changes are so drastic that the design will be ruined, it is often best to discard the sample. Even the most successful designer will always have a certain number of discards, samples that for one reason or another are never shown to the buyer.

Most firms schedule a final general meeting for the entire sales staff when the line is about 90 percent completed. This is a crucial meeting for the designer, who must be able to convince the sales people that the line incorporates the latest fashion trends and meets the needs of the market which the manufacturer has targeted.

Let us assume now that the line is complete and is slated for production. Each sample is immediately sketched and assigned a style number by which it will be identified from now on. Next, the patternmaker begins his work. He drafts a complete pattern for production. When his pattern is completed, a duplicate sample is made, which is then checked against the original sample. The duplicate should be approved by the designer, and any changes in proportion must be corrected.

Estimate	DATE	INT'L		

COST CALCULATION
DOMESTIC PRODUCTION

Standard			Season/Year	Style #:

Volume Budgeted			Description	

MATERIAL COST

Piece Goods and Lining Source and Description	Mill No.	Our No.	Width	Cost/ Yard	Yardage			Cost per Dozen		
					Est.	Std.	Act.	Est.	Std.	Act.
Freight In										
Total Piece goods and Lining Costs										

TRIMMING

Description and Source	Heckler No.	Unit Cost	Yards or Quantity			Cost per Dozen		
			Est.	Std.	Act.	Est.	Std.	Act.
Waste Allowance %								
Total Trimming Cost								

OTHER COMPONENT COST | ### MANUFACTURING COST

Description	Cost per Dozen			Cost Center	Fact'y Mult.	Labor	Cost per Dozen		
	Est.	Std.	Act.				Est.	Std.	Act.
				Cutting					
				Sewing					
				Finishing					
Total				Total					

TOTAL COST		Est.	Std.	Act.
Per Dozen				
Provision for Inter-Plant Trucking	% of Piece Goods			
Provision for Factory Loss	% of Sewing and Finishing			
Subtotal				
Provision for Shrinkage	% of Subtotal			
Provision for Merchandising Losses	% of Subtotal			
Total Cost Per Dozen				
Total Cost Per Unit				
Standard Sales Price	Less % Discount			
Gross Profit	Amount			
Gross Profit	%			

A design student at the Fashion Institute of Technology in New York working with CDI fashion design software on a Silicon Graphics Iris work station. (Photo by Irving Schild).

The Gerber Camsco patternmaking system design room. (Courtesy of Health-Tex, Inc. Photo by Max Hilaire.)

When the pattern has been perfected, it is graded into the various sizes of its particular size range. The person who does this job is called a grader. A recent development in this area is computerized grading. Digital data, representing the proportional changes in size, is programmed into a computer and translated by the computer into directions for a cutting machine, which in turn cuts the pattern automatically.

A patternmaker using the Gerber Camsco patternmaking system. (Courtesy of Health-Tex, Inc. Photo by Max Hilaire.)

The graded pattern, now including all the pieces necessary for every size in its range, is arranged into a cutting layout called a marker. We also refer to the person who performs this task as a marker. He works on paper as wide as the fabric used for the garment, and manipulates the pattern pieces so that all fabric is utilized with as little waste as possible. Markers are from 50 to 100 feet long in order to accommodate all the pattern pieces necessary for a size range. Some large firms have photographic equipment that reduces all the pattern pieces to a fraction of their original size, so that the marker is planned in miniature. This gives a more efficient overview of the marker and allows for better utilization of fabric. Of course, the completed marker must be enlarged again to full size before it can be used for cutting. Computers are also utilized for marker making, and a steadily increasing number of manufacturers use computers for both the grading and the marking function.

When the marker is completed, it is sent to the cutting department. Here, fabric is spread on long tables, in layers of varying thickness, depending on the amount being cut. The marker is placed on the top layer, and the fabric is cut, according to the pattern outlines on the marker, with an electrically powered cutting machine. Small, intricately shaped pieces, such as collars, are often die cut to ensure accuracy.

The cut garments are now assorted to size, bundled, and ticketed, in preparation for the sewing operations. Most progressive firms have an industrial engineer who supervises the breakdown of operations in the construction of a garment.

Operators are usually paid for piece work. That is, they are paid a certain amount, agreed upon by the union shop steward and the production manager, for each unit of work they complete. Operators are highly skilled and very fast in performing the particular task assigned to them. They need not necessarily know any of the other operations in putting a garment together.

Over the years, machines have been developed to combine many sewing operations. There are machines to gather the cap of a sleeve and set it into the armhole in one operation. Machines fold bindings and finish raw edges at the same time. Multiple-needle machines can sew on many rows of trimming simultaneously. Collars can be set to the neckline and collar bindings attached automatically. Machines make buttonholes and sew on all kinds of buttons. Wherever possible, automated procedures have been introduced into the manufacturing process, reducing the cost of production and making most efficient use of the increasingly limited numbers of skilled workers in the labor market.

The designer should be familiar with the machinery that her firm has available for production so that she can utilize its advantages in her designs. If at all possible, a visit to the plant should be arranged so that the designer can ascertain the full range of production possibilities. This does not mean that she should limit her thinking only to making use of the machinery in the plant, but occasionally minor adjustments can be made in a design to facilitate production. On the other hand, certain embroideries, appliqués, and other trimmings, too expensive to produce for some manufacturers when sent out to special embroidery firms, become feasible when the necessary machines are owned by the plant.

After the sewing process is completed, the garments are pressed and inspected for flaws before shipment. Most garments for children are now permanently pressed. This involves the use of fabrics constructed of natural fibers blended with polyesters and then treated with a chemical finish to impart permanent press qualities to the fabric after it has been heated under carefully controlled conditions. For children's dresses, blouses, and sportswear, the heating step is usually delayed until the manufacturing process has been completed. After the finished garments have been pressed, they are placed on hangers and baked at the proper temperature so that the shape of the garment is set to last as long as the life of the fabric.

Children's garments are shipped in various ways. Outerwear, such as coats and jackets, get no special handling before being placed in boxes for shipment. Dresses are often pinned over special cardboard frames for better hanger appeal when they are placed on racks in the stores. Blouses, skirts, underwear, sleepwear, and infant's clothing are usually folded and enclosed in polyethylene bags before shipment. A complete picture of the garment, along with sizing and handling information for the consumer, is usually printed on the bag. This type of packaging keeps the product fresh and makes handling in the store much easier.

The manufacture of childrenswear is a volume business. As the designer sees hundreds of dozens of her designs being shipped out of the firm, she experiences a thrill knowing that children all over the country, and often in other lands, will be wearing her garments. Often when she is travelling, or perhaps just walking along in the local park, she will see a child in one of her things, and somehow the knowledge that she has touched this child and perhaps brought her pleasure is one of the great rewards of designing for children.

4 Out of Thin Air?

A constant flood of ideas is essential for creating new collections of garments season after season. Without creative thinking, there would be no original garments, no new ways to clothe the human form, no fashion, and no fun in getting dressed. We assume that a designer is constantly bubbling with new ideas. Design schools can only help in pointing out what constitutes good design and in giving the student the opportunity to learn the skills necessary to give expression to ideas. Along with studies in the history and critical analysis of art and design, courses are provided in sketching, patternmaking, draping, and sewing. It is quite obvious, however, that one can become an expert in all of these areas and still not be a designer.

You either have it or you don't! That is what many experts agree on when they discuss creativity, and it seems that they are correct when referring to the basic ability for original thinking. Most young children are creative. It is evident in their early art work, their original way of seeing the world and expressing their thoughts. Later, they become more inhibited, and original expression is often rejected in favor of the acceptable, proven response. Eventually, drawings of people will look like other people's drawings of people, with eyes, nose, and mouth all in the right places, and with the acceptable lines for arms and legs. Dresses with rows of buttons, collars, and sleeves look like all the other acceptable dresses. Originality is being suppressed. The child produces work as good as everyone else's, but not different.

It is the rare person who can acquire the skills of effective expression and communication without losing the talent for original creative thought. Our potential designer is this creative individual. A designer should not be afraid to express novel thoughts in new and different ways.

Assuming that our potential designer has all the creative prerequisites, let us consider the field of childrenswear design to see how this creative ability can be channeled into a commercially productive flow. Fashion design is essentially a commercial art. Free expression is acceptable only as long as it is marketable. Without a market there is no job, and in the final analysis, there is not much satisfaction in making apparel that nobody is willing to buy.

To begin with, the designer must have a feeling for the times in which she lives. Children do not live in a separate world. When the space age brings the streamlined design and functional materials of space suits to our TV screens, children's clothing will reflect some of this styling. On the other hand, when nostalgia invades the rest of the fashion field with ruffles and lace, children will be beruffled. Fashion changes constantly, but not in as capricious a way as is often supposed. There is a steady evolution, reflecting the spirit of the world in which we live. The designer must acquire a sense of which way fashion is going, and which changes the public is ready to accept. Most people look for distinctive, rather than radically different clothing. The new must somehow look right and not bizarre.

It is interesting to note that a designer may have created a new, original dress, only to find that someone else has done the same thing simultaneously. Often, copying is suspected, but in reality, both designers being exposed to the same events have responded in similar fashion and arrived at the same form of expression. As a rule, when a number of designers arrive at similar innovations in fashion as a response to current happenings, the public is ready for the change and will accept it enthusiastically.

Even the designer who is aware of the temper of current events and is basically a creative person can have lapses of creativity, finding herself without any new ideas with which to work. In an industry where she is supposed to be productive on a regular basis, and where a sample room full of workers depend on her creative output for their jobs, a creative slump can cause a major catastrophe. It is at these times that some deliberate analysis of the sources of inspiration can be helpful. Ideas do not come out of thin air. Gazing at the walls of a design room hardly produces anything but panic. So then, what are some of the sources of inspiration to which we can turn for childrenswear?

■ Fabrics and Trimmings

Fabrics and trimmings inspire many designers. Various textures, colors, and prints may suggest ways in which they can be used effectively. A tweed texture might suggest a coat or a jacket; crisp organdy might suggest

a pinafore; fabrics in harmonizing or contrasting colors can be used in novel combinations; a small spaced floral print could work perfectly in a victorian blouse, and rich velveteen will suggest a party dress trimmed with lace.

Every season the textile houses prepare new lines from which the designer makes her selections. Almost every year brings some new chemical wonder to the fabric field, making clothing for children ever more serviceable and comfortable. At the same time for every season, textile designers create new prints and woven patterns in fresh color combinations to give a new look to the current line. Textile stylists work with the textile designers to prepare color cards and merchandising materials that indicate suggested uses of their product. These suggestions, even if not literally followed, will start the apparel designer's creative juices flowing and will lead to interesting interpretations.

Along with fabrics, new trimmings are constantly brought to the designer's attention. Representatives from the various trimming manufacturers present the latest in embroideries, laces, braids, and buttons. One never knows how the childrenswear designer will react to a certain pattern, but this unique reaction may be the basis for a new design.

■ Functionalism

Theoretically, the best inspiration for childrenswear is the concept of functionalism, whereby garments are designed to answer the needs created by the activities of the child. This is the modern approach to childrenswear design.

What are some of these thoroughly modern garments that children wear? There are snowsuits of lightweight, waterproof materials for play in winter; swimsuits that do not impede movement in water and dry quickly; sleepers of soft, warm, stretchable material with feet attached to keep the whole child snug and warm; stretchable colorful knit tights to keep little girls' legs warm and neat. The list is endless. Just consider the developmental needs and activities of the child at school, at home, at sport and play, and certain features suggest themselves.

■ Current Fashion Trends

Current fashion trends, of course, are a major influence on childrenswear. This impact of general fashion on the dress of children can take place in two ways. In one respect, the *general* feeling of a certain look filters into children's fashions, or a *specific* fashion detail may be adapted for a childrenswear garment. For example, the simplicity of the shift silhouette is perfect for children and has won ready acceptance. This is general fashion adapted for childrenswear. There are many shifts for little girls, but although the general fashion is there, the individual interpretation may be quite different from anything done in the adult market. Again, when the nostalgia of the Edwardian look was popular for adults, little boys' and girls' clothing was designed to have the same feeling for the period without being copied from the adult models.

Capitalizing on the desire of many schoolgirls to look like their older sisters, most manufacturers of size 7–14 girls' wear like to give their lines a "Junior" look. That is, they want their designers to be thoroughly familiar with the Junior market and to capture this general feeling in their designs for the younger schoolgirl. This does not mean that miniaturized versions of Junior apparel are to be made for children. The proportions and activities of children differ vastly from adults, and although a certain flair can be retained in the adaptation, clothing for the child must be designed with the child in mind.

In contrast to the general look of current fashion that filters down to childrenswear, a designer can sometimes find inspiration in a *specific* style feature. An unusual pocket or a collar could suggest a child's outfit that doesn't resemble the adult garment in any other aspect. Sometimes a bow or a combination of colors can catch a designer's eye and then her own creativity takes over.

Of course, there will always be some specific duplication. When trench coats are "in" for mother and dad, there will certainly be trench coats for son and daughter. When college girls wear ponchos over jeans, little sister will want a copy. Certain items lend themselves to all sizes and ages and look great on everyone. But beware, little girls just don't look good in sexy satin dresses even if they are all the rage for Juniors.

To be thoroughly familiar with the current fashion picture, it is imperative that the designer gets out of her studio or design room and shop the market. For anyone who works in New York or any other of the major cities this poses no problem. The large department and specialty stores display all the important new fashions. All types of apparel, from sportswear to evening gowns, should be studied anew every season. Only by repeated immersion in the current fashion scene can new trends be identified and become part of the thinking of the designer.

Personal shopping tours should be supplemented by the current fashion publications. *Vogue* and *Harper's Bazaar*, as well as *Elle*, *Seventeen* and *Mademoiselle* for the Junior scene, should be read by every designer. *Women's Wear Daily*, the newspaper for the apparel industry, should be required reading, especially every Monday, when a section is devoted entirely to childrenswear. Trade magazines for the childrenswear industry are *Earnshaws* and *Kids*. Also helpful are the foreign fashion publications, especially *Bambini* and *Children's Vogue*.

Also available to the industry are the fashion forecast services. These services supply sketches and written reviews of all the major fashion showings worldwide. Elaborate slide shows, presenting an analysis of the latest trends are prepared for subscribers each season. These showings, as well as the presentations of the fiber and textile houses are extremely helpful to the designer as she begins each collection.

■ History

In the effort to create new and contemporary dress for the modern child, designers can also turn to the past for inspiration. Of course, we cannot really step back into history and bring back costumes as they were worn years ago. Life inevitably goes forward and the literal past is unretrievable along with the prim and proper outfits of yesterday's children.

There are, however, trends in general fashion when certain historical periods extend their influence over the current scene. Sometimes, this may be due to the success of a play or a motion picture. More often it is a combination of factors and events in our lives which cause us to recall a certain historical period with nostalgic pleasure. Then, designers will try to recreate in a new and contemporary way the fashions of that particular era. Perhaps, it is the ruffled yoke of the turn of the century, the leg-o-mutton sleeve of the Gibson girl, or the graceful lines of the French Empire which capture our fancy. It is a detail here or there, adapted from former times, which can give new charm to modern dress.

The designer can explore the past by studying the costume collections in the great museums. When no actual costumes are available, paintings and sculptures of the past illustrate the various costumes worn throughout history. Richly illustrated books on the history of costume are available in the public libraries. Some of the larger libraries, notably the main branch of the New York Public Library, have excellent picture collections featuring fashion plates and photographs of fashions for men, women, and children from early antiquity to the more recent past. Television can also be an interesting source for the student of twentieth-century fashion. Movie re-runs give us a lively view of the fashions of the 1930's, '40's, and '50's.

■ Folk Costume

Especially in designing outfits for children, ideas often come from folk costumes. Indian jackets with leather fringes, belts, and headbands have been popular. Japanese kimonos and mandarin gowns have inspired chil-

drenswear designers in the past. The Austrian peasants have lent us their aprons and puff-sleeved blouses as well as their dirndls and short leather trousers for inspiration. Dutch and Scandinavian costumes, from hats to clogs, have given us ideas for all sorts of children's apparel. The field is vast. From Africans to Icelanders, from Eskimos to the Incas, wherever individual cultures developed, people have also created their unique costumes. Children love the color and the drama, and designers have a treasure house of ideas to draw from whenever the mood is right.

■ Literature

A unique source of inspiration, especially for the designer of clothing for the very young child, is the field of children's literature. Fairy tales, from "Cinderella" to "Snow White" inspire dresses as well as designs for embroideries and appliqués. Nursery rhymes are an equally popular source of ideas. There have been countless *Alice in Wonderland* dresses and pinafores inspired by the Lewis Carroll classic.

Perhaps the most striking example in this area is Kate Greenaway, who caused a real revolution in children's dress when her charming books for children appeared in England during the last two decades of the nineteenth century. In a period of constricting bustles and stays for adults, the

children in her illustrations romped gayly across the pages in her books wearing the simple costume of the Empire period. As a result, the children of England and America, following her lead, were dressed in soft garments with tiny bodices and flowing sashes.

■ Licensing

When a special personality—literary, cartoon, movie, or TV character—captures the imagination of children, manufacturers often acquire the rights to use that character in their designs. Even when the relationship is not as obvious as it is when actual appliqués, embroideries, or prints are used, hang tags will identify the garment as especially inspired. Thus, starting with Shirley Temple and Mickey Mouse, we have seen childrenswear identified with an endless number of characters, ranging from Winnie the Pooh to the Cabbage Patch Kids.

Timing is extremely important when working under licensing arrangements. Fashion items inspired by a "hot" character will rapidly lose their sales appeal after the character has faded from popular favor. Before a licensing arrangement is agreed to by the manufacturer, he must have the resources to produce the merchandise quickly and in adequate quantities, and he should have secured retailers' commitments to promote and display the merchandise.

■ Merchandising the Line

In designing a collection, most successful designers assess the mood of the moment and work around several inspirational themes. When a certain theme is repeated in various ways throughout a collection, the designer has made a positive statement about fashion. Isolated ideas, striking out timidly in new directions, usually get passed over by the buyers and in the end are meaningless. A valid, new idea, however, repeated in various ways always makes an impression. The retailer, who in turn must sell to the consumer, has a promotional idea with which to work. Inspirational themes lead to the design of merchandising groups that can be advertised and displayed together, usually leading to multiple sales on both the wholesale and retail levels.

5 The Designer As Buyer

In a way, every designer is also a buyer. The piece-goods buyer and the trimming buyer may place the actual orders for stock, but the designer is responsible for the initial selection of the fabrics, trimmings, and notions used in the original sample garment. These basic products must be carefully chosen so that the finished garment will be truly functional as well as fashionable.

Sales offices of firms producing fabrics and trimmings are located in New York City in the general vicinity of the garment center. The large fabric mills, such as Burlington, J. P. Stevens, and Loewenstein, are housed in their own new glass-and-steel skyscraper headquarters. On the other hand, many small converters and trimming houses operate from modest space in loft buildings.

When shopping for fabrics, the designer should take periodic trips into the market. This is usually done before she begins to work on a new collection so that she can see the complete fabric lines for the new season.

Textile firms schedule the designing of their lines so that they are ready with new textures, colors, and prints when the apparel designer needs them for her collection. At the fabric house, the designer is shown the entire fabric-merchandising story for the new season. New fashion colors have been developed and incorporated into coordinated groups of prints, woven patterns, and solids. These fabrics, designed to go together, lend themselves to combinations that can be used in a single garment, or in a group of garments to be displayed and sold together.

Despite the occasional trips to fabric showrooms, most childrenswear designers select practically all of the materials needed for the line right in their own offices and workrooms. Salespeople from the apparel manufacturer's established resources come to see the designer regularly so that they can supply samples of anything that may be needed. This includes embroideries, laces, buttons, belts, and other trimmings besides fabrics. If this time were not limited, a designer could spend almost every working day looking at lines. This, of course, would not be appreciated by most employers. Therefore, it is wise to set aside only one or two mornings or afternoons a week for this purpose.

Salespeople who call are notified at what time the designer will be available, and they make their appointments accordingly. When a designer, on the other hand, needs a particular item as she is working, she calls the appropriate house and her assigned salesperson is usually only too happy to provide promptly whatever is required. It is extremely important for fabric and trimming salespeople to work efficiently with the designer. Only by supplying her with the samples that she wants can they hope to do business with the manufacturer when large orders are eventually placed for stock.

Naturally, not every sample that is ordered by the designer will be used. Sometimes, a fabric swatch looks interesting, but the same material in a large piece turns out to be unattractive and just won't work in a garment. Now and then, laces and other trimming samples are ordered without a particular garment in mind in the hope that they will provide some future inspiration.

The average sample cut may be anywhere from three to six yards of fabric, depending on the type of garment, size range, and the manufacturer's general policy. Laces or braids are most often ordered in five-yard cuts.

There is usually a charge to the manufacturer for samples of fabrics and trimmings. The small amounts involved and the extra handling required preclude any profit to the supplier. The manufacturer usually does not mind the cost, but when a designer orders indiscriminately, and large stockpiles of unused sample cuts and trimmings build up, most employers will not be very happy about their investment.

■ Fabrics

Fabrics, woven and knitted as well as urethane and vinyl films, are the basic materials of children's apparel. From the vast assortment of fabrics developed each season, the designer must select the right colors, textures, and weights for the garments that will be part of the new collection.

The wearing and maintenance properties of the various fabrics are especially important in childrenswear. Active children need clothing made from fabrics that can take rough wear and present no laundering problems. It is a rule with almost all childrenswear manufacturers that fabrics used must be unconditionally washable. In addition, most fabrics have permanent press finishes so that, with modern home laundry equipment, maintenance of children's apparel requires a minimum of time and effort.

Our discussion in this chapter will be limited to the fabrics used mostly for childrenswear. There is no attempt at general coverage of the vast field of textiles. Silks, linens, and fine woolens, as well as some of the new synthetics have been omitted here because they are hardly ever used for children's apparel.

Natural Fibers

Cotton and Cotton Blends

The natural fiber most widely used in children's apparel has traditionally been cotton. Cotton is probably the most versatile of all fibers. It can be woven or knitted into an almost endless variety of fabrics, with weights ranging from gossamer, silky organdy to heavy velveteen or corduroy coating. Cotton can be finished to have a soft hand, as in knits or flanelette, but cotton can also be crisp and starchy, as in poplin or piqué. Cotton is used for every size range at every price level in every category of children's apparel.

Fabrics made of cotton are durable. Its fibers can be twisted very tightly into yarns that are strong and particularly noted for their abrasion resistance. This is the ability of fabric to withstand the destructive effects of surface wear and rubbing. Cottons are temporarily even stronger when wet than when dry and are not damaged by hot water or strong laundry detergents. Since they also do not scorch easily and can be pressed with a hot iron, they can be laundered without special care. Although color fading and shrinkage were problems associated with cottons in the past, these disadvantages have been virtually eliminated by new dying methods that guarantee colorfastness and by shrinkage-control treatments that reduce residual shrinkage to less than one percent.

Cotton fabrics are comfortable. For summer clothing, cottons feel cool because they conduct heat away from the body. Since softly finished cotton is highly absorbent, it is particularly well-suited for knitted underwear. Where fabrics made from other fibers may be clammy and irritating when wet, cotton absorbs perspiration and still keeps the wearer comfortable. This quality also makes cotton the ideal fiber for diapers. Furthermore, cotton fabrics can be used for warmth. When short fibers are brushed, thereby raising a nap, insulation for winter wear is provided.

Cotton is plentiful in the United States, and is therefore, a relatively inexpensive fiber. This makes it particularly useful for childrenswear. Youngsters continually outgrow their clothing, and most budget-minded parents look for inexpensive, practical outfits for their families. It must be added, however, that although the great bulk of cotton fabrics on the market is popularly priced, there are luxury types that are quite expensive. These are fine fabrics made from the long, silky fibers of superior cotton plants. Although some luxury cottons are produced in the United States, the finest ones are imported. Some of the most beautiful cottons especially suited for childrenswear are loomed in Switzerland.

In addition to fiber quality, there are other factors contributing to the cost of cotton fabrics. One of these factors is the number of yarns per square inch of fabric. The rule here is, the higher the count, the more expensive the fabric. The number of processes that the fabric goes through also adds to the selling price. Thus, a fabric that has been improved by mercerizing and treated for shrinkage control and wrinkle resistance will cost more than an untreated fabric.

Many of the finished processes that are commonly applied to cottons have been developed to counteract the disadvantages associated with cotton fabrics. Mercerization is a treatment of cotton fabric to increase its luster and enhance its affinity to dyes. Various shrinkage-control treatments, such as Sanforized and Pak-Nit, among others, have been developed, and almost all cotton fabrics used for apparel now have dimensional stability so that shrinkage is a problem of the past. The development of water-repellent finishes for cotton has produced a revolutionary change in the selection of fabrics for outerwear. Lightweight cotton raincoats and jackets are now practical, and with a warm lining they are suitable for all seasons. The stain- and soil-resistant finishes are chemically similar to those developed for water repellency. They coat the surface of the fabric so that stains and soil cannot adhere and penetrate.

One of the traditional drawbacks of cotton fabric has been its tendency to wrinkle. For years, research was devoted to the development of a finish that would improve the wrinkle resistance of cotton. Various processes, each an improvement over its predecessor, were introduced after World War II. When at last a truly effective permanent press process was developed, the abrasion resistance of cotton was substantially reduced. This resulted in fabrics that survived many washings without a wrinkle, but quickly wore through at stress points, such as the knees in pants and the elbows in shirts. Scientists eventually discovered that if the cotton fibers were blended with polyester fibers in the spinning process, the permanent press features remained and were even improved, and excellent abrasion resistance was retained in the fabric. Woven fabrics blended of 65 percent polyester and 35 percent cotton are now a staple in the childrenswear industry. For knits, a blend of 50 percent polyester and 50 percent cotton is effective. When treated, these fabrics have excellent permanent press properties and combine the abrasion resistance of polyester with the comfort and versatility of cotton.

Other man-made fibers that have been successfully blended with cotton are nylon and high-wet-strength rayon. Nylon adds strength, abrasion resistance, and dimensional stability as well as a softer hand, better elasticity, and quick-drying qualities to cotton. Fabrics of nylon and cotton are especially effective for snowsuits and outerwear. When the high-wet-strength rayon fibers are combined with cotton in a 50/50 blend, it is possible to achieve a fabric with the beauty, the hand, and the general quality of luxury cotton at a lower price. Both these blends take permanent press finishes effectively and combine exceptionally good looks with the practical performance features required of all fabrics used for children's apparel.

Some of the cotton fabrics most often used for childrenswear are listed below. All can be made in 100 percent cotton or blended with man-made fibers for increased strength and wrinkle resistance as well as more effective easy-care performance.

Batiste   A sheer, fine fabric, woven of combed yarns and given a mercerized finish. It is used for lingerie, blouses, and infant's wear. A heavier type may be used for linings.

Organdy   A light transparent fabric with a crisp finish. It may have a watermarked or moiré effect. The better qualities are made of pima or Egyptian cotton and are given a permanent swiss finish. It comes in white or solid colors and can be printed. In childrenswear, it is used most frequently for party dresses, alone or in combination with other fabrics.

Chambray   A smooth, durable cloth made of a dyed warp and unbleached or white filling. It is distinguished by an all white selvage. It handles and wears well with excellent results in laundering. Chambray may be woven in stripes as well as solid colors. It is used for sportswear, dresses, or loungewear.

Gingham   Medium or fine yarns may be used to obtain the plaid, checked, or striped effects characteristic of gingham. The fabric is usually yarn dyed. Gingham is strong and serviceable. Depending on the finish, it has a wide range in price. Designs range from conservative checks to traditional clan plaids and large bold patterns. Plaid gingham is a classic for back-to-school clothes and is used for dresses, skirts, jumpers, and other items of apparel.

Denim   This staple cotton cloth, both rugged and serviceable, is recognized by a steep twill on the face. Standard denim is made with blue warp yarn and gray or white filling. More recently, other colors have also been used. It is available in various weights and with permanent press and, occasionally, water-repellent finishes. Denim is a classic for sportswear and boys' wear. It is used for pants, jackets, skirts, and even coats.

Broadcloth   Cotton broadcloth is a soft, closely woven fabric with a slight filling rib. Good quality cloth has a smooth and satin-like finish. There is a wide variety of qualities in broadcloth, depending on construction, and care should be used in selection. It is used for dresses, blouses, shirts, and slips.

Percale   A staple cotton cloth of good fine texture. This compact, plain-weave fabric comes in white, solids, or prints. It withstands rugged wear and finds use in dresses, sportswear and boys' wear.

Poplin   Cotton poplin has a more pronounced rib filling effect than broadcloth. The cloth is mercerized and usually additionally treated for a lustrous effect. It may be bleached or dyed with fadeproof colors; printed poplin is also popular. Heavy poplin is given a water-repellent finish for outdoor use. This versatile fabric is used in every area of childrenswear, from pajamas to raincoats.

Piqué   A fabric characterized by heavy corded, ridged, or ribbed wales in the warp direction. It may also be woven into a waffle effect. Since it is closely woven, it is relatively expensive for cotton material. Piqué is used in childrenswear whenever a firm fabric with some surface interest is desired. Traditionally, it has been used for contrasting collar and cuff sets.

Seersucker   A fabric with a pucker stripe effect that is achieved in the weaving process. Colored stripes are often used. This fabric launders well and needs no ironing. The crepe effect is permanent. It is used for lounge and sleepwear, boys' suits, and sportswear.

Plissé   Cotton fabric treated in a striped motif or in spot formation with a caustic soda solution, which shrinks part of the goods to provide the crinkled effect. This effect may or may not be removed after washing, depending on the quality of the fabric. Ironing, if done, should take place only after the fabric is thoroughly dry and with minimum pressure.

Flannel   A heavy soft cotton material that is given a napped finish on one or both sides. In a lighter weight with the nap on only one side, it is known as flannelette. It launders and handles well, but in the cheaper qualities, the nap may wear off after repeated washings. Flannel is made in solids, stripes, plaids, and prints. It is mainly used for shirts, and linings.

Velveteen   A rich, low-pile cloth that comes in all colors, is mercerized, and has a durable texture. This strong fabric can be laundered, but will retain its beauty better when dry-cleaned. Velveteen provides warmth and tailors well. It is used for party dresses and jumpers as well as coats in all size ranges. Velveteen pile sheds at the cut edges; therefore, all seams should be carefully finished, preferably with a binding, or the garment should be lined.

Corduroy   A hard-wearing pile fabric with a velvety, ribbed surface effect. Corduroy may be woven with a plain-weave back or a twill back. The best corduroy has a closely woven twill back. There are several types of corduroy, depending on the weight of the fabric and the width of the wales. Pinwale corduroy has very narrow wales and is relatively light-weight. Wide-wale, constitution, and cable are other descriptive terms for corduroy with wales of various widths. Corduroy is also available with no wales at all. It launders well. When corduroy is lined with thick pile or quilted fabrics, it is suitable for winter outerwear. When lined with flannel, its weight is ideal for jackets. Corduroy is also used for all other sportswear items as well as dresses and robes in all size ranges.

Cotton Suede Also known as duvetyne. The cloth is napped on one or both sides and is then sheared and brushed carefully in order to obtain the closely cropped nap that is characteristic of suede finishes. Cotton suede is an inexpensive substitute for suede leather. When the cloth is closely woven and the finish is good, it resembles suede so closely that it can be mistaken for the real thing. It is used in sportswear for jackets and coats as well as for slacks and skirts. It is also very effective as a trimming.

Terrycloth This absorbent cotton fabric has uncut loops on both sides of the cloth. Its base may be woven or knitted. Woven terrycloth has a firmer hand and tailors well for bathrobes. Knitted terry will stretch; it is used for infants' wear, sweatshirts and polo shirts. The cloth is of lighter weight and even more elastic when knitted of nylon or nylon blended with cotton.

Cotton Knits Knit fabrics are becoming increasingly important in all types of apparel. The nature of the basic construction makes knit garments more comfortable, easy to maintain, and relatively inexpensive. Knitting produces a stretchable cloth, which makes garments that impose no restrictions on movement and usually provide some room for growth. Knit fabrics are porous and more absorbent than woven goods. Cotton knits vary in weight and texture from lightweight, smooth T-shirt material to the heavy, napped fabrics used for sweatshirts.

Knits are made rapidly and the manufacturing process is flexible. Childrenswear designers work closely with the mills in developing new patterns and effects. Special samples can be made up much more easily and quickly than with woven goods.

There are two basic types of cotton knits: single-knit fabrics and double-knits.

Single-knit fabric is knitted from one system of yarn. Several yarns may be combined, however, and passed into the machine as a single or individual yarn. Single-knit cotton fabric is absorbent, but usually lightweight and does not hold its shape. Given a finish for shrinkage control, it is suitable for knitted underwear or polo shirts. When single knits are used for dresses, they are usually bonded to an acetate backing in order to improve their hand and dimensional stability.

Double-knits are knitted by interlocking loops on a double-needle machine so that it has double thickness. Both surfaces are somewhat riblike in appearance. Double-knits are firmer and less stretchable than single knits. They drape well and are used for dresses and all items of sportswear.

Woolens and Wool Blends

Woolens have traditionally been used in children's apparel to provide warm clothing for winter wear. Woolen fabrics have body and resiliency. They are made with an endless variety of textures, from deep, soft, fleecy naps for coatings to the lightweight, simple weaves used for trousers, skirts, jumpers, and dresses. Woolens have a remarkable affinity for dyes, so that colors range from deeply muted shades to the bright and light colors particularly suitable for childrenswear. Woolen fabrics are comfortable in cold weather. The short fibers and the raised surface of most woolen cloths create air pockets that provide insulation to hold in body heat in cold climates. Woolen fibers are also porous and absorbent so that they never feel clammy when wet. Woolens are naturally wrinkle resistant, they press without any difficulty, and can be easily shaped in tailoring.

Although woolens have always been popular, there had been some drawbacks associated with their use in the past. Fabrics of 100 percent wool tend to shrink in the laundry because the fibers felt when they are agitated. Various finishes have been applied to woolens in the past to make them washable, but not until blends were developed was the washability of wool fabrics substantially improved. The blending of polyester, acrylics, or nylon with the woolen fiber inhibits the felting tendency and imparts a dimensional stability which was not possible before. In addition, man-made fibers contribute abrasion resistance, strength, and durability as well as the ability to hold permanent pleats in woolen fabrics. These blends retain the hand, the warmth, and the absorbency of the woolen fiber but have brought along easier maintenance and good wearing qualities, characteristics essential for children's clothing. By and large, 100 percent woolen fabrics are used today only for children's coats, and even in this area, man-made fibers are being introduced and are readily accepted by the public.

The designer should be aware of another problem associated with woolen fabrics. Many children are irritated by the somewhat scratchy texture of wool against the skin. For these children, woolen trousers or dresses must be lined, or bonded to a smooth nonirritating fabric. Skirts, jumpers, or coats cause no difficulty, because they do not touch the skin directly.

Some of the woolen fabrics most often used for childrenswear are:

Plaid Wood   When the patterns are authentic clan plaids these fabrics are also known as tartans, or Scotch plaids. Other novelty plaids might be muted or pastel. These cloths are woven from woolen, worsted, or blends in either plain or twill weave.

For permanently pleated skirts, blends or combinations of wool with acrylic, nylon, or polyester give the best results. When combination yarns are used and the pleats are formed on the lengthwise grain, the yarns containing the synthetic fiber should be used in the filling to ensure permanent press. If the synthetic yarns were used in the warp, running in the same direction as the pleats, they would be ineffective, for woolen filling yarns do not respond to permanent pleating.

Plaid woolens are traditionally used for back-to-school clothes, in skirts and jumpers for girls, and in trousers and sport jackets for boys.

Wool Flannel A lightweight, soft woolen cloth with a dull finish. The napped surface conceals the weave. It is dyed in many colors, but gray and navy are perennial favorites for blazer jackets, pleated skirts, and trousers. The wool flannel used in childrenswear is now mostly blended with nylon to improve the wearing quality and help maintain good press.

Wool Melton A heavy coating with rigid construction that affords excellent wear. The heavy fulling or felting finishing treatments cover up all interlacings of the warp and filling, thereby making a genuinely "solid" cloth. Melton is used for peacoats and other outerwear for both boys and girls.

Chinchilla The chief characteristic of this coating is its nub texture. In the finishing process, the fibers are actually curled into these chinchilla nubs. This closely woven fabric is warm and wears well. It is used for winter coats and heavy jackets for both boys and girls.

Wool Fleece A heavy, compact, long-napped coating. Interlacings are well covered by the nap. The fabric is usually a good grade and provides excellent warmth. Children like the soft surface texture of fleece. The fabric is popular in all fashion colors, but particularly in camel and navy.

Wool Knits Both single and double knits are available in wool and various wool blends. These fabrics are rarely used for childrenswear because they are relatively expensive. Bulky woolen knits, however, are still used for children's sweaters, but even in this area, acrylics and bulky cotton knits are replacing woolens to a large extent.

Rayon and Acetate

Rayon and acetate are man-made cellulosic fibers. Both have natural plant materials, such as wood pulp and cotton linters, as their basic ingredient. Therefore, rayon and acetate have some of the same characteristics as natural fibers. They are absorbent and pleasant to wear. They feel soft, are cool in warm weather and comfortably warm against the skin in winter. They are the least expensive fibers available, and are widely used alone and in combination with other fibers.

Rayon is the oldest man-made fiber. Although its inventors originally sought to create artificial silk, rayon has its own useful and desirable characteristics and has nothing in common with silk. It blends beautifully with all other fibers. The new modified, high-wet-strength, and high-tenacity rayons are strong and wrinkle resistant, and they launder well. Rayon can be obtained in an unlimited range of colors.

In childrenswear, rayon's primary importance derives from the ease with which it is blended with cotton or wool. The versatility and generally desirable qualities of the natural fiber are retained, while the addition of rayon may reduce the price of the fabric considerably. By itself, rayon is also used in tricot for inexpensive girl's underwear and sleepwear.

Acetate is similar to rayon in that it starts out with the same cellulosic raw materials, but otherwise it has entirely different characteristics. Acetate has a particular soft, luxurious hand. A brushed jersey of acetate feels soft, warm, and cuddly and is used for infants' receiving blankets, robes, and gowns.

Acetate tricot is important as a backing in bonded fabrics. Single knits of all fibers acquire dimensional stability when bonded to acetate. Tweedy woolens that might feel scratchy against the skin feel smooth and comfortable with acetate bonding. Openwork fabrics, which are too loosely structured to be either cut or sewn, become practical when bonded to acetate tricot.

New processes are continually being developed that give additional dimensions to the uses of rayon and acetate. As their practical features of wearability are improved, and since their use in bonding and blending is constantly becoming more important, these fibers will probably have an important place in the future of children's apparel.

Synthetics

Synthetics are textiles constructed from fibers that are made by chemical processes. Basic chemicals are the raw materials for this wide variety of fabrics noted for their outstanding wearability and easy maintenance.

Synthetics are rapidly becoming the most important fabrics for children's apparel. Alone or in combination with natural fibers, they are used in every type of garment available for children. There are many reasons for this phenomenal acceptance. Synthetic fibers soften at high temperatures, and fabrics may therefore be heat treated to set pleats, develop shape retention, or receive embossed designs. They are generally highly abrasion resistant and resilient. Since synthetic fibers are relatively nonabsorbent, they all dry quickly. Synthetic fibers are nonallergenic, and they are not affected by moths or mildew.

The general advantages gained when synthetics are blended with natural fibers have already been mentioned. We shall now discuss the particular characteristics of some of the more widely used synthetic fibers in childrenswear.

Nylon

First commercially produced in the United States in 1939, nylon is the oldest of the modern synthetics. The introduction of nylon brought with it an entirely new concept of what a fiber may be expected to do.

Nylon filaments may be made fine or coarse, according to the needs of the fabric desired. Since nylon is exceptionally strong and yet lightweight, fabrics can be sheer and delicate, but still practical. Nylon's abrasion resistance is three times that of wool. In addition, nylon is resilient: it springs back to its original dimensions after being stretched or compressed. Since nylon filaments are smooth and nonporous, they do not soil easily. Nylon is also nonabsorbent; therefore it dries rapidly.

Nylon fabrics made of filament yarn (the fine, smooth yarn made from continuous fibers with only a slight twist) have a silky, soft hand. On the other hand, nylon staple (filaments that have been cut into short lengths) can be spun into yarns that are used to create bulky, warm sweaters or lightweight, textured fabrics.

Nylon has excellent dimensional stability, which is retained after repeated laundering. The ability to heat-set nylon makes permanent pleats and other surface effects, such as plissé possible.

Nylon does have some drawbacks. The appearance of little balls on the surface of the fabric after repeated wearing is called pilling; it is a common fault of nylon and blends containing nylon. White nylon tends to turn gray unless it is rinsed repeatedly in the laundry process. Static electricity, which causes nylon blouses or sweaters to cling when the humidity is low, is a nuisance. This problem has been somewhat lessened by antistatic chemical finishes that can be applied to nylon. Lastly, the clammy feel of filament-nylon fabrics against the skin limits the uses of this fiber to some extent.

Nylon is used extensively in tricots for lingerie and sleepwear. Stretch nylon is used in children's hoisery and swimsuits, as well as in infants' stretchable garments. Tightly woven fabrics made from nylon fibers are used in water and wind-repellent snowsuits, ski apparel, windbreakers, raincoats, and sleeping bags. Outerwear is often designed with a shell of waterproof nylon fabric enclosing a polyester fiberfill interlining. This lightweight combination is warm and washable.

Acrylic

Acrylic is the generic name for all fibers made from a chemical compound called acrylonitrile. Acrylic fibers were first commercially produced in the United States in 1950.

Acrylics are soft, warm, and bulky, somewhat wool-like in texture. They are lightweight, but not as strong or abrasion resistant as nylon. They have excellent pressed-crease retention and are moth resistant. They wash well with no special care and need little or no ironing.

Acrylics can be used for the same type of apparel as woolens. Sweaters, socks, and accessories are knitted with acrylic yarn. Acrylics are used for double knits as well as for single knits bonded to acetate in all types of children's dresses and sportswear.

Modacrylic

Modacrylic fibers are similar to acrylics in that they also have acrylonitrile as their basic ingredient, but modacrylics have a similar percentage of this compound with other chemicals added. Modacrylics are used in apparel, primarily for furlike fabrics. Many variations have been developed. Some imitate natural furs, but others are unique in their construction. Children love the furry textures and lightweight warmth. The extremely low softening point of the fiber and its relative weakness require special care in handling. Garments should be dry-cleaned or washed in cool water by hand. Ironing, when needed, must be done at a low temperature.

Polyester

Polyester is the generic name for the fiber that has made permanent press a possibility. Although its commercial production dates back only to 1953, it has rapidly become what is possibly the most widely used synthetic fiber in childrenswear. Some of the familiar trademarks for polyester are: Dacron (Du Pont), Fortrel (Fiber Industries), and Kodel (Eastman Kodak).

Fabrics made from polyester fibers may be smooth or nubby; in compact weaves; sturdy, textured knits; or loose, open knits. When tested for automatic wash- and-wear, polyester is rated excellent. Polyester fabrics retain their dimensional stability after repeated laundering, and pleats remain permanently pressed.

Polyester staples blend easily with other fibers, and they are commonly combined with cotton, wool, rayon, and acrylics to impart easy maintenance, strength, abrasion resistance, wrinkle-free appearance, and shape retention, while the natural fibers contribute dyeability, comfort, and absorbency.

Aside from the endless variety of blends available, lightweight, woven, 100 percent polyester fabrics are used for dresses, blouses, and boys' shirts. Most important, however, is 100 percent polyester double knit. This fabric is widely used in girls' dresses and sportswear. It has excellent body, drapes well, and comes in solid colors as well as stripes. Jacquard knits in several colors and interesting surface designs have also been developed. Polyester double knit washes easily and needs absolutely no ironing to retain its new look even after numerous launderings.

Polyester is also widely used as a lightweight filling for insulated outer garments and in quilting for robes. This material is warm, maintains its whiteness, does not absorb odors, and is nonallergenic.

Vinyl and Polyurethane Films

Although in a precise sense, vinyl and polyurethane films cannot be classified as textiles, they are becoming increasingly important for use in many items of children's clothing. Textiles, by definition, are constructed from fibers by weaving, knitting, crocheting, felting, or lacemaking. None of these processes applies to film, a thin plastic sheeting that is flexible and drapeable. Film may be transparent and colorless, but it is also available in colors and prints.

Since it is nonporous, vinyl film is absolutely waterproof. This makes it very useful as a material for diaper covers, babies bibs or aprons, and also for really practical raincoats. Soft and flexible vinyls can be easily stitched on regular sewing machines, but since vinyls have a very low melting point, seams can also be fused together with applied heat, thus creating a truly watertight garment. Since vinyls are completely nonabsorbent, they may be irritating to the skin. Therefore, it is advisable that they be lined with fabric when used as raincoats or bibs.

Polyurethane films are now replacing vinyl films in many areas. Polyurethane does not become rigid and crack as easily as vinyl at low temperatures. Polyurethane also has porosity, that is lacking in vinyl, and makes for more comfortable garments. Thin polyurethane film bonded to woven or knitted fabric provides certain features that are not possible with vinyl. For example, transparent polyurethane film bonded to the face of cotton makes this fabric waterproof. The shiny surface coating enhances the colors and patterns, and gives the fabric enough body to make it suitable for outerwear. Clear polyurethane film bonded to the back of fake fur keeps the wearer warm and dry. Even simple knits can be made waterproof when bonded to polyurethane film and are then suitable for diaper covers and other protective items.

Laminates

Laminated fabric is fabric that has been bonded to polyurethane foam. Any fabric can be bonded to foam and be transformed into a warm coating material. The foam acts as insulator. New laminating techniques make these fabrics washable so that coats or jackets need no longer be dry-cleaned. In the past, these fabrics tended to be somewhat stiff, but the new methods are producing a more flexible, drapeable fabric. Laminated fabrics are relatively inexpensive. They are warm and lightweight.

"Sandwich Bond" refers to fabric in which a layer of polyurethane foam had been laminated between two fabrics. One is the face cloth and the other the lining. This eliminates the need for a separate lining and cuts down on labor costs.

Laminated fabrics are being constantly improved. New bonding adhesives are becoming more permanent and flexible. Polyurethane foam now comes in a variety of weights so that the finished fabric can be soft and drapeable or have a firm body, depending on the garment for which it will be used.

■ Trimmings

The great variety of design in children's clothing is to a large extent dependent on the use of trimmings. Once the basic shape of a garment has been developed, it is often repeated in various fabrics using different trimmings. A basic dress might be cut in gingham trimmed with eyelet; in knitted fabric trimmed with braid; in velveteen trimmed with lace; and in organdy trimmed with embroidery.

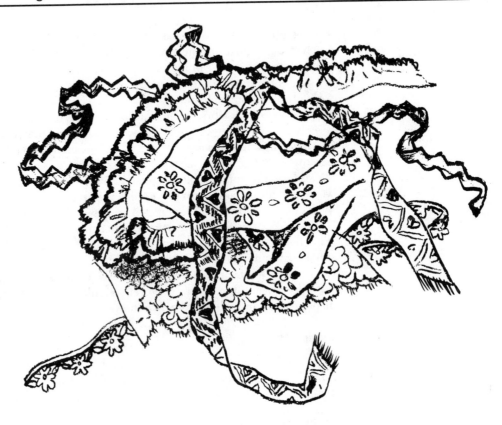

Trimmings set the tone of a garment. A restrained, neatly tailored look can be achieved by using appropriate trimmings sparingly. Ruffles and lace give a feminine dressy air to a garment. Appliqués or embroideries can be whimsical or educational. Contrasting colors may be introduced with trimmings. Examples are: white eyelet ruffles framing the neckline of a dark dress or bright appliqués on serviceable overalls.

Trimmings, when carefully used, can emphasize or underline certain design features of a garment. A pocket may be outlined with braid. Unusual seaming may be emphasized with lace or stitching. Trimmings may also be used to give a dainty finish to what might otherwise be troublesome raw edges, such as the lace edgings outlining ruffles, necklines, or sleeves where hems are clumsy or impossible, and facings would be inappropriate.

There are certain types of trimmings that are generally considered suitable for particular categories of children's apparel. On the whole, trimmings for boys' wear tend to be conservative. Excitement is created by contrasting colors and general cut. For small boys, appliqués and embroidery motifs depicting the objects in which boys are interested are commonly used. Airplanes, trains, whimsical animals, balls, and balloons, as well as sailboats and anchors, have always been popular. Stitching, creating a tailored effect, is used to trim shirts and pajamas.

For infants' wear, trimmings should be dainty and delicate. Narrow lace edging, delicate embroideries in pastel colors, smocking done by hand or by machine, very fine tucking and shirring, as well as narrow braids, are used to embellish babies' garments. Special care must be exercised in selecting trimmings for clothing worn by very young children so that they do not create a safety hazard. Decorations must be securely attached, and any loose ribbons or ties must be avoided.

For older girls, trimmings may be bolder. Bright contrasts give sparkle to garments. Certain trimmings can create a special look or effect. The use of rustic lace and colorful braid can make a peasant dress; fringe on a jacket gives an Indian look; and frog closings create an Oriental air. Although trimmings on garments for older children may be colorful and more emphatic, they must nevertheless be in carefully chosen proportion to the finished garment and the child. Trimmings should never be overdone.

Embroidery

From earliest times, man has used fancy stitching to embellish fabric. Embroidery was done with painstaking patience by hand. Considerable skill and artistry were developed to create beautiful designs, many of which are displayed in museums among the treasures of the world.

Children's fashions in clothing, in many periods of history the exact miniatures of adult finery, have often made use of embroidery. Paintings, dating back many centuries, show children dressed in elaborately embroidered garments. Heirloom christening dresses are lavish with intricate handwork.

Childrenswear today still makes use of hand embroidery. Some luxury items are imported from countries where handwork is still available at a cost that is not too prohibitive. There are hand-embroidered infants' sweaters from Italy, christening dresses from France, and hand-smocked dresses from Puerto Rico and the Philippines.

The demands of modern mass production, however, here and abroad, are responsible for the development of machine-made embroidery that compares favorably with the handmade product. Many types of machine embroidery lend themselves to children's apparel. We shall here attempt to discuss the types of embroidery that are generally suitable, pointing out in which area of childrenswear they are commonly used.

Smocking

Smocking is the use of embroidery stitches to hold gathered cloth in even folds. This type of embroidery has, for years, been typical of children's dresses, but it has also been used in adult fashions. Often, the entire bodice of a child's dress is smocked. Designs are worked in over the gathered material. French knots, rosebuds, and other tiny motifs are used. Fabric can be gathered in even rows or in a diamond design.

Hand Smocking

Smocking is still done by hand to a large extent. Some childrenswear firms specialize in hand-smocked garments and manage to produce them at competitive prices. A "hand smocking" machine may be used to facilitate the gathering and folding of the fabric. Machine smocking is available and much less expensive for volume production, but it hardly compares in beauty to the handmade product.

Machine Smocking

Handloom

One of the earliest types of machine-made embroidery, handloom is identical in appearance to hand embroidery. Heavy embroidery thread is used, and many colors can be incorporated in a design. Handloom embroidery is usually worked on the fabric section after it has been cut out. The front of the dress, the pockets, or the skirt, whichever piece the designer has chosen to embroider, is sent to the embroidery firm after cutting.

Handloom embroidery motifs are limited in size to 3½ inches × 7 inches. That is the span of the handloom machine. The fabric is spanned on a frame and embroidered with a single stationary needle that goes back and forth through the fabric while the frame moves according to the design.

Handloom Embroidery

Schiffli

By the middle of the nineteenth century, the development of the schiffli embroidery machine in Switzerland caused a major revolution in the production of embroidery. The schiffli machine can stitch 10 to 15 yards of fabric at a time, using approximately 682 to 1,030 needles simultaneously. The Swiss word *Schiffli* (translated "little boat") refers to the shape of the shuttle that is used in the machine. Its movements, in coordination with the needles, form a lockstitch that cannot ravel. The machine itself is a

Schiffli Embroidery

double decker, 10 to 15 yards long, and it operates somewhat like a sewing machine. The design is controlled by punched jacquard cards. This machine can embroider almost any pattern on either woven or knitted cloth as well as net. Schiffli embroidery has also been applied to leather and lightweight plastic film.

The schiffli machines can create an amazing variety of embroideries. Many fancy stitches are possible. Flat and relief work can be done. Eyelet embroidery as well as many types of laces can be produced. Eyelet embroidery is particularly popular for childrenswear. In this type of embroidery, holes of various shapes are first punched into the fabric and then finished along the edges with small, close stitches. These openings are worked in decorative designs and make lacy, dainty trimming.

Using schiffli embroidery naturally adds additional cost to the garment. Close, fine stitches create a clean looking pattern and are expensive. In order to save production costs, embroiderers often space stitches far apart leaving frayed edges and fuzzy patterns. This is a particular problem with eyelet embroidery. The number of different colored threads used in the design will also increase or decrease the price of the embroidery. Varigated thread is used in cases where the designer wants more than one color in the design without increasing the price of the garment. All types of schiffli embroidery are sold in various forms:

All-over Embroided Fabric

All-over   This is a continuous pattern that covers the fabric from selvage to selvage with embroidery. All-over patterns are sold on white batiste or may be worked on the manufacturer's fabric. For the dress designer, the stitching of samples may present a problem. Schiffli machines require 10½ yards of fabric to make a 10 yard sample. The extra half yard will not be covered with embroidery, but is needed to fasten the fabric to the machine. The machines cannot operate with less fabric. This means that extra large sample cuts have to be ordered from the fabric house when schiffli embroidery is desired. Some schiffli producers have solved this problem by stitching various short lengths of fabric together to make up the 10½ yard piece required by the machine. Others supply matching plain goods with their embroidery samples. In this way, the designer orders the exact yardage needed for the sample garment from the embroidery house. Later, fabric for stock is supplied by the usual resources.

If the designer wants to create her own pattern for embroideries of this kind, she works out the design on tracing paper for approval before samples can be made in fabric.

All-over embroidered fabric can be used for an entire garment or for only a small part, such as the front, or the collar and sleeves. Since embroidered fabric is more expensive than plain, combinations work out best when garments have to figure into a limited price range.

Edges   Embroidered edging is sold in various widths. These are narrow strips of embroidered fabric, usually batiste, which are finished with a continuous scallop on one side and left raw on the other. The raw edge may be gathered to create narrow, lacy ruffles, or be inserted flat into the seam.

Embroidered Edging

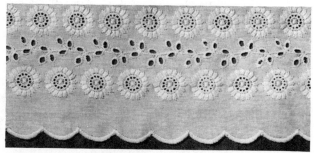

Galloon   An edge of varying widths that is decoratively finished with scallops on both sides of the embroidery.

Galloon Edging

Insertion   A trimming of varying widths that is sewn into the garment. Both sides of the embroidery are left unfinished for seam allowance. Sometimes, there is a straight line on each side as a guide for sewing.

Insertion Trim

Band   A scalloped edge with a straight line on one side. The straight line serves as a sewing guide. When the fabric of the edging is cut close at the straight line, the edge is called a steel edge. Steel-edge finishes prevent ravelling and permit sewing the band on top of the fabric rather than inserting it into a seam.

Band Edging

Beading A specially prepared edging, insertion, or galloon that has oblong eyelets through which ribbon may be run. Weaving ribbons by hand
through beading is an expensive labor process. Therefore, beading has
been developed in which the eyelets are shaped so that the ribbon is
merely stitched behind the beading, but the effect is just like laced ribbon.

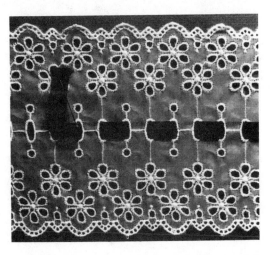

Beading

Border A design that consists of an embroidered motif along one side of
the fabric. The fabric is not cut, but used full width. Scallops, which may
or may not be cut, are sometimes used to finish the edge of the border
design.

   Borders, whether they are embroidered or printed on the fabric, are
always a challenge for the designer. In order to avoid costly fabric waste,
the garment designed from the border fabric must utilize the decorated
and plain parts of the fabric in the right proportion so that there is no
excess of either after the dress has been cut.

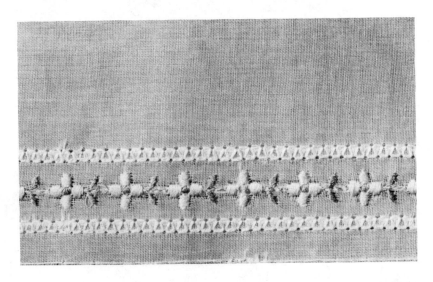

Border

Medallion

Medallion A single figure or design that has been stitched with reenforced edges to be cut out completely. Cutting is done by hand or machine. Medallions may be applied anywhere on a garment, singly or in groups. Embroidered emblems and patches are also medallions.

Application to the garment may involve high-frequency fusing, bonding, or conventional sewing methods. Improved bonding methods achieve adhesion that remains permanent throughout repeated washing and dry-cleaning.

Bonnaz Embroidery

The bonnaz machine was invented in France. It resembles an industrial chain-stitch sewing machine except that it has an open round presser foot. The embroidery design is stamped on the fabric with powder. The operator follows the powdered outline by maneuvering a handle underneath the machine. There is no limit on the size of the embroidery. The machine can be adjusted to create a chenille look giving the design a three-dimensional effect.

Jacquard Embroidery

This type of embroidery looks like schiffli embroidery. The process of execution, however, is entirely different. The electronic jacquard embroidery machine consists of a group of lockstitch or chainstitch multi-needle sewing machines joined together with a common shaft, and guided by an electronically read jacquard device. The operation of the machine is simple and does not require the use of a highly skilled operator. Therefore these machines are ideal for manufacturers who wish to do their own embroidery in their own plants. This eliminates the cost of shipping and saves valuable time in the production process.

Designing embroidery for the multi-head jacquard embroidery machine is usually done with the aid of a computer. A computer enables the embroidery designer to create or edit a design while entering the stitching instructions into the computer's memory. Designs can be enlarged and reduced to facilitate this process. The design computer interfaces with an electronic embroidery machine for the stitching of finished samples or it can be used to punch the designs on jacquard tape. This paper tape controls the execution of the stitches on the multi-head embroidery machines.

Appliqué

Appliqué embroidery is very popular in children's clothing because it is often bright and attractive, it may cover a relatively large area and it usually becomes the main feature of the garment. A combination of embroidery machines can be used in a single design to achieve coverage and color within the price allowed for the garment. Usually appliqué embroidery is designed to amuse the child. Therefore, cute scenery, silly animals, or educational motifs are very popular with younger children. Ideas for appliqué embroidery can be obtained from greeting cards, wrapping paper, toys, or anywhere an idea is born.

The following traces the development of appliqué embroidery for the designers' sample. After the idea has been conceived, the designer visualizes the appliqué work on the area of the garment where the embroidery is to be placed. Appliqués must be designed in proportion to the rest of the garment. The size of the appliqués, colors and combinations of embroidery stitches must be carefully thought out so that the best design at the lowest cost is created. Consultation with the embroidery salesperson always facilitates the process.

After the design has been completed, each piece of the appliqué is traced and cut in tracing paper to provide a pattern. (Dies are made from these pattern shapes for production.) Each appliqué pattern is then placed over a piece of fabric large enough to accommodate each shape. Glue paper or stitch witchery is placed underneath the fabric and both layers are cut following the appliqué shape. Before the appliqué pieces are ironed onto the garment, they must be carefully arranged and checked for last minute changes.

The parts of the design not requiring appliqué may be stitched using any of the various types of embroidery machines discussed earlier in this chapter. Each appliqué piece is sewn onto the garment with a close zig-zag stitch. The color of the stitching can match or contrast with the appliqué fabric. When keeping down price is important, all pieces of the appliqué may be stitched with the garment's background color.

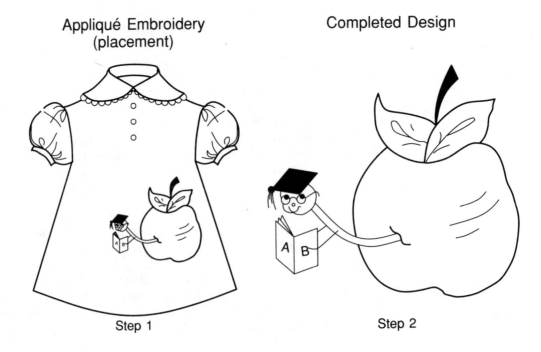

Appliqué Embroidery
(placement)

Completed Design

Step 1

Step 2

Pattern Shapes Development

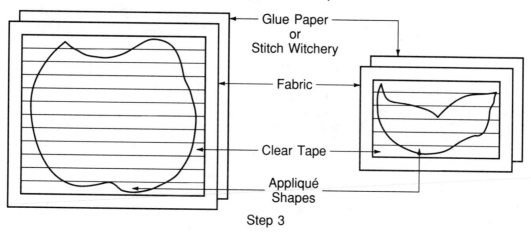

Glue Paper
or
Stitch Witchery

Fabric

Clear Tape

Appliqué
Shapes

Step 3

Appliqué Pattern Shapes

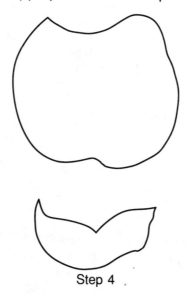

Step 4

The designer must realize that the use of embroidery will always add substantially to the cost of the garment. Shoddy embroidery is hardly worth any price, for it cheapens the garment on which it is used. When price is the primary consideration, it is best to keep embroidery to a minimum or eliminate it altogether. As mentioned earlier, the quality of embroidery is primarily determined by the number of stitches in the design. When embroidery stitches are small and close together, they form a solid clean-looking pattern that will maintain its fresh, crisp appearance through rough wear and repeated laundering.

Lace

By definition, lace is an openwork fabric produced by a network of threads twisted together, sometimes knotted, to form patterns. Traditionally, all lace was made entirely by hand from linen thread. By the nineteenth century, cotton thread was more commonly used. Although lace-making machines had been invented by that time, handmade or "real" lace was still used in preference to the machine-made product. Today, however, handmade laces are considered collectors' items. The laces that are used in the various branches of the fashion industry are now all made by machines.

A machine patented in 1813 by John Leavers in England was able to produce laces that resembled the handmade product very closely. Today, the Leavers machine is still used, and in its modern form, it can create designs of infinite variety.

Val

For childrenswear, the most commonly used leavers-type lace is Val, short for Valenciennes lace. This dainty, light, and airy lace, usually in the form of edgings, is used on all types of children's apparel. It is particularly suitable for infants' and toddlers' wear, and is almost indispensable in trimming children's lingerie.

Val lace is now mostly made with nylon thread. When cotton thread is used, it is generally given a drip-dry, no-iron finish. Val is a flat bobbin

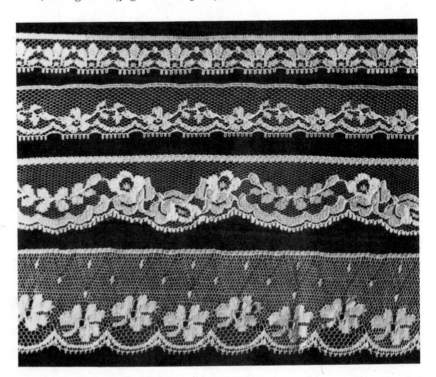

Val Trimming Laces

lace with a diamond- or lozenge-shaped mesh ground. The lace is worked in one piece, and just one kind of thread is used for the outline of the design and every part of the fabric. The pattern is usually spriglike or floral. In addition to the narrow edgings, Val is also available in the form of insertions, galloons, and beading.

Although traditional laces are always created with thread alone and without ground fabric, many laces used for children's apparel are embroidered by the schiffli machine on a temporary ground fabric that is later removed by a chemical or heat process. Only the embroidered stitching remains. A large variety of laces can be imitated by the schiffli machine. Most popular for childrenswear are Venice, tatting, and Irish.

Venice

Venice lace is usually wide and quite heavy. The pattern is in the form of flowers and is united by bars. The design may be given a three-dimensional effect by raised embroidery stitching. Venice is available in galloons and edgings of various widths.

Venice Lace

Tatting

Tatting was originally a knotted lace, it is now imitated by machine. Tatting is usually produced as a narrow edging, to be used as a dainty finish for ruffles, necklines, collars, and cuffs. It is particularly useful in the finishing of girls' lingerie.

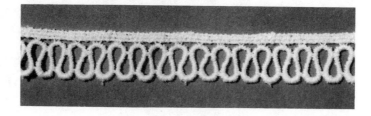

Tatting Lace

Irish

Irish lace is a fine crocheted lace with rose or shamrock patterns that stand out from the background. Although Irish lace can be easily crocheted by hand, good-looking machine-made imitations are available for childrens-wear.

Irish Lace

Braids

Many types of trimming for children's apparel can be classified under the general category of braids. By definition, braids are narrow fabrics, sometimes ropelike, sometimes flat like ribbons, that are formed by weaving or plaiting together several strands of cotton, rayon, or other material. There are trimming houses that specialize in braids, and they supply the designer with the various trimmings listed below.

Peasant Braid

Peasant braid comes in various widths. It is usually flat like a ribbon with textures that may be basically smooth or more rough and rustic. Peasant braids are usually embroidered with floral designs or other ethnic patterns in bright, clear colors. Sometimes, the patterns are woven directly into the braid. When the peasant look is in fashion, which seems to be a recurring phenomenon every few years, peasant braids are used to trim every kind of apparel for both boys and girls of all ages.

Peasant Braid

Rickrack

Rickrack is a perenial favorite, an inexpensive trimming that is available in a wide range of sizes and can be dyed any color to match or contrast with all fabrics. Rickrack is woven into a zigzag shape.

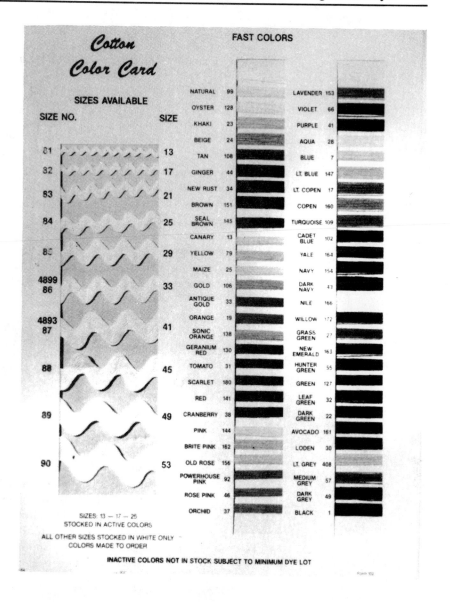

Rickrack Trimming

When rickrack is sewn on top of a fabric, it can be applied in several rows simultaneously with multiple-needle machine, giving a bold but inexpensive trimming. It should be remembered that this type of application can only be done in straight lines, because multiple-needle machines cannot turn corners or stitch curves in one operation. However, rows of rickrack or other braids can be stitched around a skirt as a border or down the front of a blouse without any difficulty. Rickrack can also be inserted into seams or into the edges or collars and cuffs. When this is done, only the points of the rickrack will show to provide a dainty edging.

Soutache

Soutache is a narrow, rounded, shiny, braid, commonly woven of rayon or silk. Cotton braid of the same width is also available, and is more often used for childrenswear. The cotton braid is flatter and has a herringbone effect in the weave.

Soutache braid is so narrow, usually no wider than an eighth of an inch, that it can be curved and sewn around yokes, collars, and pockets. The traditional sailor collar is usually trimmed with two or three rows of soutache. These are applied with a multiple-needle machine and, therefore, must be stitched in straight lines without corners. Soutache braid is also often used to emphasize unique design features, such as the pockets and yoke on a cowboy shirt.

Soutache

Fringe

Fringe is a decorative border of yarn or thread, hanging loosely from a raveled edge of fabric or a separate band. Fringe may also consist of narrow strips of leather or plastic. The fringe that is sold as trimming is always attached to a band and sold by the yard. It is finished in various widths and thicknesses. The loops of yarn that form the fringe are sometimes left uncut for a novelty effect. All fringe should be securely attached to the band so that the lose yarns do not come off after washing and wearing. Fringe is effective in imparting an ethnic or nostalgic look to fashion.

Fringe

■ Fasteners

The selection of fasteners required to finish garment openings can be either routine or carefully considered by the designer. Often, dress or jacket closings are handled as vital design features. There are numerous types of fastenings available for children's apparel. The designer has a choice of traditional or novelty buttons, a wide variety of zippers, Velcro®, and many kinds of gripper fasteners as well as grommets or eyelets for buckling and lacing.

Two-Hole

Four-Hole

Sew-Through Button

Buttons

Buttons that are passed through buttonholes or loops have been used traditionally to close garments. When used on garments for children under three years old, buttons must be sewn on very securely, so that they cannot be pulled off by the child and thus present a choking hazard.

There are two basic types of buttons. A sew-through button has two or four holes through which it is sewn to the garment. A shank button has a small projection or knob at the underside of the button which contains an opening, through which the button is attached. The shank may be of one piece with the button, made of the same material, or may be a wire loop.

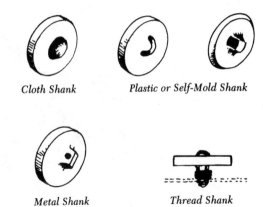

Shank Button

Cloth Shank   *Plastic or Self-Mold Shank*

Metal Shank   *Thread Shank*

Although shank buttons are considered more decorative than sew-throughs, since the buttons themselves are solid and the sewing thread is hidden from view, there are times when a shank button should not be used on children's apparel. By and large, the shank projection will cause discomfort when these buttons are used for back closing of a garment. On sleepwear also, a flat sew-through button is deemed to be more comfortable. Both sew-through and shank buttons are attached by special machines that can sew and space buttons automatically.

Buttons, whether shank or sew-through, come in many sizes. The diameter of a button is measured in lignes. A ligne is equal to 1/40 inch. Thus a sixteen-ligne button, a fairly common size for small garments, is equal to 2/5 inch in diameter; a 24-ligne button equals 3/5 inch; and a 30-ligne button equals 3/4 inch.

Buttons can be both ornaments and fastenings. They are made from a large variety of materials, but for childrenswear most buttons are made of plastic. Cellulose, casein and polystyrene, and the polyvinyl resins are used to manufacture buttons that are molded into all sorts of decorative shapes. Molding machines can produce from 50,000 to 250,000 plastic buttons in a twenty-four-hour period. Plastic buttons can be clear and glasslike, or they can be dyed in a wide variety of brilliant colors. For the back opening on dresses or sportswear, a clear plastic sew-through button can be used on all types and colors of fabric. Plastic buttons are also made to simulate pearl, wood, metal, and other natural materials.

Silver- and gold-toned metal buttons are used on all sorts of childrenswear. Metal sew-through buttons are available but metal shank buttons are much more widely used. The face of the button may be smoothly polished with a shiny or brushed finish, or the metal can be embossed with all sorts of decorative designs. Anchor buttons for sailor suits are a typical example.

Real pearl buttons are still used on luxurious infants' garments, but for the most part, they have been replaced by the simulated pearl plastics. Nevertheless, real pearl buttons, especially ocean pearls, have a beautiful irridescence that cannot quite be duplicated by the more common materials. Fresh-water pearls are somewhat less expensive than ocean pearls, but they do not have this highly irridescent quality. Pearl buttons can be white or dark gray. The dark gray pearl buttons are called "smoked" pearls. Sew-through pearl buttons or simulated pearls are used to fasten blouses and shirts. Tiny pearl shank buttons decorate little girls' party dresses, and larger pearl buttons are typical on toddler boys' suits.

For an occasional novelty effect, leather or wood buttons may be used. Since neither is washable, they are only suitable for outerwear that is normally dry-cleaned. Large, oblong buttons of leather or wood are called toggles. They are passed through loops rather than buttonholes, and they are typically used on duffle coats or on other rugged winter jackets. Toggles made of plastic materials are also available, but although practical, they lack the style impact of the natural materials.

Zippers

There are a number of reasons why a designer might choose a zipper rather than buttons to close a child's garment. Zippers can be more easily managed by a young child just learning to dress alone. Once a zipper is properly closed, it will not pop open as buttons might do. They provide a smooth, unobtrusive closing when used on the back of a dress. Zippers

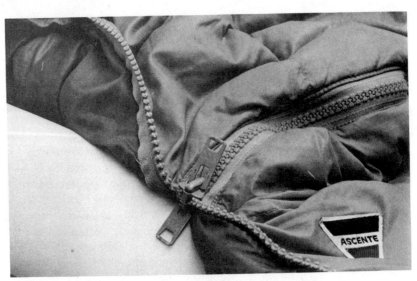

Reversible Zipper

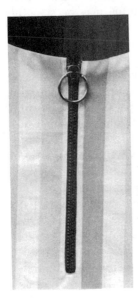

Decorative Zipper

can close outerwear so that it is airtight and waterproof. Decorative zippers give apparel a modern, streamlined air. Zippers can be designed with decorated tapes. Colorful patterns are printed on or woven into these tapes. The zipper itself may be in bright, contrasting colors. Separating zippers are used on jackets and coats. Regular zippers, which have one end securely fastened together, are used on neck openings, slacks and skirt plackets, and even on pockets.

Zippers were originally made of metal, but now nylon and other plastic materials are also used. Nylon zippers are lightweight and very fine, but after repeated laundering and use, the teeth of the zipper tend to become misshaped and the slide cannot move easily over the damaged part of the zipper. Zipper producers claim that by moving the slide, the nylon zipper can easily by repaired. But the average consumer seems to have difficulty with this, and for a sturdy longlasting product, nothing has yet been able to outwear the traditional metal zipper. Especially on outerwear, the separating metal zipper is most often used.

Wide plastic zippers are very decorative and come in several colors. They often do not work as smoothly as metal zippers, and since they are usually imported, there are occasional problems with delivery. They do, however, provide a bright splash of color and are a very effective trimming.

Grippers

Gripper-snap fasteners are sturdy, modern snaps that are used on all types of garments for children. They are impossible to pull off and they cannot get caught like a button; nor can they get stuck like a zipper. Grippers, therefore, are safe for small children and their use is highly recommended where a good, functional closing is desired.

Originally, the use of gripper-snap fasteners was confined mostly to sleepers, jeans, and the crotch openings in infants' pants, but today they are used on all sorts of clothing from robes to raincoats and every type of sportswear.

The front heads of the grippers may be decorated with all kinds of fancy designs from embossed metal emblems to colorful enamel or jewellike plastic inserts. Gripper heads are usually round, but interesting shapes are also available.

There are hand gadgets available for attaching grippers in the design room. Fastener producers usually supply these tools to the designer. In factories, efficient machines do the application. Gripper-snap fasteners are also sold spaced evenly on tapes, so that they can be easily sewn into garments without special machinery. Diaper pants, sleepers, and infants' wear crotch openings are often closed with these gripper tapes.

No-sew Snap Tape

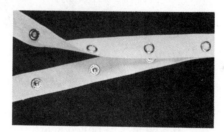

Eyelets and Grommets

Eyelets and metal grommets for lacing, hooking, or buckling fabric together can be inserted into garments. An eyelet, by definition, is a small hole, usually round and finished along the edge. Although stitching may be used to finish eyelets, as in embroidery, metal rings or grommets are more sturdy and are, therefore, generally used when the eyelet serves as part of a fastening device.

Eyelets with laces or ribbons help to give a period or peasant look to garments, but are difficult for children to manipulate when used as the actual closure. For this reason, lacing is usually used as a decorative feature and is supplemented with a more practical garment closure. On the other hand, larger eyelets, finished with grommets and paired with buckles or hooks are easy for children to manage and are often used on raincoats and other outerwear. The method used to insert grommets is similar to that for the insertion of gripper-snap fasteners.

Metal Eyelet

Grommet

Velcro

Of all fasteners, probably the safest and easiest for small children to handle is Velcro®. It consists of bands with fibers projecting from the surface, which when pressed together form a closure that can only be opened when the bands are pulled apart.

Velcro® is available in long strips of varying widths or patches of various sizes. The patches work well for small garments, because they do not affect the flexibility or reduce the stretch properties of the fabric on which they are used.

Velcro is washable at moderate temperatures, but must be carefully closed before washing in a washing machine because the rough fibers of the Velcro surface will catch on other garments and cause damage. A warning regarding this washing problem should be included on the label describing care instructions when Velcro is used on washable garments.

The intelligent selection of fabrics, trimmings, and fasteners is vital to the success of the designer. In order to produce marketable garments continuously, the designer must make every effort to know all the recent developments in the ever-changing field of textiles. As a result of the constant emergence of new products, fashions evolve and have become increasingly functional.

Velcro® Tape

The future will probably again bring more new and exciting fabrics—fabrics that will lend themselves to more efficient mass production. With the constant decline of skilled personnel available, the cutting and stitching of garments by conventional methods will give way to new methods of production. Developments in the use of robotics, along with the development of fabrics that can be molded and fused, will eventually lead to more cost-efficient manufacturing methods. Trimmings and fastenings must also keep pace with these new methods and materials.

The designer will have the opportunity to create truly modern garments by taking advantage of the advances in the new technology. This is only the beginning. Fashion will continue to change until the ultimate in good looks, comfort, ease of care, and economical production is achieved. Whether or not this stage will ever come to pass is anybody's guess, but until then, designers must continue to work towards this goal.

PART 2

BASIC PATTERNMAKING

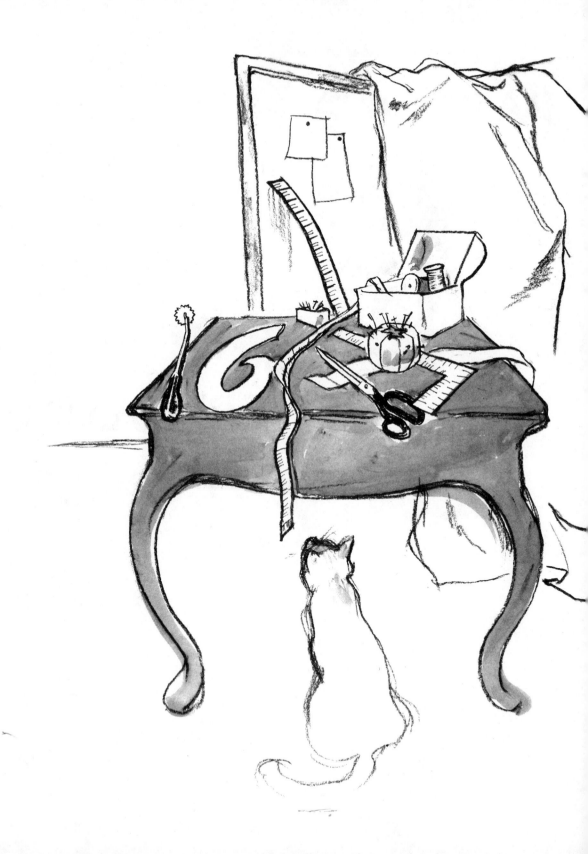

6 Preliminary Considerations

Part 2 of this text is devoted to the basic patternmaking techniques used in childrenswear design. Although designing with the flat pattern is universally accepted in the industry, it has become increasingly evident that certain shapes are more easily developed when draped directly in the fabric on the model form. Therefore, many designers use both draping and patternmaking to translate their ideas into garments. Whereas most designers of adult fashions drape in muslin, in childrenswear, muslin is rarely used for this purpose. Most firms do not even have muslin available, but this is no particular disadvantage, since draping directly in the fabric of the finished garment gives the designer a clearer picture of the developing style as she drapes and cuts. Instructions for fabric draping can be found in Chapter 10.

Every designer should be familiar with basic patternmaking as it applies to childrenswear. Once the foundation pattern has been draped, the styling of the basic bodice and skirt can be accomplished faster and more efficiently on the flat, rather than by redraping every variation. Basic sleeves and collars are easily drafted. Later, refinements of line can be achieved by trying the drafted pattern on the model form and making corrections.

Since most firms employ a patternmaker to draft the perfect stock pattern, it is usually permissible for the designer to work with a fairly rough pattern, frequently making corrections as the sample is developed. When pattern shapes turn out to be unusual, such as a new collar or a unique pocket, most designers submit this pattern to the patternmaker along with the finished sample. This eliminates much trial and error for the patternmaker, and assures the designer of accurate reproduction of the design.

Although instructions for patterns in this book do not mention seam allowances, they must be added to all pieces before they are cut in fabric. The general rule for seam allowances is ½ inch for all basic seams. Necklines or enclosed seams, such as the inside seams in collars and cuffs, are ¼ inch. Some manufacturers prefer ⅜ inch seams, and others want ⅝ to ¾ of an inch on certain items. This depends on the price level of the garment and the special type of machinery used in production.

■ Tools for Patternmaking

Before beginning the specific instructions for patternmaking, a discussion of the required tools is in order.

Scissors and Shears

Two pairs of scissors are needed. One pair should be reserved only for fabric cutting and draping. For this dual purpose, medium-weight scissors with a 5-inch blade are usually satisfactory. Another pair of scissors should be used for paper cutting only. Scissors used for paper, become too dull for cutting fabric and draping. The paper shears may be somewhat heavier and larger.

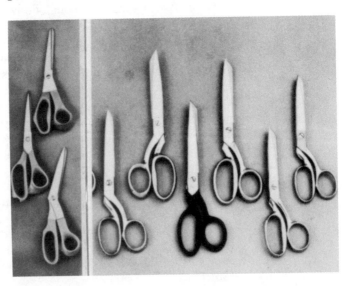

Scissors and Shears

It is easier to develop the steady hand needed to achieve a smooth edge, essential for patterns, with generously proportioned shears. Good quality scissors and shears are worth the additional cost. They must be kept sharp and in good working order.

The L Square

This is an L-shaped ruler with arms at a perfect right angle. It is essential for marking grain lines on paper, for squaring off style lines and for general patternmaking.

L-Square

The French Curve

This clear plastic, curved shape is engineered to facilitate the shaping of necklines, armholes, and other curved lines on patterns.

French Curve

The Skirt Curve

Also known as a HIP CURVE, this curved metal ruler is particularly engineered to shape the side seams of skirts and shifts. It is also useful for shaping waistlines and other shallow curves in the pattern.

Skirt Curve

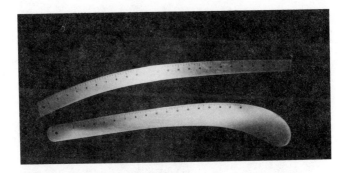

The Clear Plastic Ruler

These flexible rulers come in 1- and 2-inch widths, and are marked off in ¼-inch squares. They are very useful for adding seam allowances and are convenient for all sorts of measuring jobs.

Clear Plastic Ruler

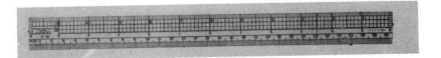

The Tape Measure

This flexible tape is mainly used for measuring children or the model form.

Tape Measure

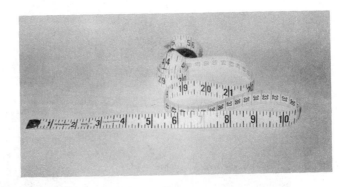

Pins

Pins used for draping and general purposes should be lightweight and of good quality. Number 17 steel satin pins are recommended.

Pins

The Needle-Point Tracing Wheel

This is used to trace lines when developing a paper pattern.

Needle-Point Tracing
Wheel

■ The Model Form

The model form is a facsimile of the human body used for the fitting and draping of garments. It is modeled according to the specific body measurements of each size. There are forms consisting of only the torso on a stand, and there are full-length forms that reproduce the human body from neck to ankle. Full-length forms are essential for designing sports wear and boys' wear. Some designers prefer a full-length form for all types of childrenswear, since it gives a clearer picture of the proportions of the garment in relation to the size of the child. Full-length forms are considerably more expensive than torso forms. Therefore, some manufacturers are likely to have only torso forms available in sample sizes.

Model forms are molded of papier-mâché, covered with a layer of wadding and jersey, and finished with an Irish linen canvas. The canvas cover is seamed in a conventional way, in order to serve as a guide for the placement of darts and seams in the garment.

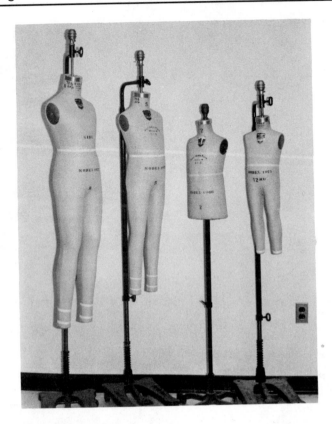

Model Forms

All forms have a seam at the center front and the center back. There is a seam at the base of the neck and at the shoulder. The canvas cover is joined at the side seam with a whipstitch, creating a ridge, which is easily located when draping. The conventional waistline is indicated with a tape. This is somewhat arbitrary in the smaller sizes, since young children do not have a natural waistline.

Model forms in the larger sizes, beginning with the 7-14 size range, have a vertical seam separating the center front from the side front panel, and the center back from the side back. This seam is sometimes referred to as the princess seam, since it is the characteristic fitting line of princess dresses, jackets, and coats, etc.

The place where the arm joins the body is indicated on most forms with a metal plate, usually referred to as the armplate. Instead of an armplate, some forms, especially those used for outerwear, have a padded extension to indicate the top of the arm. Model forms can be ordered with collapsible shoulders to facilitate the putting on and taking off of finished garments. Model forms can also be ordered with detachable arms. Additional parts of the form, such as heads and feet, can be ordered separately.

7 The Foundation Patterns

The Basic Waist Draped in Muslin

Every manufacturer has his own foundation patterns. These are basic patterns, fitted to the figure and perfected in the various sample sizes. These foundations, or slopers, as they are called in the industry, are jealously guarded by most manufacturers, because they reveal his unique refinements in sizing and fit. Nevertheless, it is important for the designer to be able to develop new slopers when necessary.

Slopers can be drafted from measurements, but are usually more quickly and accurately draped in fabric on the model form. The usual group of slopers for dresses includes a basic waist, fitted with darts; a dartless shift; and a basic sleeve pattern. The basic sleeve pattern is drafted from measurements. Then, it is cut in fabric and fitted to the waist for any necessary adjustments.

Unbleached muslin is the fabric used to drape the foundation pattern. It is a relatively inexpensive fabric with clearly visible grain. In fabric, grain is the direction of the threads in relation to the selvage. In draping and fitting a sloper, accuracy is essential, and muslin readily reveals any flaws in grain position and fit.

■ The Basic Waist

The basic waist foundation is used when developing any garment that is closely fitted to the waistline. Dresses with fitted waists and full skirts, as well as garments that are designed with princess seaming, are developed with the basic waist foundation.

Preparation of Muslin

All body measurements required for the preparation of muslin are established by measuring the model form.

1. Tear two pieces of muslin measuring as follows:
    a. Length—center back from neckline to waistline + 4 inches.
    b. Width—across back at underarm + 3 inches.
2. Straighten grain so that length and cross grain in muslin are perfectly perpendicular, and press carefully.
3. Draw a grain line 1 inch from edge of muslin for center front and center back.
4. On center back, measure down 2 inches from top of muslin to establish the location of the neckline.
5. From this point, measure down on the center back line the distance from neckline to waistline.

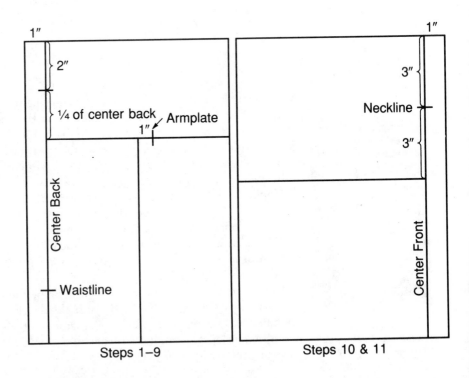

Steps 1–9   Steps 10 & 11

6. Measure down from neckline one quarter of the distance from neck to waist at center back to establish the location of the shoulder blade level.

7. Draw a cross-grain line at this level.

8. On this cross-grain line, mark off the distance between the center back and the armplate plus¼ inch for ease.

9. On the cross-grain line, measure 1 inch toward center back from the armplate. From this point, drop a grain line to lower edge of muslin.

10. On center front, measure down 3 inches from top of muslin to locate the neckline.

11. From this point, measure down 3 inches for level of cross-grain line across chest.

Draping Front

1. Pin muslin to model form at center front and neckline intersection.

2. Pin at center front and waistline intersection.

3. Smooth muslin cross grain across upper chest area and pin at armhole.

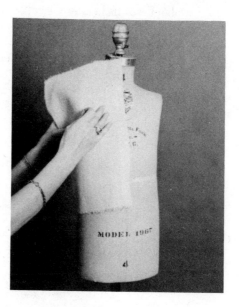

Steps 1-3

4. Smooth down around armhole and pin at intersection of side seam and armhole.

5. Smooth lightly, with grain, down along side front section of bodice, and pin at the center point between side seam and dart, taking in a slight pinch of muslin for ease.

6. Take in excess muslin for waistline dart. The distance between finished dart and center front at waistline should range proportionately from

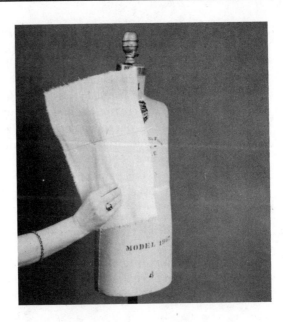

Steps 4-6

about 2 ¼ inches for a size 2, to 3 inches for a size 10. Actual dart pick-up may be very small on sizes 3-6x, and even smaller on 1-3. Infants' garments need no dart at all. (If the basic waist is draped on the newer forms, no waistline dart is needed for a size 4 or smaller.) Locate vanishing point of dart with a pin.

7. Slash and shape neckline, making sure that grain is not stretched in the neckline area. (Always smooth in the direction of the grain as muslin is slashed for neckline.)

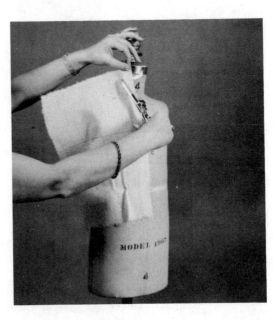

Step 7

8. Pin shoulder into place at neckline and armhole intersections.

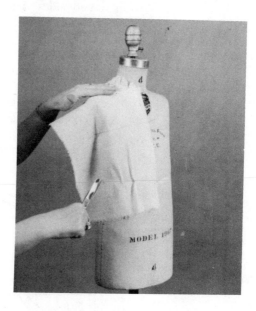

Step 8

9. Mark with a sharp pencil on muslin:
   a. Dot neckline.
   b. Crossmark at neckline and shoulder.
   c. Crossmark at armhole ridge and shoulder.
   d. Dot to screw level along armhole ridge.
   e. Crossmark at underarm and side seam.
   f. Crossmark at waistline and side seam.

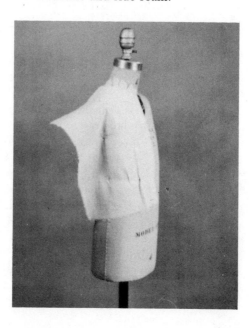

Step 9

g. Dot waistline to dart.

h. Crossmark both sides of dart at waistline.

i. Crossmark at center front and waistline.

10. Remove muslin from form.

11. True:

Trueing the muslin is drawing the lines that define the exact dimensions of the finished pattern.

a. Extend center of dart on grain from waistline to level of vanishing point. Adjust position of vanishing point if necessary. Connect both

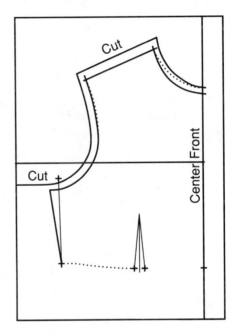

Step 11 a to g

sides of dart from waistline to vanishing point.

b. Lower neckline ¼ inch at center front. True neckline with French curve.

c. Establish shoulder line by connecting crossmarks at neckline and armhole ridge.

d. Connect crossmarks at side seam from armhole to waistline.

e. To enlarge the armhole for a set-in sleeve, measure down from armhole ridge at shoulder, over the center of the plate, to the side seam. Armhole depth should measure 4 ½ inches for size 10, 4⅜ inches for size 8, 4¼ inches for a size 6, 4⅛ inches for a size 5, 4 inches for a size 4, and 3¾ inches for size 2. The size of the armhole plate varies according to the manufacturer and the year that the form was manufactured. Therefore, the distance between the bottom edge of the plate and the recommended armhole depth may vary from nothing to 1½ inches on some older models. Lower the armhole at side seam accordingly.

Step 11e

    f. Extend side seam ½ inch at lowered armhole for ease in all size ranges. From this point, connect new side seam to waistline and original side seam intersection.

    g. True armhole with French curve, connecting shoulder, dotted ridge, and lowered armhole.

12. Pin dart.

13. Add ½-inch seam allowance on all seams except at neckline. Necklines need only a ¼-inch seam allowance.

14. Cut out front of waist at neckline, armhole, and shoulder.

15. Replace on form as illustrated. Shoulder seam should be marked with a dark pencil line and pinned down smoothly so that back of waist can be draped over the front in the shoulder area. Instead of pinning side seam to form at side seam, pin 1 inch away from side seam toward front so that side seam area on form is exposed for draping the back.

Step 15

Draping Back

1. Prepare muslin for back as illustrated on page 95.
2. Pin muslin to form at center back.
3. Smooth grain across shoulder-blade area, leaving a slight amount of ease, and pin at armhole plate.
4. Smooth grain downward at indicated grain line and pin at waistline with a pinch for ease.
5. Pin excess fullness at waistline for dart, placing back dart the same distance from center back as front dart is from center front. Back dart pick-up will be greater than front dart.
6. Indicate the level of the vanishing point of the dart with a pin. The vanishing point of the dart should be at least ½ inch below the level of the armhole plate.
7. Smoothing in the direction of the grain, slash and shape the back neckline. Pin at the intersection of shoulder and neckline.
8. Smooth muslin up over front shoulder. Place two pinches (about ¹⁄₁₆ inch deep) along shoulder line. The back shoulder seam measures ¼ inch longer than the front shoulder seam. Pin at armhole and shoulder intersection over front.

Step 8

9. Locate backside seam by pinning to original (no ease) front side seam at underarm and waistline.

Step 9

Step 10

10. Mark:
   a. Dot neckline, shoulder, and waistline.
   b. Crossmark intersections at: neckline and shoulder, shoulder and armhole, waistline and center back, armhole plate at shoulder blade level, and both sides of dart at waistline.

11. True:
   a. Leave side seam pinned together and remove both front and back waist from form.

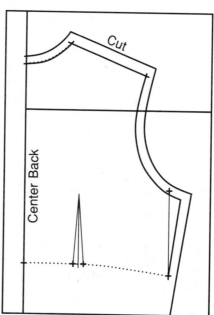

Step 11 a to e

    b. Trace original and extended side seam from front to back waist.

    c. True back waistline dart same as front. Center of dart must be on grain.

    d. Connect dots for neckline and shoulder seam.

    e. Shape armhole by connecting crossmarks at shoulder, armhole plate and side seam with French curve. Armhole should follow the grain for about 1 inch below the shoulder blade.

    f. Pin dart.

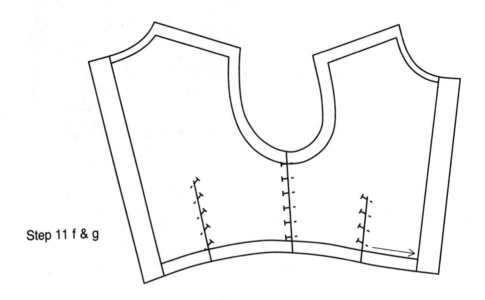

Step 11 f & g

    g. Pin side seam together, and true the waistline of front and back with one continuous line. Grain should be straight from front dart to center front at waistline.

    h. Pin shoulder seam together, easing back shoulder.

12. Replace on form; check fit; make any necessary adjustments.

■ The Basic Shift Without Darts

Eliminating darts provides a smooth foundation, which simplifies pattern-making for almost any type of unfitted garment. This does, however, throw off the grain in the chest area, a factor that can be troublesome in the larger sizes of the 7-14 size range. The dartless shift is *not* suitable for sub-teens unless cut in knits or other stretch fabrics. Another exception might be when an oversized, loose, shirt-like garment is desired.

The Basic Shift Draped
in Muslin

Preparation of Muslin
for Basic Shift

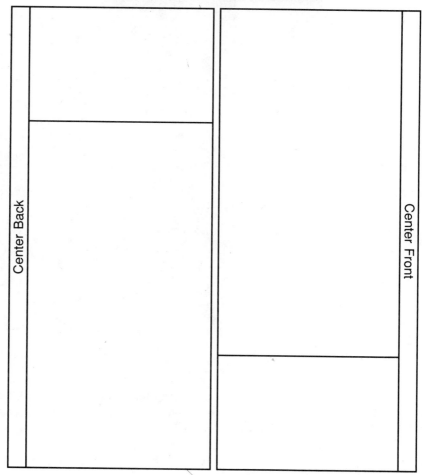

Preparation of Muslin

1. Tear two pieces of muslin measuring as follows:
    a. Length—center back from neckline to hem + 2 inches.
    b. Width—across back at underarm + 4 inches.
2. Straighten grain so that length and cross grain in muslin are perfectly perpendicular, and press carefully.
3. Draw grain line 1 inch from edge of muslin for center front and center back.

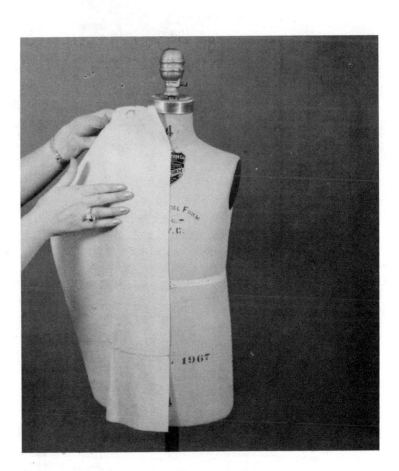

Steps 1-3

4. Divide entire length of muslin into quarters.
5. Draw a cross-grain line at upper quarter of back.
6. Draw a cross-grain line at lower quarter of front.
7. On center back, measure down 2 inches from top of muslin to locate neckline.
8. On center front, measure down 4 inches from top of muslin to locate neckline.

Draping Front

1. Pin center front of muslin to form at neckline, chest, and indicated grain line.
2. Smooth across grain line and pin 3 to 4 inches from center front.
3. Pick up a ¼ inch pinch for ease along grain line.
4. Smooth up towards shoulder and place a row of pins across chest. The grain will be slightly higher at armhole than at center front.
5. Smooth up to neckline and shoulder; shape neckline.
6. Pin shoulder into place at neckline and armhole intersections. There will be a slight amount of ease in the armhole.
7. Mark:
    a. Dot neckline.
    b. Crossmark at neckline and shoulder.
    c. Crossmark at armhole ridge and shoulder.
    d. Dot armhole down to the screw level on armplate.
    e. Crossmark at bottom of armplate and side seam.

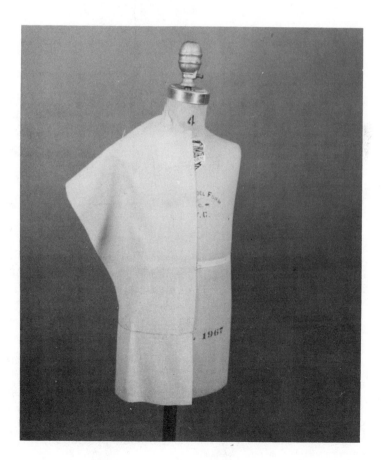

Steps 4-7

8. Remove muslin from form.
9. Lower neckline ¼ inch at center front; true neckline and shoulder.

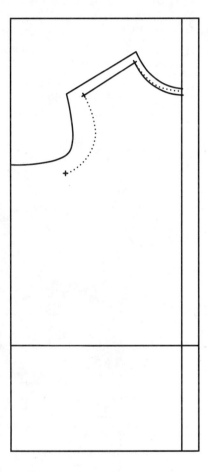

Steps 8 & 9

10. Leave seam allowance and cut out neckline and shoulder.
11. Leaving about 1 inch, roughly cut out armhole.
12. Return muslin to form and pin down center front and shoulder.

Draping Back

1. Pin center back of muslin to the form at neckline, grain line, and lower torso.
2. Letting back fall straight down, smooth along grain line to armhole; allowing ¼ inch ease, pin along shoulder blade grain line.
3. Without disturbing the back grain, pin back and front together at side seam and armhole intersection.

4. Shape neckline and pin back shoulder over front. There will be ¼ inch ease in the back shoulder.

5. Mark: same as front of shift.

6. Remove both back and front muslin from form.

7. *True on back and front*

    a. Lower armhole for set-in sleeve (see pages 94–95, step 11-e) and extend ½ inch beyond side seam crossmark.

    b. From enlarged armhole, drop a grain line to hem.

    c. Add 1 inch flare at hem. (This is not really a flare, but necessary ease for movement.)

8. Shape armhole front and back with French curve.

9. True back neckline and shoulder.

10. Pin side seam and shoulder together.

11. Replace finished muslin on form; adjust hemline; check fit; make any necessary corrections.

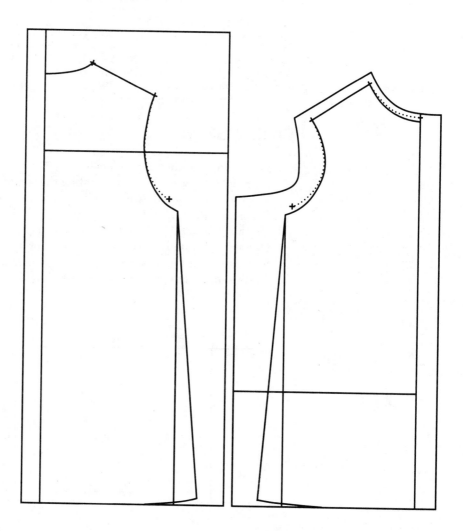

Steps 7-11

■ The Sleeve Sloper

For most designers, the most efficient method for creating a foundation pattern for a sleeve is to draft it from measurements on paper. It is possible to drape a sleeve sloper in fabric, but since most firms don't have arm forms available in all sample sizes, and since drafting a sleeve from measurements is relatively simple and accurate, drafting is the preferred method. Table 1 provides all of the measurements required to draft the sleeve sloper for various sample sizes. These measurements are *not* arm measurements. Minimum ease required for basic fit has been included.

Table I—Sleeve Measurements for Sample Sizes in Childrenswear

SIZES	12 MO	2	4	5	6	8	10	SUB-TEEN 8	10	12
Cap Height	2⅞	3¼	3½	3⅝	3⅞	4¼	4½	5¾	5⅞	6
Biceps Circumference	8½	9¼	9¾	10	10⅛	11¼	11½	11	11½	12
Underarm	6	7⅝	9½	9¾	10	13¼	13¾	15¼	15⅝	16
Wrist Circumference	6¾	7	7½	7¾	8	8¼	8½	8	8¼	8½

Drafting Sleeve

1. Fold patternmaking paper in half.
2. From fold, square a line representing the top of the sleeve.
3. Measure cap height down on fold to determine the level of the biceps.
4. Square a line from fold for biceps.
5. On this line, mark off one half of biceps measurement.
6. On fold, mark underarm length down from biceps level.
7. Square up line for wrist.
8. On this line, mark off one half of wrist measurement.

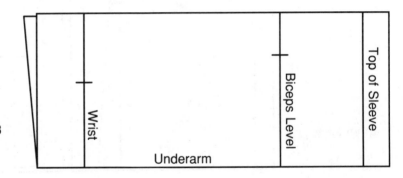

Steps 1-8

9. Connect wrist and biceps, extending line to top of sleeve.

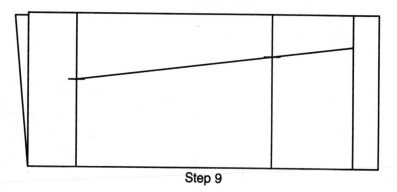

Step 9

10. Cut out sleeve.

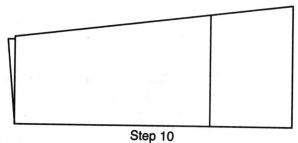

Step 10

Shaping Cap

1. Fold sleeve cap into quarters.
2. At top of cap, mark ½ inch from fold.
3. From folded intersection, mark ½ inch up toward top of sleeve.
4. At biceps level, mark 1 inch in from underarm line.
5. Connect guide points lightly.

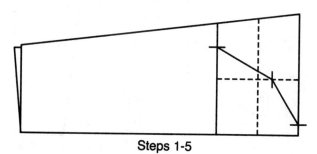

Steps 1-5

6. For final shaping, place French curve so that upper cap rounds off above guide lines.

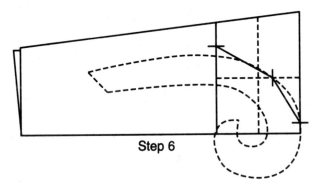

Step 6

7. To shape lower cap, trace through front armhole section from basic waist as illustrated, or use French curve.

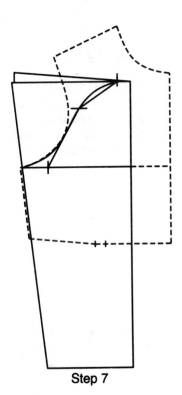

Step 7

8. Add ⅛ inch along curve of back cap for ease.

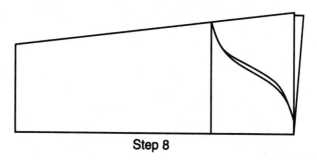

Step 8

9. Trace front of cap to other side of pattern.
10. Cut out cap.

Shaping Elbow

For most children's sleeves, a straight sloper is sufficient. When, however, a more fitted sleeve is desirable, as in a full-length dress or jacket sleeve, the elbow must be shaped and the wrist tapered.

1. Locate elbow by measuring 1 inch above the halfway point between biceps and wrist.

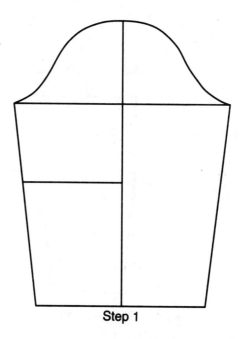

Step 1

2. Slash at elbow to center of sleeve.

3. Spread slash to a ¾ inch opening, shaping in wrist at the same time.

4. Extra fullness at elbow must be absorbed by shaping two small darts, gathers, or a tuck.

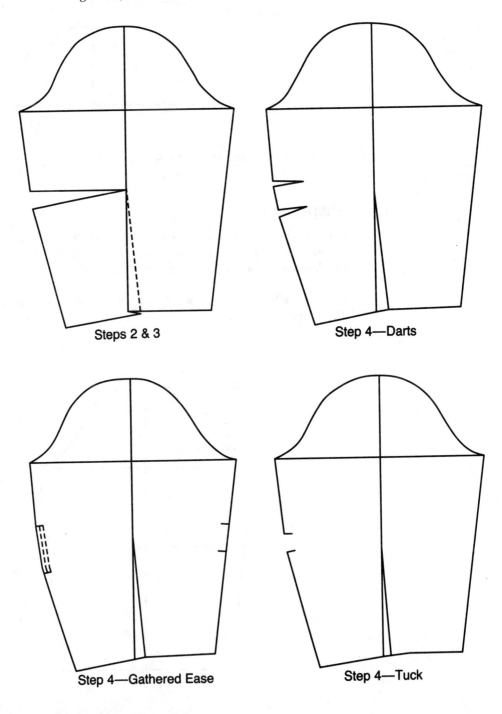

Steps 2 & 3

Step 4—Darts

Step 4—Gathered Ease

Step 4—Tuck

After the paper sleeve pattern has been completed, it should be traced to muslin and cut out with seam allowances added. The muslin sleeve is then tested for fit, as follows:

1. Run a row of machine stitching along the stitching line of the sleeve cap.
2. Pin underarm seam together.
3. Pin sleeve into armhole. There should be enough ease in the upper cap area to give the sleeve a slightly rounded look at the shoulder. (See photo on page 89.)

Sleeve Cap Adjustment

If there is too much or too little ease in the cap of the sleeve there are various ways of adjusting the relationship of sleeve to armhole. Children's basic set in sleeves require no more than ½ inch ease at the cap. Measure around the armhole and the sleeve cap, and compare both measurements. The sleeve cap should be ½ inch longer than the armhole. If the difference is slight, the armhole may be lowered somewhat to increase its measurement; or the armhole may be raised a little to reduce its measurement.

If a more considerable adjustment is necessary, the sleeve cap may be enlarged or reduced as follows:

1. Draw a vertical line for the center of the sleeve long enough to accommodate the sleeve sloper.
2. Square a line across the center of the sleeve at the biceps level.
3. Place the sleeve sloper over these lines so that the center and biceps lines are aligned.
4. Trace the sleeve sloper below the biceps level.
5. Slash the cap of the sleeve sloper down the center and along the biceps line stopping at the biceps and underarm seam intersection.
6. To enlarge the cap, spread the cap sections at the top of the sleeve as much as necessary. To reduce the cap, overlap the cap sections at the top of the sleeve. See illustrations on page 110.
7. Trace new outline of cap.

Increase Cap Fullness

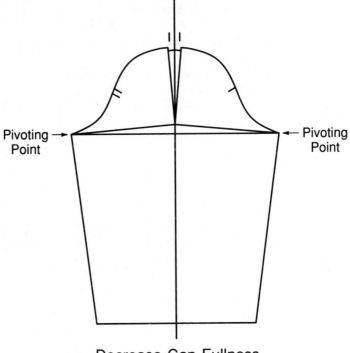

Pivoting →
Point

← Pivoting
  Point

Decrease Cap Fullness

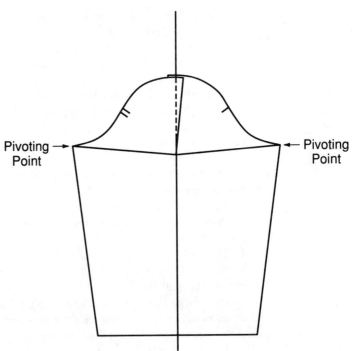

Pivoting →
Point

← Pivoting
  Point

■ Transferring Muslin Patterns to Paper

When all the foundation patterns have been completed in muslin and checked for perfect fit on the form, they are transferred to thin, flexible cardboard or plastic sheets so that they can be used repeatedly for developing other patterns.

To transfer muslin patterns:

1. Separate pattern pieces; open darts; true all corrections carefully; press flat without disturbing the grain.

2. Draw a cross-grain line across the back and front patterns at the intersection of the armhole and side seam.

3. On paper or plastic, draw two parallel lines, representing center back and center front, far enough apart so that front and back slopers can fit in between. Draw a perpendicular line between center back and center front at the level of the underarm.

4. Place muslin patterns on paper with center back, center front, and cross grain aligned. Smooth the rest of the muslin pattern into place and secure with pins or weights. Trace carefully on seam lines with the spiked tracing wheel.

5. If seam allowances are desired, add them before cutting out the basic. pattern. In the industry, most patternmakers work with seam allowances on their slopers. Many designers, however, find it easier to develop new patterns without taking seam allowances into consideration. It is perfectly acceptable to work either way. In this book, all patterns are developed from slopers without seam allowances.

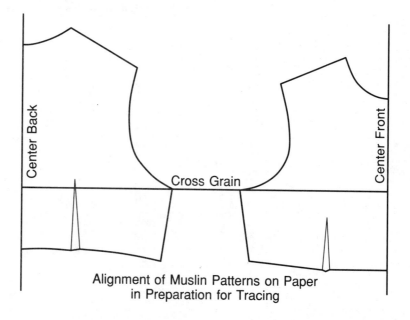

Alignment of Muslin Patterns on Paper
in Preparation for Tracing

8 Skirts

Skirts for girls are relatively simple to construct. Girls have very little hip development until they reach Sub-teen sizes, so that there is practically no difference between the waist and hip measurements. In view of the young child's anatomy, and the protruding tummy of the baby stance, the waistline of the skirt is wider at the front than at the back. Back measurements, however, increase at the buttock level, where they are equal to the front.

Children's skirts, whether they are separate or part of a dress, are usually cut with some sort of fullness for flattery. Gathers, flares, and pleats provide plenty of room for action and give shape to the silhouette of the garment. In this chapter we shall describe the development of the basic gathered and flared skirts. Pleats and pleating are discussed in Chapter 10.

■ The Gathered or Dirndl Skirt

This is the most popular skirt for children. It is the simplest to cut. Width is dictated by the design and is often influenced by the width of the fabric. When the fabric is wide enough for the front or the back of the skirt width desired, the skirt is cut in two rectangular pieces joined with side seams.

Example: All-around width desired—80 inches; width of fabric—45 inches.

When the fabric is not wide enough to cut the skirt in two pieces, the skirt is cut in three pieces with a seam at each side of the front and at center back. It is usually desirable to avoid a seam at center front.

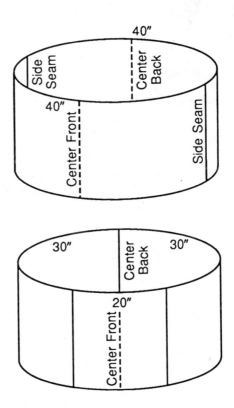

Example: All-around width desired—80 inches; width of fabric—36 inches.

The all-around width (or sweep) of a gathered skirt can range from a relatively narrow 55 inches to a full 105 inches, which is a skirt with three full widths of 36-inch fabric. When full dirndl skirts are in fashion, they are best supported with crisp petticoats to make them stand out. Since it may be difficult to gather a very full skirt, the fabric may be taken in at the waistline with small overlapping unpressed pleats.

In production, skirts are gathered with special sewing machine attachments that are set to take in fullness at a pre-determined ratio such as: 2 to 1, 2½ to 1, or 3 to 1.

Example: Waistline 24 inches, at 2 to 1 ratio = 48 inch skirt sweep.
Waistline 24 inches, at 2½ to 1 ratio = 60 inch skirt sweep.
Waistline 24 inches, at 3 to 1 ratio = 72 inch skirt sweep.

When figuring out the length of the skirt, decide on the finished length, add desired hem + ½ inch for seam allowance at the waistline.

Example: Finished length	12"
Hem and turn-in	4½"
Seam allowance at waistline	½"
Cut length of skirt	17"

Straight gathered skirts look best when they have 3- to 4-inch hems. For sheer party dresses, very deep hems of from 5 to 6 inches are used. On the other hand, some manufacturers turning out budget dresses save fabric by using only 1- to 2-inch hems.

■ The Flared Skirt

A flared skirt can vary in width from the controlled A-line to the full circle.

The A-line skirt is slightly flared at the sides and mostly suitable for sportswear and tailored dresses. Fabric for this skirt should be firmly woven or backed for shape retention.

To draft an A-line or moderately flared skirt:

1. Determine waistline measurement and sweep desired.
2. On a large sheet of paper, draw line for center front.
3. Square across one-quarter of the waistline measurement; add ¼ inch for A-line, ½ inch for moderately flared skirt.
4. On center front line, measure down the length of the skirt.

5. Square across one-eighth of sweep at hem level (one eighth of 40 inch sweep = 5 inches).

6. Place L-square so that shorter end rests on the 5-inch mark on the paper, and long end rests against the end of waistline (see illustration).

7. Mark length of skirt at long end of L-square, and draw side seam and guideline for hem.

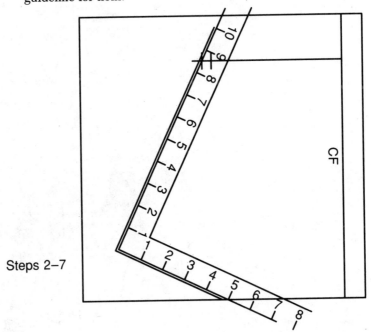

Steps 2–7

8. Reverse L-square, and square a line down to meet the waistline.

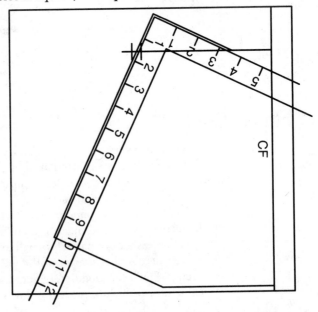

Step 8

9. Round out waistline and hem as illustrated. Check waistline measurement to make sure that it still equals one-quarter of the waist circumference. Make any necessary adjustments by raising or lowering the waistline.

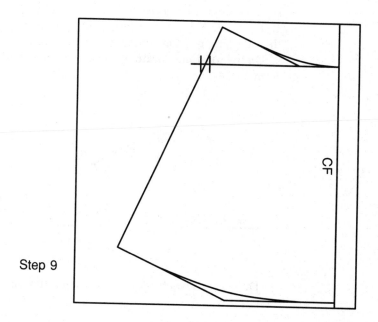

Step 9

10. To flatten flares at center front, raise waistline approximately ¼ inch as illustrated.

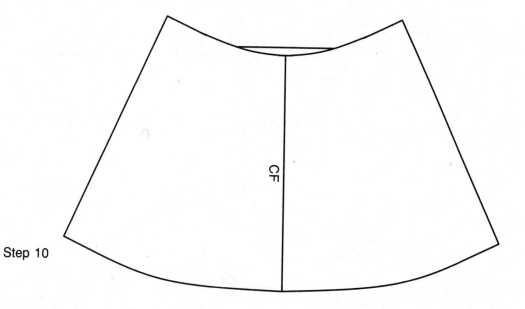

Step 10

Flared skirts usually have 1- to 2-inch hems, depending on the amount of flare in the skirt. The more circular a skirt becomes, the more difficult it is to handle a deep hem. Therefore, even ¼-inch hems are not uncommon on full circle skirts.

Once the basic width of the finished skirt has been established, the skirt can be divided into gores as follows:

1. Place skirt pattern on a large, flat surface and, with a yardstick, locate the vanishing point of center front and side seam.

2. On the waistline, locate the desired point for the placement of the gore seam.

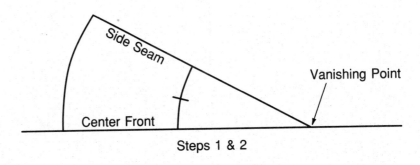

Steps 1 & 2

3. Draw gore seam from vanishing point through waistline mark to hem.

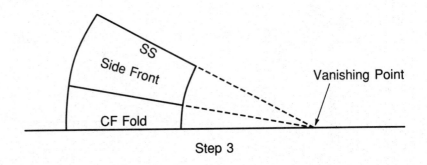

Step 3

This method can also be used to design and place pockets in proportion to the shape of a flared skirt.

Placement of Pockets in
Flared Skirts

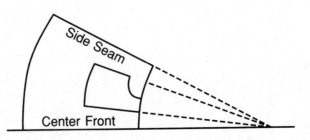

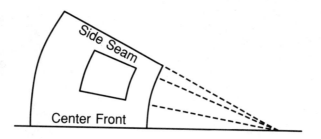

Placement of Pockets in
Flared Skirts

■ The Full Circle Skirt

A full circle skirt is developed by using a formula to determine the radius of the waistline.

1. The formula is:

$$\frac{WL - 1''}{6} = R$$

Example:

Waistline $= 22''$
$22'' - 1'' = 21''$
$21'' \div 6'' = 3\frac{1}{2}''$

Radius for waistline $= 3\frac{1}{2}''$

2. Using radius determined in step 1, draw circle for waistline on paper folded in fourths as illustrated.

3. From waistline, measure the desired length. This indicates the hemline.

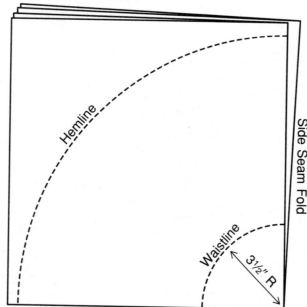

Steps 2 & 3

Table II—Slacks Measurements for Sample Sizes in Childrenswear

SIZES		2	4	5	8	10	SUB-TEEN 12
Waist Circumference Measurements	Front	5½	6	6⅛	6¼	6½	6¾
	Back	5	5½	5½	5¾	6	6¼
Hip Circumference Measurements	Front	5¾	6¼	6½	7	7¾	8¾
	Back	6	6½	6½	7½	8	9
Distance from Waist to Hip Level		3	3¼	3⅜	4	4¼	6
Crotch Level (1″ Ease)		7	8¼	8½	10½	11¼	11¼
Side Seam		17½	22	24	32	33¾	36
Inseam		10¾	14	15¾	21¾	23	25
Dart Placement	From CB at WL		2½	2½	2⅞	3	3
	Length		3	3	4⅛	4¼	5

9 Slacks

Slacks or trousers in one form or another are worn almost constantly by most children. Overalls, jeans, and shorts are worn for play. Neat slacks and jeans are also worn to school by both girls and boys. Party slacks, pantsuits, and jumpsuits are made in velvet and other luxurious fabrics for special occasions. Late in the day, children lounge, watch TV, and go to sleep in many types of pajamas.

We shall present here the basic drafting method for slacks patterns. Adjustments for infants' wear, sleepwear, and boys' wear, etc., will be covered in Part 3 of this book.

The essential measurements for drafting a slacks pattern are:

1. *Waistline Circumference*
    a. Front—from center front to side seam.
    b. Back—from center back to side seam.
2. *Hip Circumference*

This is measured at the widest part of the body below the waist—usually the outer curve of the buttocks.

    a. Front—from the center front to side seam + ¼ inch for ease.
    b. Back—from center back to side seam + ¼ inch for ease. The distance from the waist to the hip level varies according to the size range (see Table II on page 120). The back hipline measurement is usually wider than the front hipline.

3. *Crotch or Seat Level*

This is the measurement from the waist to the chair when the model is seated. One inch to 2½ inches of ease, depending on the size range and the fit desired, are usually added. The fuller the slacks, the lower the crotch. The tighter the slacks, the higher the crotch.

4. *Side Seam*

The measurement from waistline to ankle or top of shoe, whichever is preferred for the length of the slacks.

5. *Inseam*

The measurement from the crotch to the ankle or top of the shoe. The crotch level should equal the difference between the side seam and the inseam measurements plus ¼ inch.

To draft a basic slacks pattern:

1. On a large piece of paper, draw a vertical guideline.
2. On this line, mark off waistline, crotch level, and ankle.
3. Square lines across at waistline, crotch, and ankle.
4. On crotch line, mark front and back hip-circumference measurements.
5. Square guidelines up towards waistline for center back and center front.
6. Place a mark ½ inch in on waistline at center back, and ¼ inch in on waistline at center front.
7. Extend one half of back-hip measurement on crotch line.
8. Divide this extention in half, and connect the halfway mark with the point ½ inch in from the center-back guideline at the waistline. Extend the line ½ inch above waistline, and square toward the waistline as illustrated.
9. Extend one quarter of the front-hip measurement on crotch line.
10. Round out both crotch extensions with the French curve. Connect center front line to the mark ¼ inch in from the guideline at the waistline.
11. At front, square a guideline from the original hip measurement to the ankle.
12. At back, square a guideline from the halfway mark on the extension to the ankle.
13. Connect inseam line from the extension at front and back to the guideline at the ankle. Square inseam corner toward ankle line.
14. To shape the side seam, draw another guideline ½ inch toward back at ankle level, from waistline to ankle. At ankle, mark ½ inch at both sides of new guideline for the side seam. Shape both side-seam lines to meet at crotch level. This ½-inch shaping is for classic slacks; for tapered slacks, this measurement is increased. When the side seam is tapered, the inseam must also be tapered for balance.
15. The side seam need not be shaped at the waistline for Toddler sizes. For 3-6x, mark ¼ inch at each side of the side seam at the waistline, and connect to the side seam with the flat end of the French curve. For 7–14 and Sub-teen sizes, mark ½ inch at each side of the waistline, and connect to side seam as above.

16. Establish the grain line by squaring a line from the crotch line on the front. Match the side seams of both front and back from the crotch line down, and trace the front grain line to the back.

17. Compare the waistline on the pattern with waistline measurements. In most cases, there will be no need for any darts at the front. In the back, excess fullness may be shaped in with a dart or held in with an elastic waistband. For the smaller sizes, the back waist is almost always elasticized for better fit. See Table II for placement and length of the back dart. The direction of the dart should be in harmony with the center-back seam.

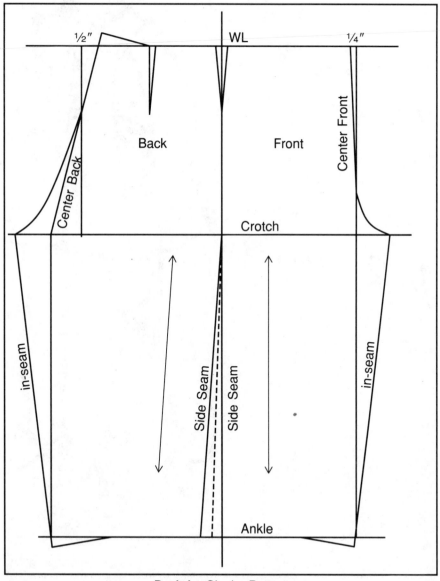

Draft for Slacks Pattern

10 Design Features

When the foundation patterns of Chapter 7 have been completed, they serve as a starting point for the development of patterns for most other apparel in childrenswear. In this chapter we will explore the drafting methods for the basic silhouettes and design features that are characteristic of children's apparel.

■ The Princess

Step 1

The seam-fitted princess garment is a classic in childrenswear. It is used in all types of apparel and for all size ranges. There are princess dresses and coats ranging from Infants' to Sub-teen sizes. Princess lines fit tennis dresses and bathing suits as well as jackets and robes.

The typical princess silhouette is fitted throughout the waist and has a flared skirt. The skirt width can vary from a modified A-line to a full circular flare. The position of the grain is crucial in developing a princess pattern. The grain must be perfectly straight in every major pattern piece, with cross grain straight at the waistline, across the chest, and at the hip level.

To draft the princess pattern:

1. Pin front and back of traced basic waist sloper on form and draw style lines as illustrated. Princess-seam style lines should pass over, or be no more than ½ inch away from the apex of the waist line dart. The style lines of the back waist should harmonize with the front. Back and front princess seams terminating at the shoulder seam should meet. If seams extend into the armhole, they should be at the same level.

2. Remove slopers from form and indicate three crossmarks, notches for matching seams, along the front princess line, and two crossmarks along the back princess line.

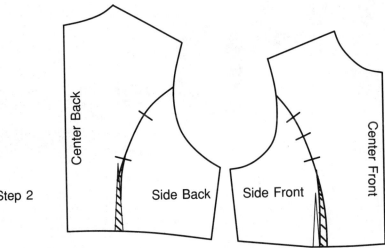

Step 2

3. Separate center front and back from side sections. Cut away dart, shifting dart to conform to princess line where necessary.

4. Working on a large piece of paper, draw line for center front.

5. Square line for waistline cross grain, from center front across the entire width of the paper.

6. Place center front panel on paper as illustrated, and trace.

7. From princess-seam and waistline intersection, extend grain line to hem level.

8. Add desired flare at hem level, and connect with princess-seam at waistline. If point develops at waistline, smooth it into a curve.

9. Place side front panel so that the waistline rests against indicated grain line on paper, and trace. Allow enough space for skirt flare.

10. Draw parallel grain lines from waistline to hem level at princess-seam and side seam.

11. Add flare to each side. Flare at the princess-seam of the side front panel must be equal to the flare at the princess-seam of the center front panel so that the seam will be balanced. Side seam flare need not equal princess-seam flare, but both sides of a single seam must be identical to assure straight position of the seams on the finished garment.

12. Place side back and center back along waistline, following the same procedure as for front panels.

13. Adjust length at all flares. The length from waistline to hem at flares should equal the length from waistline to hem at center front. Square off hemline at princess seams and blend using the French curve. Add hem and seam allowances.

14. Cut out pattern. Be sure that all notches for matching seams are clearly marked.

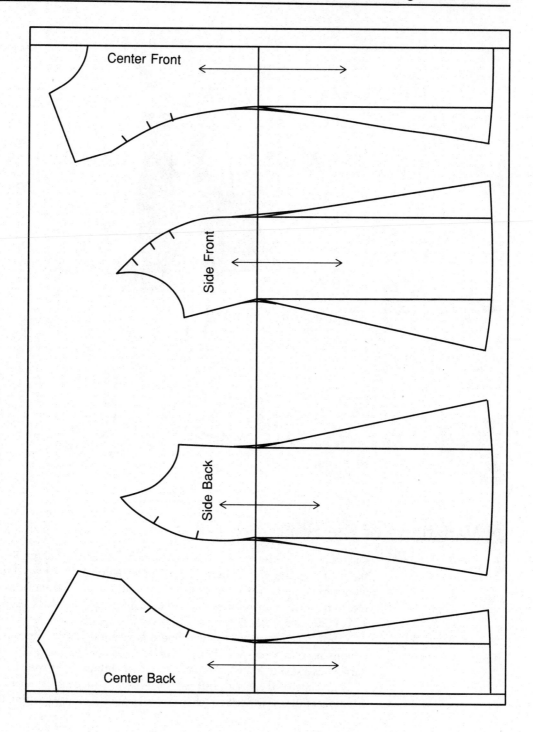

Steps 3–12

■ Variations of the Shift

Of all the silhouettes for children's dresses, the shift most naturally follows the shape of the child's body. The comfortable, easy-fitting shift dress allows freedom of movement for active children. Its simple lines do not interfere with embroideries and other trimmings, and it is used for all sorts of dresses, from beachwear to party clothes.

Fabrics used for shift dresses should have some body. The usual crisp cottons or firm wool-type fabrics are fine. Sheers or laces, suitable for party dresses, should be backed in order to maintain the shape of the shift.

The shape of the basic shift can be varied as follows. If not too much additional fullness is desired, changes can be achieved by shaping the side seam.

To Draft a Shaped A-Line Shift:

Indent side seam at waistline, and add up to 2 inches of flare at the hem level.

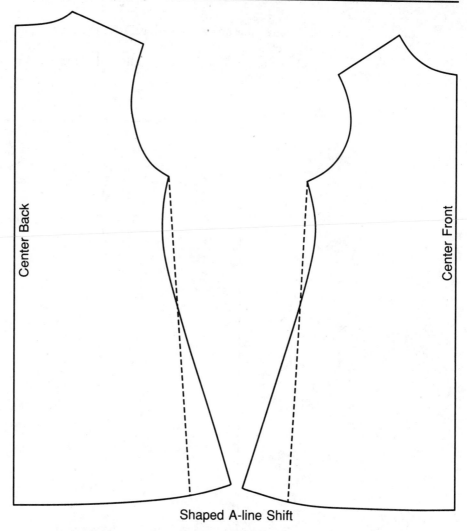

Shaped A-line Shift

To Draft a Full, Tent Shaped Shift:
1. Mark off lower third of armhole on shift sloper (front and back).

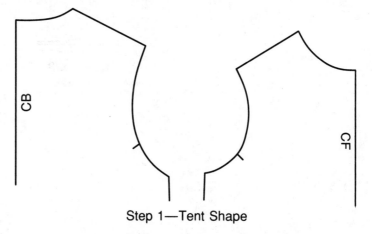

Step 1—Tent Shape

2. Place sloper on paper, and mark ¼ inch above armhole and side-seam intersection.

3. Trace center front, hem, neckline, shoulder, and upper two thirds of armhole.

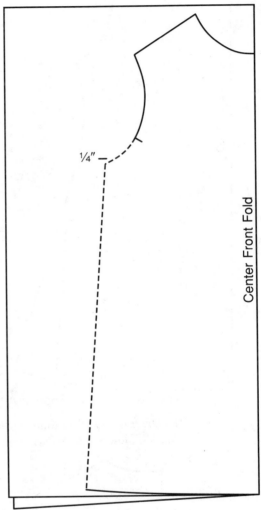

Steps 2 & 3—Tent Shape

4. Using mark on armhole as pivot point, shift armhole and side seam intersection to ¼-inch mark on paper.
5. Trace lower third of armhole and side seam.
6. Up to 2 inches of additional fullness may be added at side seam if desired.

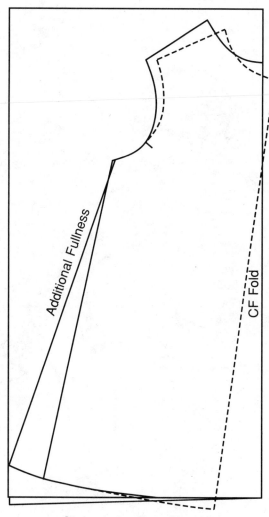

Steps 4–6—Tent Shape

■ Sleeve Variations

Since sleeves lend themselves to a variety of treatments, they are frequently the focal point of a child's garment. Sleeves can be narrow and small, or full and wide. Often they are made of contrasting fabric or adorned with trimming.

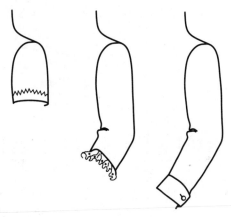

Straight Sleeves

Straight sleeves, based on the basic sloper, can be cut at various lengths ranging from short to three-quarter and wrist-length sleeves.

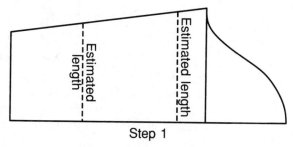

Step 1

To draft variations of the straight sleeve:
1. Estimate the length on the sleeve sloper.
2. Add hem or cuff and cut.

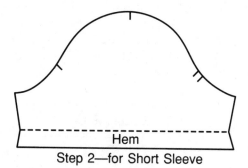

Step 2—for Short Sleeve

Very Short Straight Sleeve

For a very short straight sleeve, some of the fullness at the biceps of the sleeve sloper should be eliminated.

To draft the very short straight sleeve:
1. Mark length of sleeve at center fold of sloper. Sleeve length should be at least ½ inch at the underarm.

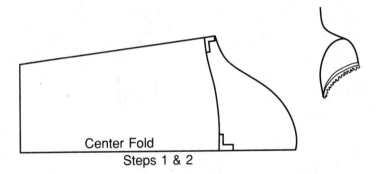

Center Fold
Steps 1 & 2

2. To draw the lower edge of the sleeve, square off 1 inch from center-fold mark and 1 inch from underarm mark on the sleeve sloper. Connect with a shallow curved line.

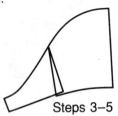

Steps 3–5

3. Cut out sleeve.
4. Slash sleeve halfway between center fold and underarm.
5. Overlap ¼ inch at lower edge. Since the lower edge will curve, it needs a facing, or the sleeve should be lined.

The Shirtwaist Sleeve

The shirtwaist sleeve is very effective for childrenswear. Basically a straight sleeve, it has enough fullness to permit easy movement. At the wrist, the extra fullness is gathered or pleated into a cuff. The sleeve cap is flattened, and almost all the extra ease is eliminated at the top of the sleeve.

To draft a shirtwaist sleeve:
1. Fold paper in half.

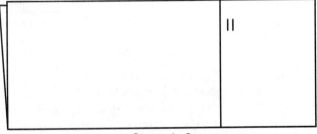

Steps 1–3

2. Square biceps line from fold.

3. Place a short guideline ¼ inch above biceps and another line ¼ inch above this first guideline. The sleeve cap will be flattened ½ inch for this sleeve. This is an arbitrary measurement that may be varied slightly according to the effect desired.

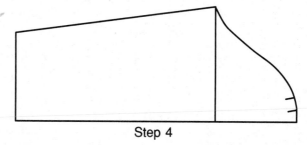

Step 4

4. Mark off two ½-inch spaces from center of sleeve cap at the top edge of the folded sloper.

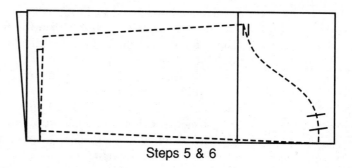

Steps 5 & 6

5. Place sloper on folded paper and trace cap to first ½-inch mark. Trace wrist.

6. Using the first mark as pivot point, swing biceps of sloper to the first ¼-inch guideline on paper.

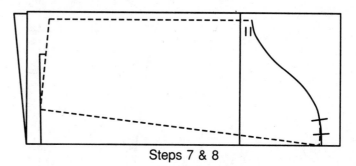

Steps 7 & 8

7. Trace cap to second ½-inch mark and pivot, using second mark as the pivot point, so that the biceps of the sloper is in line with the second ¼-inch guideline on paper.

8. Trace rest of sleeve cap. Measure cap. Compare to armhole measurement; sleeve cap should be ½ inch longer than armhole. (If cap is too large, or too small, adjust as indicated on page 110.)

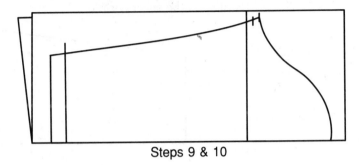

Steps 9 & 10

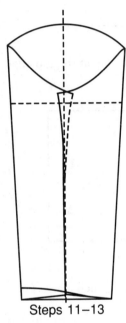

Steps 11–13

9. Connect underarm from biceps to wrist level, allowing for desired width of sleeve at wrist. When wrist is narrower than biceps, the underarm seam should be curved as illustrated.

10. Shorten sleeve ¾ inch less than the finished width of the cuff. (Example: for a 2-inch cuff, the sleeve should be shortened 1¼ inches.)

11. Cut out sleeve.

12. Fold sleeve in quarters as illustrated. When underarm seam is curved, seam will overlap at biceps.

13. Mark up ½ inch on front fold from wrist. Square a 1-inch line across; mark 1 inch from fold on back wrist. Complete wrist by connecting markings and blending into a shallow S-curve.

14. Cut out finished wrist.

15. Open sleeve, marking up 2½ inches at back sleeve fold for a placket opening.

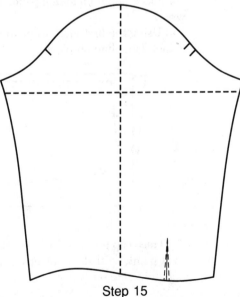

Step 15

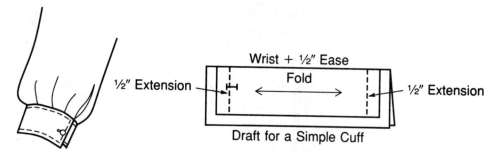

Draft for a Simple Cuff

Cuffs

Simple cuffs should be planned with ½ inch ease at the wrist plus button extensions, and grain running crosswise.

French cuffs fold up and should measure double the width of the simple cuff.

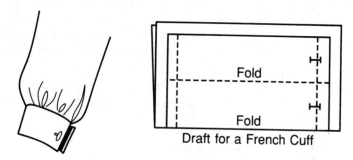

Draft for a French Cuff

The Bishop Sleeve

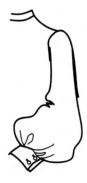

The bishop sleeve is similar to the shirtwaist sleeve, but the cap is not flattened, and there is more fullness in the lower part of the sleeve.

To draft a bishop sleeve:

1. Divide cap of sleeve sloper into three equal sections; divide wrist also into three equal sections.
2. Fold paper in half.
3. Place sloper on folded paper as illustrated.

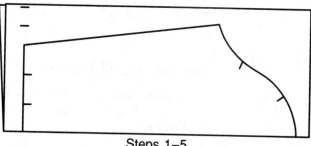

Steps 1–5

4. At wrist level, on paper, mark desired width of lower sleeve.

5. Place another mark halfway between sloper and desired width at wrist.

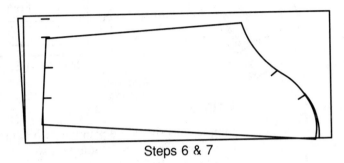

Steps 6 & 7

6. Beginning at center fold, trace first third of sleeve cap; trace first third of wrist.

7. Using first mark on sleeve cap as pivot point, swing out lower sleeve so that the underarm and wrist intersection touches the halfway mark on paper.

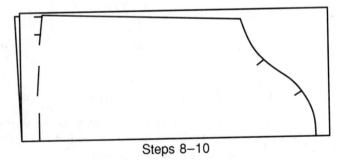

Steps 8–10

Step 12

8. Trace middle section of cap and wrist.

9. Pivot from second mark on cap so that underarm and wrist intersection touches desired width of sleeve.

10. Trace last third of cap, entire underarm, and last third of wrist.

11. Connect wrist sections.

12. Follow directions for shirtwaist sleeve to finish lower edge and cuff. (For more puffy fullness, allow 1½ inches additional length at back of sleeve.)

The Baby Doll Sleeve

The baby doll sleeve is a short version of the bishop sleeve. It is used on dresses as well as blouses and gives the effect of a soft puff with a smooth shoulder line.

To draft a baby doll sleeve:

1. Mark off desired length of sleeve on sloper.

2. Follow directions for bishop sleeve (see pages 137–138). Since this sleeve usually ends above the elbow, there is no need for special shaping of lower edge.

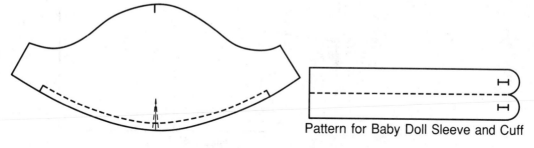

Pattern for Baby Doll Sleeve and Cuff

The Flared or Bell Sleeve

The flared or bell sleeve is drafted using the same method as for a baby doll sleeve. Gathers and cuff are eliminated.

The Puffed Sleeve

For years, the sleeve most closely identified with childrenswear has been the puffed sleeve. There are two basic types of puffed sleeves: the peasant puff, which may be constructed in any length or width; and the short baby puff, which needs no elastic or tight cuff to support it.

To draft a peasant puff sleeve:

1. Estimate length and width of desired sleeve. Sheer, soft fabrics need more width.

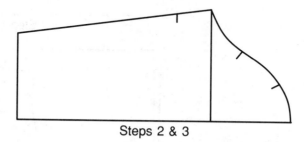

Steps 2 & 3

2. Mark off desired length at underarm of sleeve sloper. Sleeve may be short, three-quarter, or full length.

3. Divide cap of sleeve sloper into three equal sections.

4. Fold paper and square biceps line from fold.

5. At biceps, mark off half of the estimated width of the sleeve.

6. Place sleeve sloper on paper and mark off half the distance between sloper and estimated width on biceps line.

7. Trace first third of cap.

Step 1

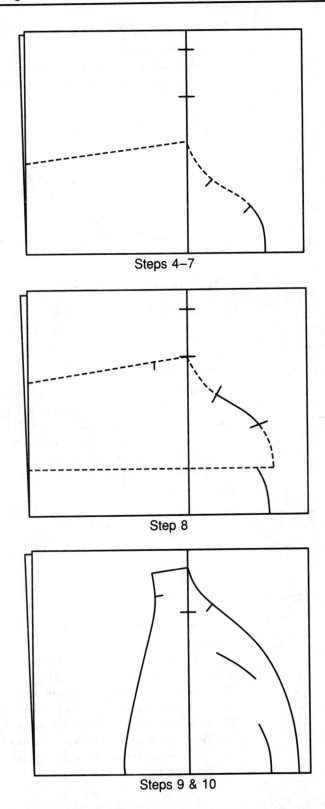

Steps 4–7

Step 8

Steps 9 & 10

8. Shift sleeve sloper along biceps to first mark; trace second third of cap.

9. Shift sleeve sloper along biceps to last mark; trace the rest of cap and underarm; and square a 1-inch line from underarm for lower edge of sleeve.

10. Taking into consideration the measurement estimated as the overall desired length of the puffed sleeve, add height at the cap and lower the bottom edge as illustrated. This will cause the sleeve to puff up at the cap and puff out at the lower edge when the cap and the lower edge are gathered to fit armhole and cuff. Lower edge may also be elasticized to fit the arm.

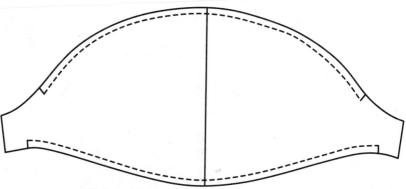

Finished Pattern for Peasant Puff Sleeve

The Short Baby Puff

The short baby puff is typically associated with baby clothes and toddler wear. It is very short and perky without causing any pressure against the upper arm. It is usually finished with a French piping or a narrow cuff.

To draft a short baby puff sleeve:

1. Estimate length and width of puff sleeve same as for peasant sleeve. (Length may be approximately 6 inches for a size four; 7 inches for a size 10.) Underarm should be no longer than 1 inch finished. (Width may be approximately 18 inches for a size 4; 20 inches for a size 10.)

2. Divide top of sleeve sloper into three equal sections.

3. Fold paper and square biceps line from fold.

4. At biceps, mark off half the estimated width of sleeve plus 1 inch.

5. Place sleeve sloper on paper, matching biceps line, and trace first third of cap.

6. On biceps line, mark off half the distance between end of sloper and indicated mark for the width of the sleeve.

7. Shift sleeve sloper to halfway mark along biceps, and trace second third of cap.

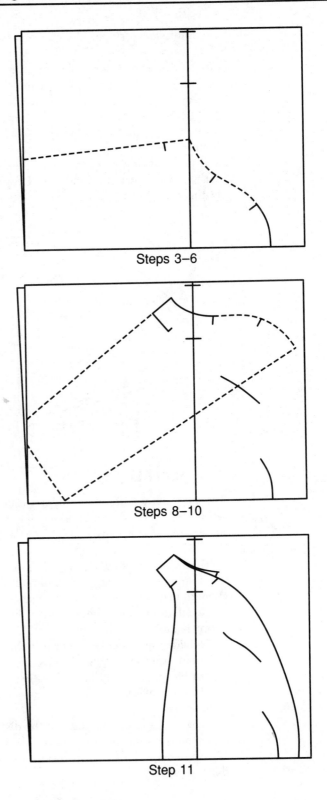

Steps 3–6

Steps 8–10

Step 11

8. Shift sleeve sloper along biceps to the full width of the sleeve. Using the last third mark on the sloper as a pivot point, drop the sloper 1 inch below the biceps line at the intersection of cap and underarm.

9. Trace the last third of sleeve cap and 1 inch of underarm seam.

10. Square 1 inch in from underarm seam for lower edge of sleeve.

11. Using estimated desired length as a guide, shape the cap above guidelines and the lower edge of sleeve as illustrated.

The Kimono Sleeve

Cut in one piece with the bodice, the kimono sleeve is a simple method of adding sleeves to a child's garment. The cap sleeve is a short version of the kimono sleeve.

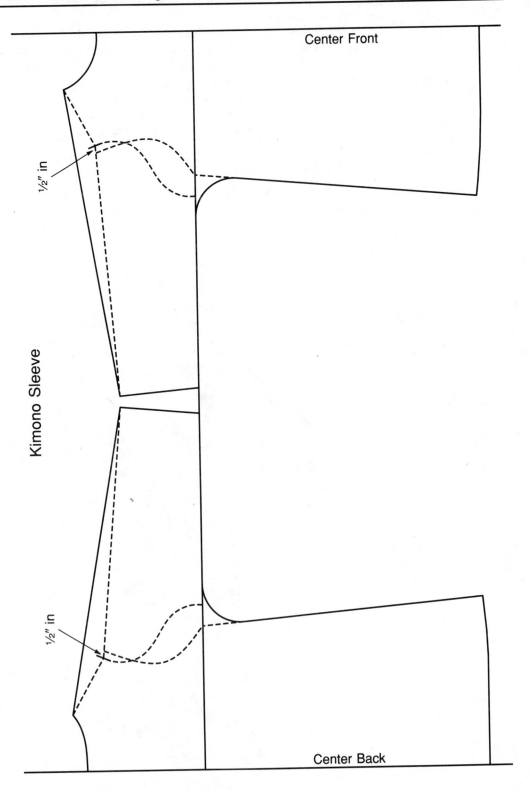

Center Front

½" in

Kimono Sleeve

½" in

Center Back

A longer kimono sleeve must fit loosely at the armhole in order to be comfortable; therefore, it is not recommended when a smooth, close fit is desired. The kimono sleeve works well for infants' gowns, knitted garments such as sweaters and T-shirts, sleepwear, and robes.

To draft kimono sleeve:
1. Trace front and back shift slopers as illustrated on page 144.
2. Extend cross-grain line at underarm.
3. Mark ½ inch on shoulder at armhole.
4. Place folded sleeve sloper so that underarm rests on grain line and top of cap touches ½-inch mark on shoulder.
5. Draw wrist of sleeve.
6. Draw shoulder seam in a straight line from neckline and shoulder intersection to wrist.
7. Draw underarm seam rounding off armpit to desired shape.
8. Shorten kimono sleeve for cap sleeve at the desired level. For a loose-fitting raglan sleeve, draw raglan seam from neckline to underarm.

The Raglan Sleeve

Raglan sleeves give a soft, rounded look to garments. Diagonal seams join the sleeves to the bodice. These seams may be straight or curved, depending on the effect desired.

In sportswear, the raglan sleeve is often used for sweat shirts and jackets.

To draft a raglan sleeve:

1. Trace front, back, and sleeve sloper on a large piece of paper as illustrated.

2. Place crossmarks at lower third of sleeve cap on sleeve sloper.

3. Transfer sleeve cap crossmarks to lower armhole on front and back sloper.

4. Draw a guideline ½ inch above sleeve cap crossmarks. Extend this line beyond the sleeve sloper at each side.

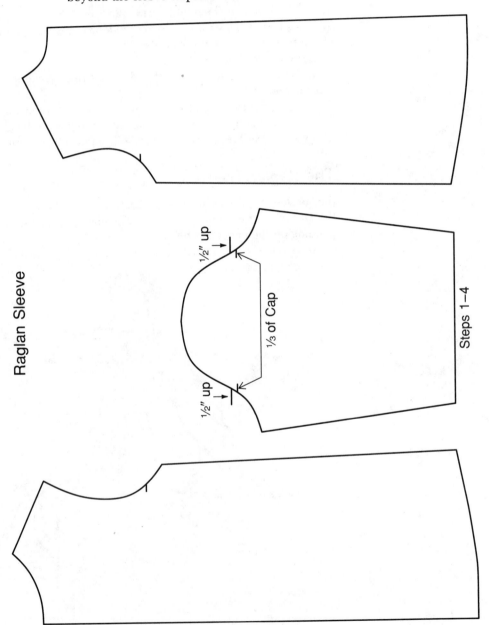

Raglan Sleeve

Steps 1–4

5. Draw a style line for the raglan seam from armhole crossmarks to neckline on front and back sloper as desired.

6. Cut on style line and place front and back shoulder sections on top of sleeve, so that shoulder seams meet at the neckline and are spread 1 inch apart at the armhole. Shoulder sections should touch the guideline, which was drawn ½ inch above sleeve cap crossmarks. Trace outline of shoulder sections.

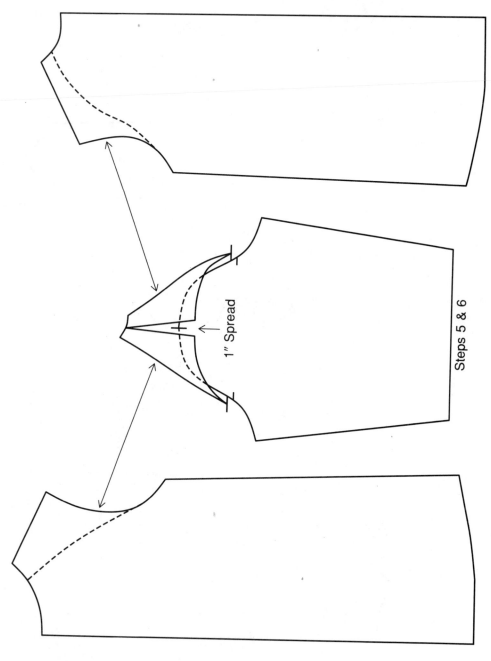

7. Raise sleeve at underarm ½ inch and draw lower third of sleeve cap as illustrated.

8. Blend armhole and sleeve cap lines into smooth curves.

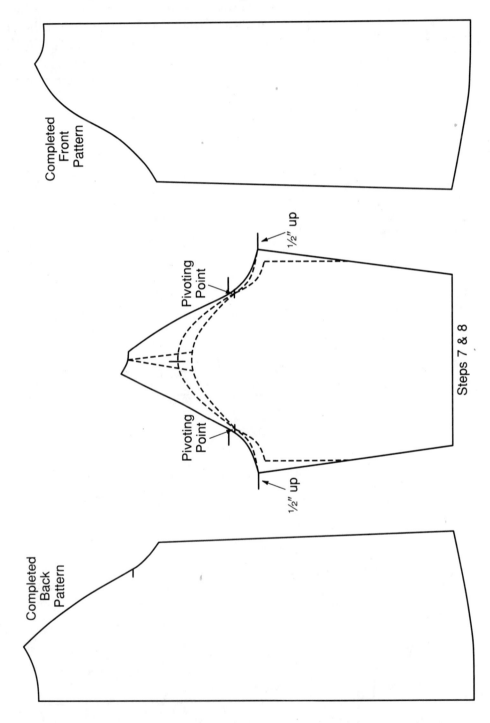

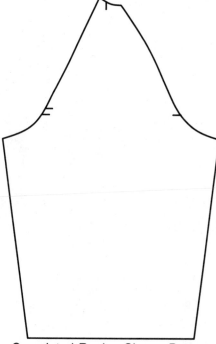

Completed Raglan Sleeve Pattern

■ Collars

Almost all children's dresses, blouses, jackets, and coats are designed with some sort of collar. There are several reasons for this. To begin with, the collar draws attention to the face. In a way, it provides a frame that sets off the child's features to best advantage. By their teens, women use make-up to highlight their features or brighten a dull complexion, but for children, this is considered in bad taste. Women may also use jewelry to transform a simple neckline. For children, collars must be designed so that they convey the flattery provided by jewelry and cosmetics.

Children's apparel of subdued or dark colors would be quite dreary if it were not for that touch of brightness near the face, often supplied by a contrasting collar. A crisp white collar of linen or piqué looks right on many dresses. There are other instances, however, when a collar should be cut from the same fabric as the rest of the dress so as not to detract from other focal points of design.

Collars are often trimmed with lace, embroidery, contrasting piping, or braid. Collars may be big like a Bertha or minute like a mandarin. They may stand high at the neck or lie flat on the shoulders. The variety is endless, limited only by the imagination of the designer. Collars fall into two basic categories—straight collars and round collars. Straight collars are drafted from measurements; round collar drafts are based on the neckline of the front and back waist sloper.

The Convertible Straight Shirt Collar

This simple collar works well on dresses and shirts. It can be worn buttoned up to the neckline or open.

To draft a convertible straight shirt collar:

1. Measure the neckline of the garment (not the dress form or the child) from center back to shoulder, and from shoulder to center front.
2. Decide on desired width of collar. (The collar will be narrower in back since almost half the width will form the height of the roll.)
3. Fold paper in half as illustrated.
4. From fold, square a line across paper for the neckline of the collar.
5. On this line, mark off the distance from center back to shoulder, and from shoulder to center front.

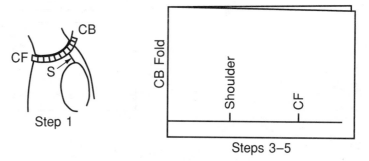

6. On center back fold, measure up from neckline the desired width of the collar.
7. Square a line from the outer edge of the collar. This will be a fold line.
8. Refold paper as illustrated.
9. Draw the front edge of the collar. A squared line will give short points to the collar. The greater the angle of the front edge, the longer the points. If the outer edge of the collar is shaped, the collar must be cut in two pieces.

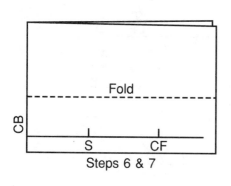

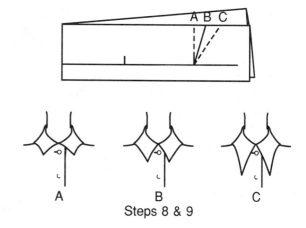

The Bias Roll Collar

This collar is similar to the shirt collar, except that it is cut on the bias grain. The back of the collar is usually split, shaped like the front, and allowed to lie flat.

When cut in one piece, the grain will not match in front.

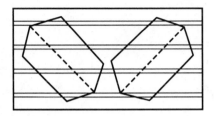

To match stripes and plaids, the collar must be cut in pairs as illustrated.

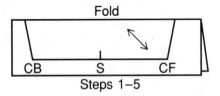

To draft the bias roll collar:

1. Fold paper in half.
2. Estimate the width of the collar. Measure width of collar from fold. Mark and draw a line for the neckline of the collar.
3. On collar neckline, indicate center back, shoulder, and center front.
4. Draw front and back edges of collar at desired angle.
5. Indicate grain line on true bias as illustrated.

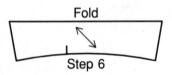

6. To make this collar conform still more to the neckline and lie a little flatter, the neck edge is curved slightly.

The Mandarin Collar

The standing mandarin collar is shaped to fit the contour of the neck. Although the traditional mandarin collar, used on authentic Chinese garments, is at least 2 inches high, mandarin collars for modern childrenswear rarely exceed 1-½ inches in height.

To draft a mandarin collar:
1. Fold paper as illustrated.
2. Square a line from fold ½ inch above the lower edge.
3. Center back is at fold. On line, mark the shoulder and center front of neckline.
4. Place a mark ½ inch above center front.

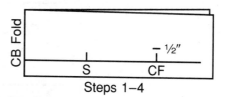

Steps 1–4

5. Blend neckline as illustrated.
6. Draw a parallel line for upper edge of collar.
7. Cut out collar pattern draft; place on the form and shape the front edge as desired.

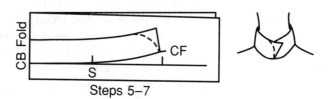

Steps 5–7

The Band Collar

The band collar fits smoothly around the neck. The opening is usually in the back. When trimmed with lace, the band collar is reminiscent of the Victorian style. When left untrimmed, the band collar is rather severe, reminding us of clerical collars.

To draft a band collar:
1. Fold paper as illustrated. The fold is center front.
2. Square a line from fold ½ inch above lower edge.
3. On this line, mark shoulder and center back.
4. Place a mark 1-½ inches above center back.
5. On line, place a mark 1 inch from center front.
6. Connect 1-inch mark with raised center back. Blend into a shallow curve as illustrated on page 154.

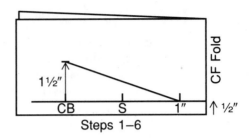

Steps 1–6

7. Square off center back from neckline.
8. Mark finished width of band and draw upper edge of collar parallel to neckline as illustrated.

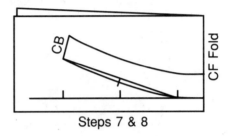

Steps 7 & 8

The Two-Piece Shirt Collar

This collar is the authentic shirt collar, and is used when a tailored effect is desired. Consisting of a band and an upper collar, it is fitted to the contour of the base of the neck. It is suitable for older girls.

To draft a two-piece shirt collar:

1. Band—Follow directions for the mandarin collar, allowing for an overlap extension at the center front. The band may be shaped so that the back of the band is a little wider than the front.

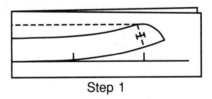

Step 1

2. Collar—
   a. Trace upper curve of band to center front.
   b. Shape collar as desired. The collar should be at least ¼ inch wider at the center back than the band.

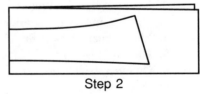

Step 2

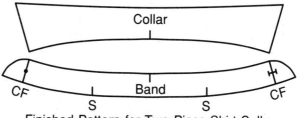

Finished Pattern for Two-Piece Shirt Collar

The Mock Shirt Collar

A simpler version of the two-piece shirt collar can be achieved by combining the band and the collar sections.

1. Trace lower edge and front extension of the band from the two-piece shirt collar.

2. Place the collar section of the two-piece shirt collar directly above the band, as illustrated. Trace outer edge of the collar. The front edges of the collar may be varied as desired.

3. Develop the under collar by making it ⅛ inch smaller at the outer edges.

Mock Shirt Collar

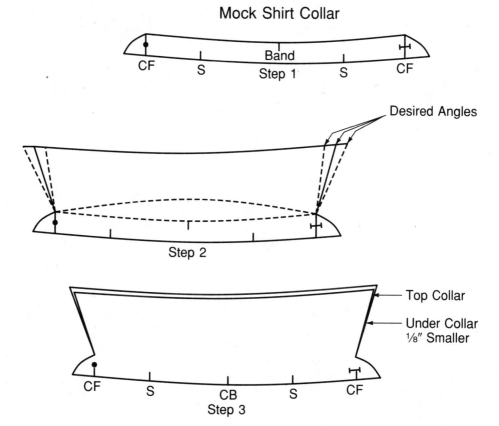

The Peter Pan Collar

By far, the most popular collar for all childrenswear is the Peter Pan collar. It curves gently around the neckline and can be finished with round or straight lines at the center front. At the center back, the collar may be split like the front to accommodate a back opening, or it may be cut in one piece.

Since the Peter Pan is a round collar, the bodice front and bodice back patterns are needed for its development.

To draft a Peter Pan collar:

1. Place front and back bodice so that shoulder seam lines meet at the neckline intersection and overlap at least ½ inch at the armhole intersection. As the overlap at the shoulder tip increases, the neckline becomes straighter. A ½ inch overlap at the shoulder tip provides a neckline curve, that results in a fairly flat collar. A 1 inch overlap will result in a slight roll. The greater the overlap at the shoulder, the straighter the neckline, and the higher the roll of the collar.

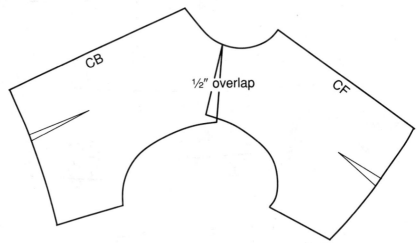

Step 1—Shoulder Overlap for a Flat Collar

2. Trace the neckline, center front, and center back of bodice patterns. Indicate width of the shoulder.

3. Shape the Peter Pan collar as desired.

4. Develop the under collar by making it ⅛ inch smaller at the outer edges.

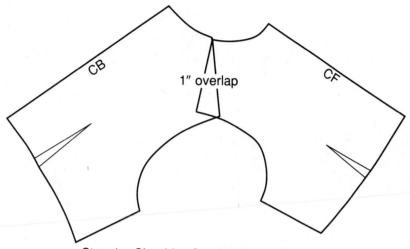

Step 1—Shoulder Overlap for a Slight Roll

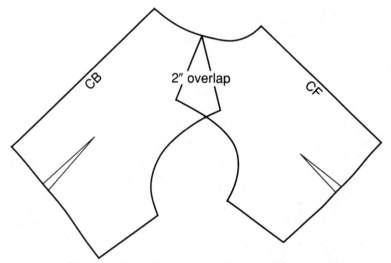

Step 1—Shoulder Overlap for a Rolled Collar

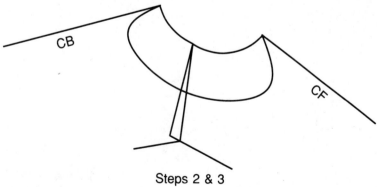

Steps 2 & 3

The Cape Collar

The Cape collar is developed by using the same method described for the Peter Pan collar above. Only the design of the outer edge is different as illustrated.

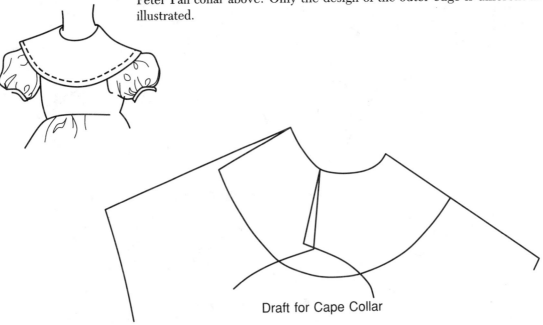

Draft for Cape Collar

The Puritan Collar

This is another collar developed by using the basic drafting techniques described for the Peter Pan collar.

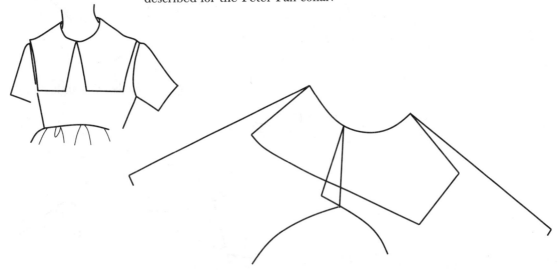

Draft for the Puritan Collar

The Sailor Collar

This classic shape is used for both boys' and girls' wear, with single or double breasting closings.

To draft a basic sailor collar:

1. Place front and back patterns together with shoulders overlapping ½ inch at armhole.

2. Measure down length of collar at center back.

3. At this point, square line across back to armhole.

4. Square line up along armhole toward shoulder.

5. Connect with center front of lowered neckline. The outer edge of the collar may have to curve in front if the neckline is not low enough. The neckline opening must be large enough for the head to go through plus ½ inch for ease.

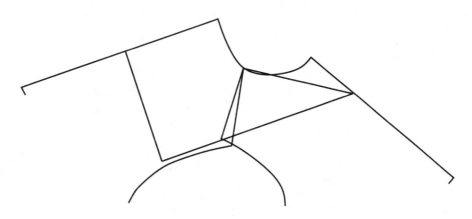

Steps 1–5

To draft a double-breasted sailor collar:

1. Outline neckline and closing on front sloper.

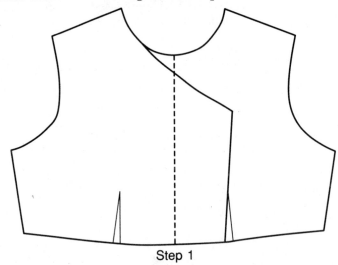

Step 1

2. Cut out front waist pattern, and place front and back together as for basic sailor collar.

3. Draw in desired shape of collar.

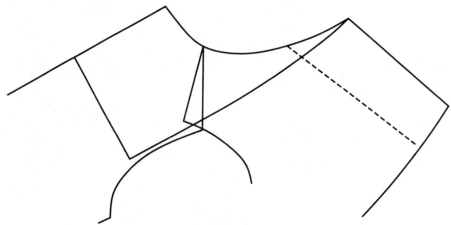

Steps 2 & 3

This method is used to draft other collars with double-breasted closings. For a higher roll, the overlap at the shoulder should increase proportionately.

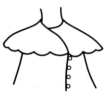

■ Style Lines and Other Design Details

Once the basic silhouette for a garment has been established, most design in childrenswear consists of adding style lines. These lines may be horizontal, vertical, or curved. The designer carefully considers the placement of style lines in order to add interest and a focal point to the garment. Seam lines for yokes and other design features must be placed in just the right proportion to the rest of the garment and to the size of the child.

To achieve the exact lines desired, trace the basic waist or shift sloper onto plain white paper. Some designers prefer marking paper for this purpose because it has crossmarks indicating grain at 1 inch intervals all over the paper. When this pattern is pinned on the model form, the designer can readily see where yokes, seams, and pockets should be.

To add style lines to a basic pattern:

1. Fold paper in half. Trace both the front and back basic patterns with center front and center back on fold.

2. Cut out paper pattern; open flat; close darts with pins.

3. Pin pattern on model form and draw in desired style lines.

4. Pockets, tabs, and all other design details that are formed of additional layers of fabric must be traced from the foundation pattern.

5. Cut the foundation pattern apart on all other seam lines; add seam allowances before cutting in fabric.

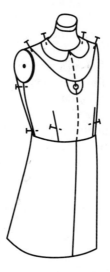

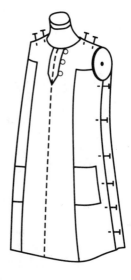

Steps 2 & 3 on Basic Waist Foundation   Steps 2 & 3 on Shift Foundation

Buttons and Buttonholes

When buttons and buttonholes or other closures are integrated into the design of the garment, the extension and the buttons should be indicated on the foundation pattern along with the other style lines. Using this procedure, one can easily determine the width of the extension, and the size and placement of the buttons. Facings are needed wherever buttons and buttonholes are used.

Gathers

Extra fullness may be added to either a basic waist or a shift by adding gathers.

To add gathers to a basic pattern:
1. Draw style lines on basic pattern as above.
2. Indicate gathers where desired.
3. Place crossmarks at seamline where gathers begin and end.
4. Cut pattern apart at seamlines.
5. Slash pattern where gathers are indicated.
6. Spread pattern to desired fullness and trace new outline.

Pleats

Fullness with a more tailored look is achieved with pleats. The fabric is folded and pressed into place, so that the effect is straight and simple when the garment is at rest. With movement, however, there is plenty of fullness and a play of pattern.

When planning an all-around pleated skirt, a good rule of thumb is to allow three times the waistline measurement for the width of the entire skirt. Each pleat will then lie smoothly at the waistline without bulky overlap. Sometimes, lightweight fabrics are planned with deeper pleats, when extra fullness is desired. On the other hand, when manufacturers are cost-conscious, they often resort to very shallow pleats. Skimpy pleats usually do not hold their shape, and the results are not satisfactory.

Most sample garments are sent out to be pleated by a professional pleater. There are, however, rare instances when the pressure of time or other considerations require hand pressing in the sample room. Stock garments are always pleated by the specialist unless the manufacturer has his own pleating plant.

To prepare a skirt for the pleater, join all but one seam and finish the hem. The pleater will want to know the finished width of the waistline, the type of pleating desired, and the width of each pleat. He will plan the pleating pattern, allowing the right amount to underlap for each pleat and, for the older girl (Sub-teen), providing the necessary shaping over the hipline so that the skirt will fall smoothly from waist to hem.

Permanent pleating, which lasts through many launderings, is achieved by pressing and heating garments made of man-made fibers to just under the melting point of the fiber, and thus molding the fiber to the shape of the pleat. This process is just as effective for textiles consisting of blends of natural and man-made fibers, such as wool and nylon, or cotton and polyester.

Following is an analysis of the pleats most often used in childrenswear:

Side Pleats

All pleats are pressed to one side, as in the traditional kilt. When pleats are no wider than 1 inch, they are often called knife pleats.

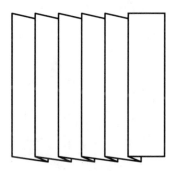

Box Pleats

Pleats are pressed in alternate directions, forming a box.

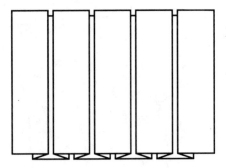

Cluster Pleats

Pleats are folded into clusters and pressed.

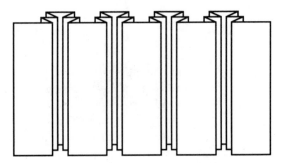

Accordian Pleats and Sunburst Pleats

These pleats both resemble the folds of an accordian.

Accordian pleats are cut on the straight grain and are the same width throughout. In childrenswear, they are used for ruffles and other trimming. Accordion pleats are rarely used for a skirt because they tend to cling too unflatteringly close to the body for children.

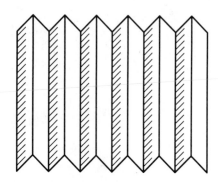

Sunburst pleats are used to pleat circular skirts. Radiating from the waistline to the hem, they increase in width in proportion to the rest of the skirt.

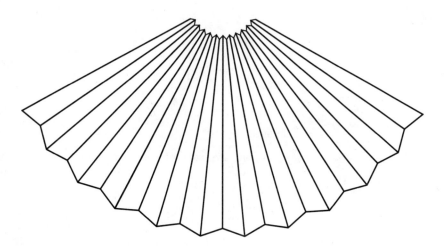

Both accordion and sunburst pleats are not suitable for hand pressing and are always done by the professional pleater. To prepare a circular skirt for the pleater; join all but one seam; let the skirt hang for one or two days so that the necessary adjustments in length can be made to compensate for stretch in the bias grain; finish hem.

Inverted Pleat

Two folds are brought together, often at the center front or center back of a garment, to give interest or room for movement.

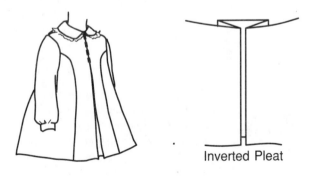

Inverted Pleat

Inverted pleats, as well as side pleats and box pleats can be used anywhere in a garment. To make the pattern, fold pleats as desired in paper,
and then place the basic pattern over the folded pleats as illustrated.

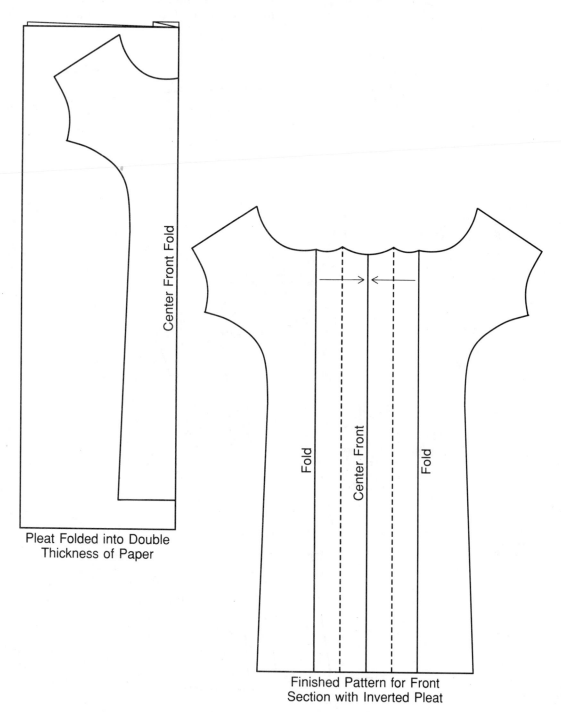

Center Front Fold

Pleat Folded into Double
Thickness of Paper

Fold

Center Front

Fold

Finished Pattern for Front
Section with Inverted Pleat

Pleated Side Panels

Follow the same directions as for inverted pleats. Although pleats pressed by hand will hold their shape better when cut with all creases on grain, it is sometimes preferable to cut pleats deeper at the hemline, following the flare of the skirt.

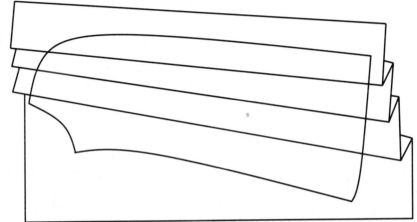

Paper Folded into Side Pleats. Pattern for Side Panel of Garment Placed Over Folded Paper.

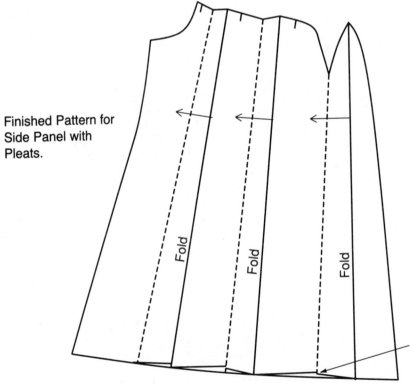

Finished Pattern for Side Panel with Pleats.

Fold

Fold

Fold

Smooth out hemline if points form at pleats.

■ Draping in Fabric

The best way to achieve the line of a new fashion is to drape and shape the fabric directly on the model form. Fabrics vary in texture: some have body and a certain amount of stiffness; others are soft and pliable. By draping, it becomes immediately obvious how much fullness is needed to achieve a certain line or where the precise placement of a styling detail should be.

To drape in fabric:

1. Cut a rectangle of fabric to the approximate dimensions of the particular piece being draped.
    a. Allow fabric for seam allowances, hems, and neckline shaping.
    b. Some facings can be cut in one piece with the garment. Allow approximately 3 inches for facings wherever needed.
    c. Allow enough material for both sides of front or back when there is no seam or closing at center back or center front.

2. Prepare fabric for draping.
    a. Block fabric by pulling grain into straight, perpendicular position where possible. There is no way of changing the alignment of grain after the finishing process for wash-and-wear or permanent press is completed; therefore, these fabrics should be cut as straight as possible, with the grain more or less ignored.
    b. Press fabric.
    c. Mark center front and center back with thread or chalk line. Stone chalk, which can be easily removed from the fabric without leaving stains, may be used for marking. Test chalk on all fabrics to make sure that no stains remain after removal.

3. Pin center front or center back to model form. Drape only on one side of the form.
4. When draping and pinning are complete, mark seam lines, darts, and pleats, etc., with chalk or pins and remove from form.
5. True all lines by connecting chalk marks or pins with thread tracing or chalk lines. Some designers merely add accurate seam allowances and cut out. To do this, one must be sure that all markings are perfect.
6. Fold on center and cut out other side, transferring any necessary markings with pins and chalk.
7. For future reference, cut a paper pattern of the draped garment before it is sewn together.

PART

3

SPECIAL PROBLEMS

11 Infants' Wear

Clothing for children during the first year of life must meet many unique requirements. Infants need body coverings that protect against extremes of temperature without causing discomfort. It is essential that all garments be easily washable at high temperature and need little or no ironing. Openings should be large enough so that changing diapers and clothing will be pleasant and not a frightening struggle for the baby.

Since the skin of infants is sensitive, fabrics used for clothing should always be soft and nonirritating. For example, scratchy organdy or coarse wool is most unsuitable. The most widely used fabrics for infants' wear are made of cotton, or blends of cotton and polyester or acrylic, either knitted or woven, but always finished so that the fabric is soft to the touch.

Modern child experts agree that, for optimum development of the infant, clothing should be constructed so that it is not restrictive. There should be plenty of room for movement, but garments should not be so large that they cause uncomfortable folds and bunches.

Certain safety factors must also be considered in designing infants' wear. Using drawstrings around the neck as a fastening is a hazard. So is the use of buttons that could be pulled off and swallowed. Instead, gripper fasteners, soft nylon zippers, or velcro provide safe and efficient closings.

■ The Basic Layette

In view of the rapid development of the infant, many garments are outgrown both physically and functionally in a relatively short time. Stretch

173

fabrics provide room for growth and extend the use of some garments. Nevertheless, the baby's first wardrobe, the layette, may be outgrown within the first three months of life. For most babies, the layette is kept simple and includes only the bare necessities for the first few months.

Absolutely essential are: diapers, shirts, and lightweight, cotton receiving blankets. In cool weather, gowns, kimonos, or stretch coveralls provide another layer of clothing. A sweater and cap with a warm blanket are needed for outdoor wear in colder weather.

Shirts

There are several types of baby shirts. For cold climates, there are double-breasted shirts that either snap or tie at the sides. Some parents prefer shirts that slip over the head. These shirts have adjustable, overlapping necklines and no fastenings to fuss with. For warm weather, there are sleeveless shirts with built up straps over the shoulders. All shirts are made of cotton knit for comfort and absorbency. Table III gives the garment measurements for infants' and children's shirts as recommended by the United States Department of Commerce. These measurements were developed for shirts of ribbed (1.1) knit cotton.

Table III
Garment Measurements for Infants' and Children's Shirts

SIZE		3 MO.	6 MO.	12 MO.	18 MO.	24 MO.	36 MO.
Width of garment:	(C–D)						
Sleeves		7	7½	7½	8	8½	9
Sleeveless		6½	7	7	7½	8	8½
Total length	(A–B)	10	11	12	14	16	17
Sleeve length:	(E–F)						
Long		7	7½	8	9	10	11
Short		2¾	3	3½	3¾	3¾	4
Armhole length:	(G–E)						
Sleeves		4	4¼	4½	4¾	5	5¼
Sleeveless		4¼	4½	4¾	5	5½	5¾
Neck opening:							
Flat		9½	10	10½	11	11½	12
Stretched		17½	18	19	19½	20	20½
Sleeveless shirt		16½	17¼	18	18¾	19½	20¼
Sleeveless shirt:							
Shoulder-strap length	(H–I)	2¾	3	3¼	3½	3¾	4
Shoulder-strap width		1¼	1¼	1¼	1¼	1¼	1¼

Method of Measuring

- Width of garment—Measured across the garment, 1 inch below the bottom of the armhole. Shirts with sleeves need ease for movement at the underarm.

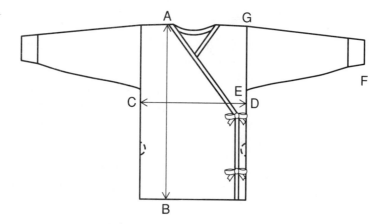

- Total length—Measured from the point where the shoulder joins the collarette or neck opening to the bottom of the shirt.
- Sleeve length—Measured in a straight line from the point under the arm where the sleeve is seamed to the garment to the lower edge of the sleeve, or sleeve cuff, if a cuff is used.
- Armhole length—Measured from the point where the sleeve is attached to the shoulder to the lowest point under the arm.
- Neck opening—pullover styles: Flat—measured by taking the circumference at the top edge with the fabric relaxed and smooth. Stretched—measured by taking the circumference of the neck at the seam with the fabric stretched.
- Sleeveless shirt—shoulder strap: Shoulder-strap length—measured from the point where the shoulder strap joins the body of the garment to the top of the strap. Shoulder-strap width—measured across the strap at the top edge of the strap.

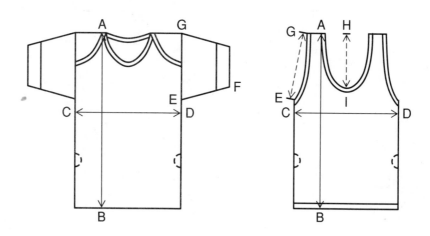

Diapers

By far, the majority of parents prefer disposable diapers. Designers are constantly improving these diapers for increased absorbency and more comfortable fit. Disposable diapers have a waterproof covering so that the need for diaper pants is eliminated. Nevertheless, some parents prefer washable fabric diapers. These are made of gauze or bird's eye cotton and are available in flat, prefolded, or fitted styles.

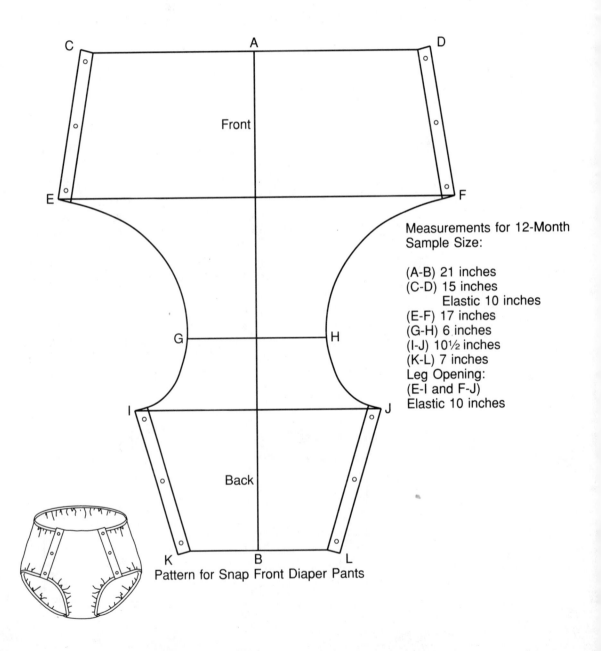

Measurements for 12-Month Sample Size:

(A-B) 21 inches
(C-D) 15 inches
      Elastic 10 inches
(E-F) 17 inches
(G-H) 6 inches
(I-J) 10½ inches
(K-L) 7 inches
Leg Opening:
(E-I and F-J)
Elastic 10 inches

Pattern for Snap Front Diaper Pants

Diaper Pants

When washable diapers are used, a waterproof covering is needed to protect bedding and other clothing. Plastic pants serve this purpose. Some diaper pants are made of knitted or woven fabric and lined with plastic. They are usually fastened with grippers at the sides so that they open flat for easy changes.

Gowns and Kimonos

These are the garments worn for sleeping, the activity infants are engaged in 80 percent of the time during the first few months of life.

Gowns are long garments with a placket opening at the neck and a drawstring or envelope fold at the bottom. Their main advantage is that they keep the baby's feet warm during cold weather.

Kimonos are also cut long, but they open all the way down the front and are easier to get in and out of.

Many gowns and kimonos are designed with raglan sleeves, a style which provides a comfortable armhole and seems to fit for a longer period of time than the set-in sleeve. Sleeves may be long or short. Long sleeves may have drawstrings or flaps covering the hands, preventing infants from scratching themselves.

Table IV gives the garment measurements for infants' size gowns and kimonos as recommended by the United States Department of Commerce. These measurements were developed for gowns and kimonos of flat knit cotton fabric.

Table IV-Garment Measurements for Gowns and Kimonos

SIZE		6 MO.	12 MO.
Width of Garment	(C–D)	12	12½
Total Length:	(A–B)		
Gowns		28	30
Kimonos		21	23
End of Sleeve to End of	(G–H)		
Sleeve Across Garment			
Open Sleeve		26	28
Closed Sleeve		30	32
Short Sleeve		18	19½
Width at Bottom:	(K–L)		
Gowns		19	20
Kimonos		16	17
Neck Opening		10	10½
Opened up		18	19
Armhole Length	(F–N)	5½	5½

Method of Measuring

- Width of garment—Measured across the garment, 1 inch below the bottom of the armholes.
- Total length—Measured from the point where the shoulder meets the neck opening to the bottom of the garment.
- End of sleeve to end of sleeve across garment—With the neck fastening closed and each sleeve fully extended as the garment lies flat, the measurement is taken from the outer end of one sleeve across the body of the garment to the outer end of the other sleeve.
- Width at the bottom—Measured between the outside edges of the extreme bottom of the garment.
- Neck opening—With neck fastening closed, measure the circumference of the neck at the top edge, with fabric relaxed and smooth.
- Armhole length—Measured from the point where the sleeve is attached at the shoulder to the lowest point under the arm.

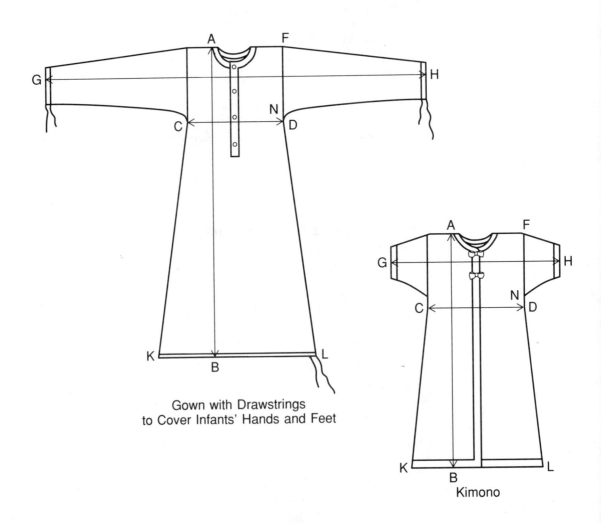

Gown with Drawstrings
to Cover Infants' Hands and Feet

Kimono

Stretch Coveralls

Stretch terry coveralls are practical garments for new babies. Made of soft, knitted terry cloth, these garments cover the baby from neck to toe and stretch a size or two so that they are comfortable and nonrestricting. They keep the infant covered without being bulky, and snap open down the front or back of the garment and along one leg for easy diaper changing access. They are usually knitted of 100 percent nylon.

Table V gives the garment measurements for nylon stretch coveralls in Infants' sizes. Since the amount of stretch in fabrics varies considerably, sample garments should be tested on babies to insure that proper fit is maintained.

Table V—Garment Measurements for Infants' Nylon Stretch Terry Coveralls

SIZE		SMALL	MEDIUM	LARGE	X LARGE
Width of Garment:		9¾	10¼	10¾	11¼
Chest	(C–D)				
Seat	(E–F)	10¼	10¾	11¼	11¾
Thigh	(G–H)	5	5¼	5½	5¾
Total Length	(A–B)	17½	20	22½	24½
Trunk Length	(A–G)	13	14½	16	17
Inseam	(G–M)	5	6	7	8
Sleeve Length:					
from center back	(N–O)	11¼	11⅞	12½	13⅛
from neck seam	(A–O)	10	10½	11	11½
Armhole Length	(J–D)	8½	9	9½	10
Sleeve Opening		5	5¼	5½	5¾
Neck Opening		10	10¼	10½	10¾
Foot Length	(P–Q)	4	4¼	4½	4¾
Foot Width	(M–R)	3	3⅛	3¼	3⅜

Method of Measuring

- Width of garment—chest—Measured across the garment, 1 inch below the bottom of the armhole.
- Width of garment—seat—Measured across the garment, 3 inches above the crotch level.
- Width of garment—thigh—Measured across the leg at the bottom of the crotch.
- Total Length—Measured from the point where the shoulder joins the neck opening to the heel of the garment with the heel extended as the foot is folded back over the ankle of the garment.
- Trunk length—Measured from the point where the shoulder joins the neck opening to the bottom of the crotch.

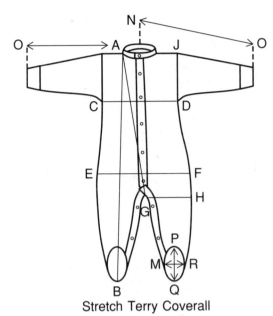

Stretch Terry Coverall

- Inseam—Measured from the bottom of the crotch along the snap opening to the sole of the foot.
- Sleeve length—from center back—Measured from center back at the neckline to the upper outside edge of the sleeve.
- Sleeve length—Neck seam—Measured from the point where neck and shoulder seams meet to the upper outside edge of the sleeve or cuff.
- Armhole length—Measured from the point where the sleeve is attached at the shoulder to the lowest point under the arm.
- Sleeve opening—Measured by taking the circumference of the sleeve at the wrist with the fabric relaxed and smooth.
- Neck opening—Measured by taking the circumference of the neckline at the seam with the fabric relaxed and smooth.
- Foot length—Measured from toe to heel at the sole of the foot with the foot laid out flat.
- Foot width—Measured across the sole at the widest point.

Since gowns, kimonos, and stretch terry coveralls are used primarily as sleepwear for babies, these items are covered by the government regulations that require all children's sleepwear to be flame resistant. Please refer to pages 210–211 for government regulations for children's sleepwear.

Sweaters and Hats

These are needed for outdoor use. Knitted or crocheted of nylon, acrylic or cotton, they should be washable, warm, and nonirritating to the baby's skin.

Bibs

Bibs are needed to protect baby's clothing at feeding time, and later when the baby is teething, to absorb some of the moisture from drooling. They are usually designed in some soft, absorbent fabric, such as terrycloth or several layers of gauze, and backed with plastic.

Other Layette Items

To complete the baby's layette, baby blankets, crib sheets, and pads are needed. Although these items do not necessarily fall into the category of clothing, they are often manufactured by the same firms that produce the shirts, gowns, and kimonos. Several large infants' wear firms produce all the above items except diapers, which are manufactured by specialists.

The designs for layette garments are fairly standard, placing emphasis on comfort and function. Modifications are usually the result of some new development in textiles or construction, which increases comfort for baby or reduces work for parents. Nevertheless, designers add appeal to layettes by working out color-coordinated groups and presenting them in attractive packages. Delicate prints are often used for kimonos, gowns, and stretch terry coveralls. Dainty or colorful appliqués, stitching, or embroidery are used for trimming rather than bunchy ruffles. A good sense of proportion is essential when designing these tiny garments. Very little else is needed to make them attractive and appealing to the consumer.

■ Clothing for the Growing Baby

After the first few months, when babies are awake for longer periods of time and become more active, their clothing requirements increase. Parents usually like to dress up their baby for company and for his daily outings, and more items are likely to be added to his wardrobe. Since these garments are often purchased as gifts, they are designed to be appealing as well as practical.

Sample size in this group is usually 12 months. Although body measurements are included in the Appendix, the foundation pattern is most easily developed on the model form (see Chapter 7). It is advisable to work with a full-length form when designing for infants, because it gives a somewhat better concept of the proportions of the infant's body.

Using a model form, however, is no substitute for the actual child. A rigid form cannot approximate the posture and flexibility of a baby. It must be remembered that, for practical reasons, the legs of the form must be straight, whereas children's legs are always bent at the knees before they learn to walk. The form is upright, suspended from a stand, but babies must be visualized lying or sitting in the crib, playpen, baby seat, or carriage.

The body shape of the infant eliminates the need for any darts. Although a waistline level is indicated with a tape on the model form, it is mainly useful for locating the upper edge of trousers. When designing dresses or toppers for infants, if a waistline is desired, it is arbitrarily placed to suit the proportions of the finished garment.

Topper Sets and Panty Dresses

Some manufacturers refer to these popular outfits for boys and girls as diaper sets. In any case, they consist of pants, long or short, and matching top. For boys, there are matching tailored shirts, and for girls, there are more feminine tops or dresses. Sometimes the dresses are paired with stretch tights. Embroidery, appliqué, and lace edgings are used for trimming, and the fabrics vary, but should meet the requirements for easy washability and comfort for the baby.

There are many variations on the topper set. For cool weather, there are knitted outfits for outdoors, consisting of leggings with feet, sweater, and hat. In summer, the topper set is often a sunsuit with a matching cover-up.

Crawlers

For the second half of the first year, the crawler becomes an important item in the baby's wardrobe. The classic crawler consists of pants with gripper fasteners along the crotch, held up with straps that button to a built-up front. These are usually worn with a long- or short-sleeved polo shirt. Sometimes, crawlers are designed as a coverall, a one-piece garment with sleeves and collar.

Fabrics for crawlers should be sturdy: denim or other firm cottons for summer and corduroy or flannel for winter. Three-piece sets, consisting of crawler with matching jacket and hat, are popular for spring and fall outdoor wear. Knitwear manufacturers also produce three-piece coordinated outfits consisting of sweater, hat, and leggings.

Patterns for Crawlers or Coveralls

Draft a basic slacks pattern (see Chapter 9). The side seam may be eliminated for infant's wear to simplify construction. The measurements necessary to draft the size 12-months crawler pattern are:

Side seam	15″
Inseam	8¾″
Crotch level	6¼″
Hip circumference	21″
Hip-front measurement	5¼″
Hip-back measurement	5¼″

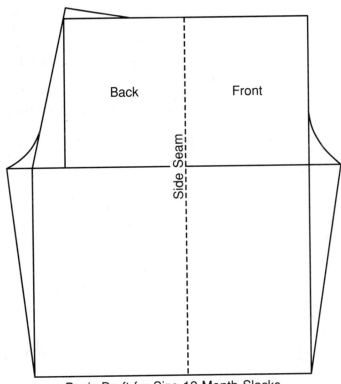

Basic Draft for Size 12-Month Slacks

For a one-piece coverall or to design a crawler with built-up front and back sections:
1. Establish side seam on crawler pattern so that the front waistline measures 5½ inches and the back waistline measures 5 inches. This corresponds with the waistline on the front and back waist pattern.
2. Separate front and back of the crawler pattern.
3. Place the front and back waist patterns so that the waistlines of the crawler and the top meet at center front. There will be a space at the side seam and center back between the pants and waist patterns. See page 254 for basic jumpsuit pattern development.
4. Draw in any desired style lines.

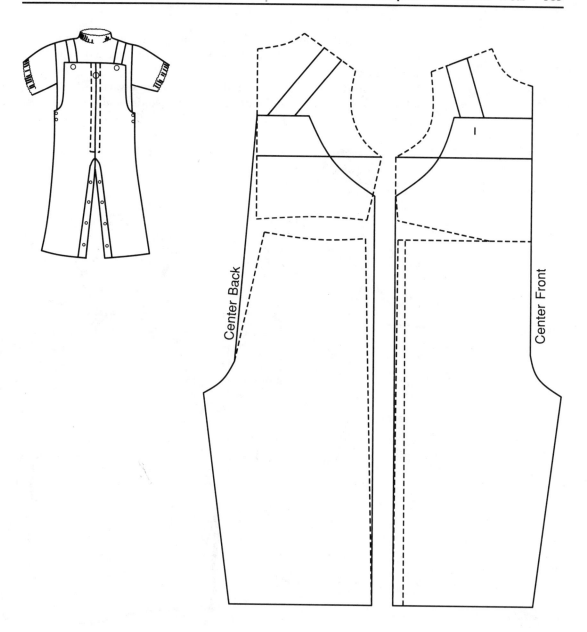

Pram Bags, Buntings, and Pram Suits

For really cold winter weather, babies need warm outfits for their carriage rides. Pram bags are easiest to get in and out of. They are loose, bag-like coverings fitted with sleeves that cover the hands, and a hood.

Buntings come in two or three pieces: a jacket with a separate or attached hood, and a simple blanket bag which covers the baby up to the chest and shoulders.

The pram suit is mostly sold for babies in the second half of their first year. It is a one-piece coverall-type garment with attached feet and a matching hat or hood.

Fabrics for these outfits vary, but they are always warm, lightweight, and washable. Nylons, polyester and cotton blends, and corduroy, together with acrylic pile or quilted linings, are usually used.

Blanket Sleepers or Pajama Blankets

These are warm, coverall garments of blanket fabric, usually a brushed acrylic, that is soft and washable. As the baby gets older and tends to kick off his covers, these blanket suits keep him warm through the night. They are usually designed with a zipper that opens from neck to crotch and along the leg to facilitate diaper changes.

The Luxuries

Beyond the necessities for an infant's wardrobe, there is a good market in out-and-out luxury items for the baby. These are rarely purchased by parents, but are often irresistible to grandparents and other doting relatives when selecting gifts.

Among these luxury garments are dresses sweaters lavish with hand stitching and embroidery. Important in this category are elaborate, long christening dresses embellished with exquisite laces and other delicate trimming. The fabric for these dresses is almost always the finest silky cotton batiste. Hand-knit sweaters are still fashioned from very fine soft wool, although acrylic yarns are also used because of their nonallergenic and easy-care properties.

These special garments cannot be mass produced and are usually imported from other countries, such as France, Switzerland, Italy, the Philippines, and China where skilled labor is still readily available. Some American manufacturers design these garments in the United States, but use production facilities in other countries.

12 Sportswear

More sportswear is sold than any other kind of children's apparel. Sportswear is worn for all occasions. In school, at play, and even for parties we see children wearing separates that are produced by sportswear manufacturers. One reason for the popularity of sportswear for children is that separates fit for a longer period of time than one-piece garments. The separation at the waistline allows for growth. Another advantage is that skirts, slacks, blouses, sweaters, and jackets can be worn in any number of combinations, creating a variety of outfits.

Every year, the typical children's sportswear house manufactures three seasonal collections of separates for all occasions. The fall line consists of outfits for school wear. Blouses, shirts, sweaters, and jackets are teamed with skirts, jumpers, and slacks in coordinated fabrics. Acrylics, blends of wool with acrylics or nylon, cotton corduroy, and other sturdy cottons are traditional fall fabrics. For blouses and shirts, blends of cotton and polyester are most commonly used.

The holiday line is more dressy with a generally softer look. Trimmed sweaters and frilly blouses are popular gift items. Fabrics may be somewhat more expensive for holiday separates with velveteen a perennial favorite. The selling period is short but intensive before Christmas, and for children's sportswear this is a very lively season.

On the other hand, the selling period for spring and summer sportswear is a long one. A preliminary group of summer clothing has already been included in the holiday line for resort- or cruise-wear selling. As family weekend vacations occur throughout the year and indoor swimming pools

are featured at most resort hotels, there is a constant market for bathing suits and cover-ups. Also, family winter holidays in the tropics are not as rare as they used to be, and of course, the children who live in Florida or Southern California need summer sportswear the year around. Consequently, spring and summer separates are sold in most stores from November to July. For only a few months, starting in mid-August, do most children's sportswear departments limit their stocks to winter merchandise.

Spring and summer sportswear consists of shorts, slacks, skirts, and tops of light, bright fabrics. Tennis dresses and bathing suits are included in some lines. Most of the bathing suits, however, are manufactured by the large swimsuit houses that produce swimwear for adults as well as for children. In addition, children's knitwear manufacturers also produce bathing suits for summer selling. Fabrics for warm-weather sportswear are mostly cottons, or blends of cotton and polyester for easy washing with no ironing.

Most styles for girls' sportswear are cut from sizes 3 or 4, to 14. Garments are cut in sizes 4–6x at one price, and in sizes 7–14 at a slightly higher price to cover the additional fabric requirements. Size 3 is often eliminated from the smaller range because typical separates do not seem to work for the child who is smaller than a size 4. Therefore, Toddler sportswear is usually cut in sizes 2T–4T. On the other end of the size scale are the Sub-teens, sizes 6–14, with their own more sophisticated styling.

■ SEPARATES

Following is an analysis of the special problems of which a designer must be aware when creating the various items included in a sportswear collection.

Blouses and Shirts

Blouses are soft and dressy. Shirts are tailored. Blouses fit the same way as a dress around the shoulders and armholes, whereas shirts may have a straighter armhole and a flattened-cap-type sleeve. Although blouses may be styled to look neat and tailored, they usually are trimmed with ruffles, lace, or fancy stitching. On the other hand, shirts may also have frills for trimming, but they usually have tailored design features such as back yokes, two-piece shirt collars, long sleeves with cuffs, pockets and double-needle stitching.

Adjustment of the Basic Pattern for a Blouse
1. Add 5 to 7 inches (depending on size) below the waistline at the side seam.
2. Square a line from center front and center back for lowered hem of blouse.

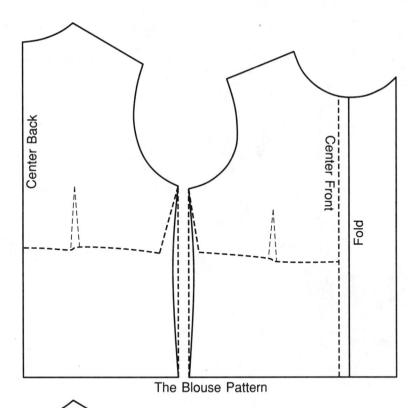

Center Back

Center Front

Fold

The Blouse Pattern

Center Back

Center Front

The Shirt Pattern

3. Square a line up from the hemline to the intersection of the armhole and side seam.

4. If desired, shape the new side seam, as illustrated, to eliminate some of the waistline fullness.

5. Add extension and facing at the center front.

Adjustment of the Basic Pattern for a Shirt

1. Straighten and lower the armhole as illustrated. Lower the armhole to the extent that the straightened armhole remains the same size as the original armhole.

2. Add length below the waistline and shape the side seam the same as for the blouse.

3. Add extension and facing at center front.

4. Flatten the cap of the basic sleeve (see shirtwaist sleeve, page 134).

5. Measure the sleeve cap. The cap should not be more than ½ inch longer than the armhole.

Blouse-Slips

Blouse-slips combine the blouse or shirt with a petticoat. They are particularly useful for active little girls who have difficulty in keeping their blouses tucked neatly inside their skirts. Blouse-slips may be manufactured by blouse specialists or by the firms producing slips and underwear. The pattern for a blouse-slip may be based on a basic waist foundation with a flared skirt, or on the basic shift. Ruffles or lace edging usually substitute for a hem.

Skirts

Separate skirts for children may be pleated, gathered, or flared. For the toddler, skirts must be suspended from the shoulders with straps or buttoned to the waist of the blouse. The very young child's body does not have enough shape to hold up a skirt at the waistline. Older girls can manage with a waistband, especially when it is elasticized at the back, so that it can adjust to individual differences of waistline measurements. To cut gathered, flared, and pleated skirts, see pages 113–119 and 162–168.

To cut a waistband for a skirt:

1. Length—
   a. Measure the waistline and add ½ inch for ease.
   b. Add 1 inch underlap at placket as illustrated at top of page 193.
2. Width—
   Two times the width of the finished waistband.

Special elastic for children's waistbands is 1 inch wide, soft, and has a great amount of stretch. It may be sewn in at the center back of the waistband or in two sections, at each side back.

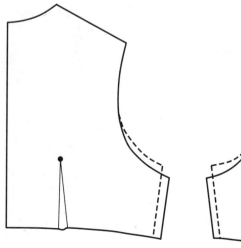

| Back | | Front |

Side Seam   Fold   Side Seam

Jumpers

Jumpers are sleeveless garments designed to be worn over blouses or sweaters. There are many reasons for their popularity in all size ranges. Blouses remain neatly in place regardless of how active the child is. In cold climates, jumpers add extra warmth. Since there is no need for a waistband, they are often more comfortable than a skirt.

Jumpers can be styled in many ways. They may have a waistline at the normal, empire, or lowered level. They can be fitted with princess seams or cut like a shift. There is really no end to the possible varieties of jumpers. Fabrics can range from the familiar blue serge of the school uniform to bright cottons, corduroy, or velveteen. Almost anything is suitable except sheer fabrics.

Since the jumper must fit over a blouse or sweater, the foundation pattern must be adjusted. The amount of adjustment depends on the weight of the fabric of the jumper and the type of garment over which it is to be worn. For example, the adjustment of the pattern for a cotton jumper to be worn over a sheer blouse is not as great as the adjustment of a wool tweed jumper to be worn with a sweater.

To make an average adjustment of the basic pattern for a jumper:
1. Lower the armhole ½ inch.
2. Extend the side seam ¼ inch.

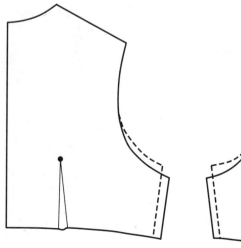

Pattern Adjustment for a Jumper

Slacks

Trousers are worn by both boys and girls of all ages, year in and year out. Occasionally, fashion changes require the development of new patterns to conform to the current silhouette. Slacks may taper close to the leg, hang straight from the hips, or flare out from the waistline, hip or knee. They can vary in length from very short shorts to any point above or below the knee, depending on the fashionable length of the season. Over the years, trousers of varying lengths and shapes have been identified by fashion writers as illustrated on pages 194–199.

Tapering Slacks

It is best to taper slacks by adjusting the basic pattern on the slacks form and taking in the desired amount at the side seam and the inseam. When slacks are very tapered and fitted to the buttocks, the back of the crotch must be lowered, raising the grain along the back inseam. In this way, more fullness is taken from the back of the slacks leg than from the front.

To adjust the basic slacks pattern for moderately tapered slacks, when a slacks form is not available:
1. Lower the back crotch ½ inch for size 10, ¼ inch for size 4.
2. Taper the side seam, beginning just above the crotch level, to 1¼ inches at the ankle for size 10, ¾ inch for size 4.
3. Taper the back inseam, beginning at the crotch level, to 1¼ inches at the ankle for size 10, ¾ inch for size 4.
4. Lengthen the back inseam ½ inch for size 10, ¼ inch for size 4.
5. Taper the front inseam ¼ inch at the ankle for all sizes.

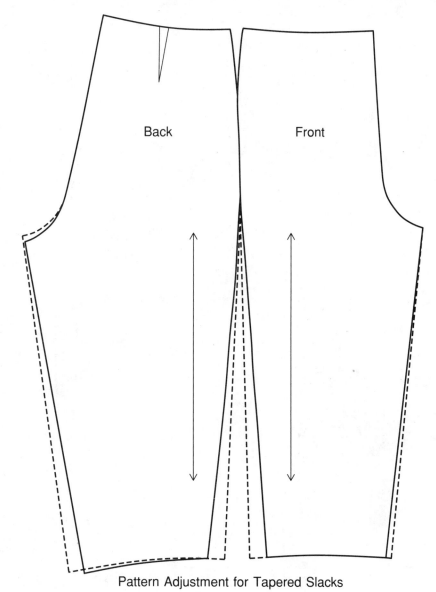

Pattern Adjustment for Tapered Slacks

To adjust the tapered slacks pattern for a moderately flared lower leg:
1. Lower the back crotch another ½ inch for size 10, ¼ inch for size 4.
2. Bring the back inseam in another ¼ inch at the ankle.
3. Beginning at the knee level, add desired amount of flare. For moderate flare, add 2 inches at the side seam for size 10, 1¼ inch for size 4. Add 1 inch at the inseam for size 10, ¾ inch for size 4.

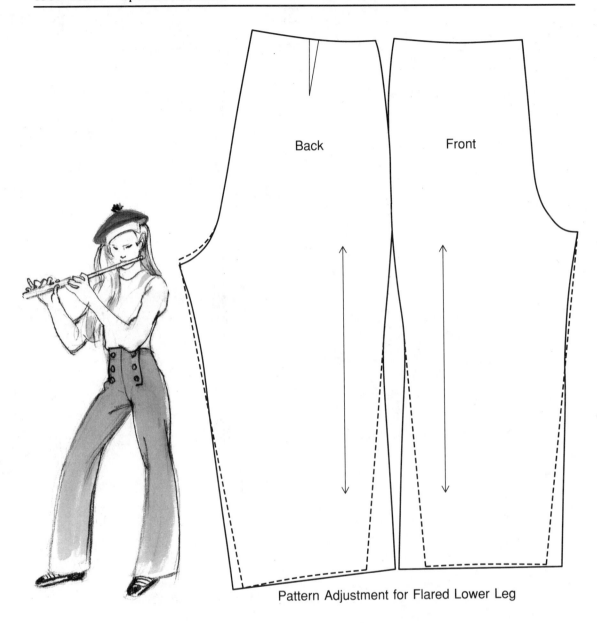

Pattern Adjustment for Flared Lower Leg

To adjust the basic slacks pattern for jeans (tapered or flared pattern may also be used):
1. Mark off the shape of the yoke below the waistline on the back pattern.
2. To eliminate the back dart, slash the pattern on the yoke line from the side seam to the dart. Close the dart in the yoke area. When the dart extends into the lower part of the pattern, take off the necessary amount at the center-back seam as illustrated.
3. Mark off the pocket opening on the front pattern.

4. Indicate the shape of the inside pocket.

5. Add the placket for the fly front to the center-front seam. The placket may be cut in one piece with the front or separately. For an inexpensive method of construction, see pages 278–280.

Back   Front

Pattern Draft for Jeans

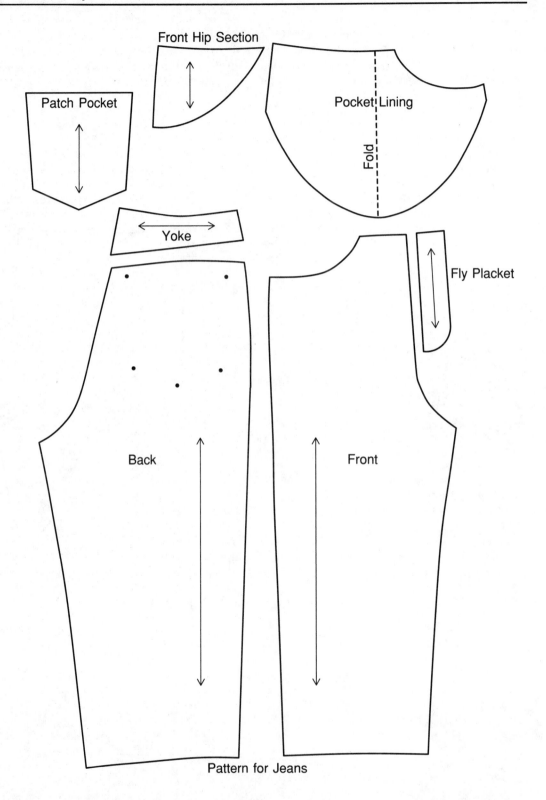

Front Hip Section

Patch Pocket

Pocket Lining

Fold

Yoke

Fly Placket

Back

Front

Pattern for Jeans

Shorts

Shorts are a perennial favorite for children. In summer, they are a staple providing freedom from unnecessary clothing; all year, they are worn for sports; and in heavier fabrics, paired with warm tights, shorts are a fashion item for fall and winter.

To adjust the basic pattern for shorts:
1. Cut off at desired length.
2. Add hem or facing.

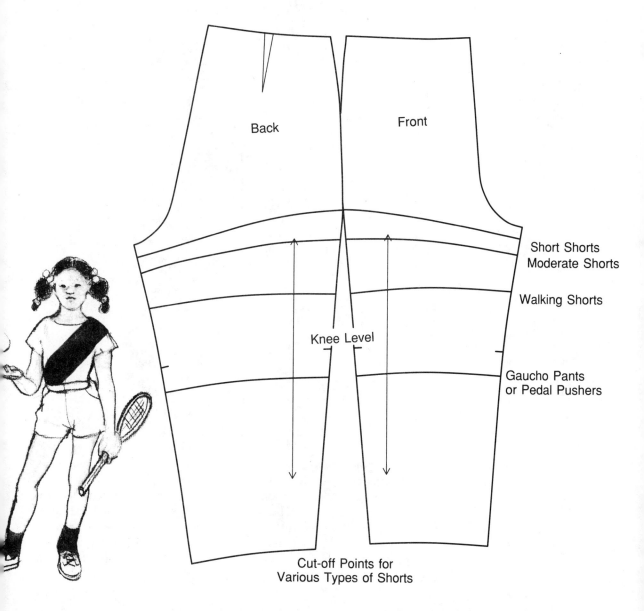

Back   Front

Short Shorts
Moderate Shorts

Walking Shorts

Knee Level

Gaucho Pants
or Pedal Pushers

Cut-off Points for
Various Types of Shorts

Culottes

Culottes combine the look of a skirt with the comfort of pants. Sometimes they are referred to as a split skirt.

To adjust the basic slacks pattern for culottes:

1. Construct desired skirt pattern. See Chapter 8.
2. Superimpose the crotch seam area from the basic slacks pattern at the center-front and the center-back seams of the skirt. The crotch extension may be lowered for cullottes. The general rule is: the fuller the garment, the lower the crotch; the tighter the garment, the higher the crotch.
3. Draw the inseam of the culottes parallel to the center-front and the center-back seams of the skirt.

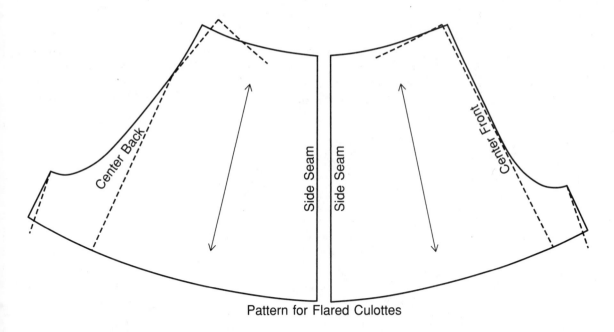

Pattern for Flared Culottes

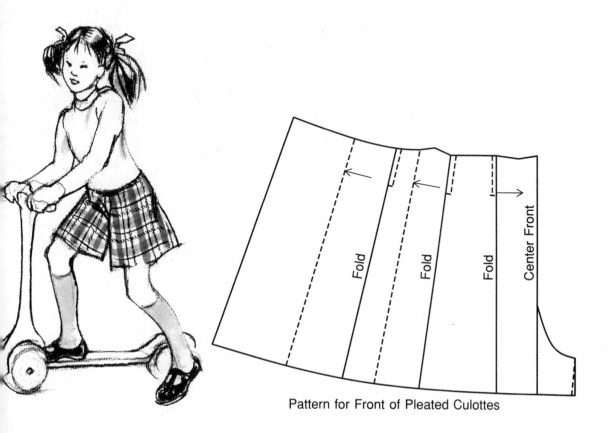

Pattern for Front of Pleated Culottes

Jackets

A jacket may be designed as a unit in a group of coordinates or in combination with a specific skirt and blouse to form a suit. A jacket may also be designed to be worn with a dress as an ensemble. Since jackets usually must fit over another garment, the foundation pattern should be adjusted.

To adjust the basic pattern for a jacket:
1. Lower the neckline ⅛ inch all around.
2. Raise the shoulder ⅛ inch at the armhole.
3. Extend the shoulder ⅛ inch at the armhole.
4. Lower the armhole ¼ inch.

5. Extend the side seam ¼ inch.

6. Slash the sleeve as illustrated. Spread ¼ inch at the vertical slashes and ⅛ inch at the horizontal slashes.

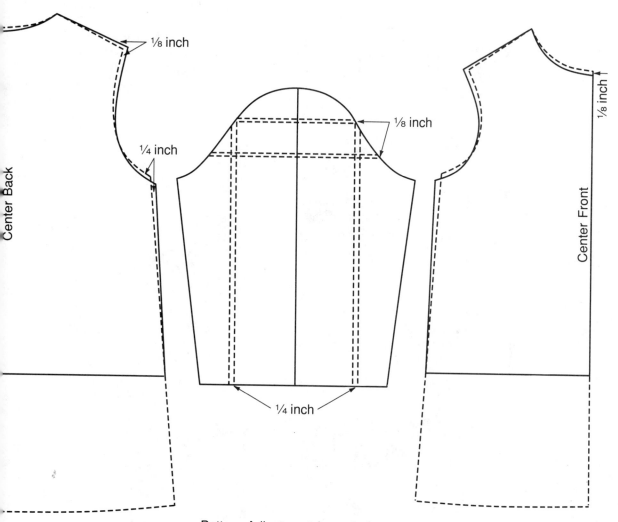

Pattern Adjustment for a Jacket

These measurements may be varied according to the type of fabric used or the purpose of the jacket. For example: the pattern for lined jackets of heavy fabrics will need more adjustment than the pattern for unlined cotton jackets. The foundation pattern, to be used for a jacket or a cover-up designed to be worn over a sundress or a bathing suit, may need no adjustment at all.

■ Sweaters

The job of designing sweaters is unique. The designer not only determines the cut and trimming of the garment, but also creates the actual fabric.

The first step is the selection of the yarn. Color and yarn texture vary from season to season and must be selected to meet the requirements of climate and fashion.

After the color and type of yarn are selected, stitch patterns are determined which will create the effects desired by the designer. The possibilities for surface interest in knitted fabrics are endless. In addition to simple flat knits; ribs, cables, openwork, and endless jacquard designs are possible. The term "jacquard" is used in knitting to include not only patterns using various colored yarns, but also patterns created by intricate stitching repeats.

Technicians, rather than designers, handle the knitting machines and work out samples from the designer's diagrams. The manufacturers of knitting machinery maintain large libraries of swatches which illustrate the design potential of their machines. Most fashion designers use these samples freely. Beginning with a swatch of fancy stitching, they develop a new fabric in fashionable colors and the weight that is currently desirable. Usually several samples are knitted before the designer gets exactly the fabric that she wants. The weight of the yarn, the tension of the stitch, and the combination of colors all influence the end result.

Sweaters and other knitted garments can be roughly divided into two categories: *fully fashioned* and *cut-and-sew*. Fully fashioned sweaters or dresses are knitted to the shape of each individual pattern piece and then sewn together, whereas the cut-and-sew method involves cutting the garment pieces from knitted fabric, and then sewing them together. The development of the overedge machine, which firmly overcasts the cut edge of each pattern piece as seams are being stitched, has made the cut-and-sew method practical. Without this secure method of locking in the edges of each cut piece, there is the likelihood that the garment will unravel.

Most large firms use both methods of production to achieve varying effects. However, fully fashioned sweaters are usually somewhat costly to produce. Consequently, the large bulk of American knitwear is cut out from knitted fabric, which has been either finished flat like woven yard goods or knitted in tubular shape. Almost all knitting machines produce yard goods in a circular fashion, producing a tube of fabric that is pressed flat and rolled for shipping.

When knit garments are cut from yard goods that have been finished so that they retain their shape in handling and wear, the methods of production are not much different from those used in manufacturing apparel from woven fabrics. Therefore, some general sportswear and dress manufacturers are also producing sweaters and other knit garments. It must be said, however, that manufacturers specializing in sweaters have the various machines required for the smooth finishing of necklines and closings, and usually produce a better finished product.

■ Swimwear

Sometime in March, usually after a good vacation, the children's swimwear designer begins work on a new collection. This collection will reach its peak selling season in the retail stores a year and a half later. In contrast to other childrenswear areas, there is only one collection every year. Its selling season in the wholesale market extends through several seasons. The first group of samples must be ready in June, when the mail-order houses place orders for next year's summer catalogues. Specialty shops and department stores buy swimsuits for cruise-wear selling in late August and early September. Then, in January, the complete line is shown and

the bulk of the business is placed for summer selling. Fill-in orders and re-orders continue well into spring, while the designer is busy with the following year's models. This is the tempo of swimwear, an area that has many unique problems and demands an extraordinary amount of expertise from the designer.

Most swimwear designers cut their own samples. Sketches can only give a rough approximation of a finished swimsuit. The stretch and general behavior of the fabric will affect the proportions of the suit. Each design is a three-dimensional problem that must be carefully worked out.

The designer and the patternmaker usually work together to develop the foundation pattern for each type of fabric. Although a full-length leg form is used in the design room, all new patterns must be tested on a child before they go into production. The amount and direction of the stretch in fabric, the type and amount of elastic used in a cotton suit, and the general silhouette of the suit all affect the fit and function of the garment and must be tested. Ideally, the swimsuit should not only be tested for fit in the design room, but under conditions of normal use, immersed in the swimming pool and the ocean.

The sample room of a swimsuit house is equipped with the machines necessary to turn out a sample that is finished just like a stock garment. Special overedge and elastic-covering machines as well as many attachments are available to turn out a professional product.

Designing swimwear is probably the most challenging of all the specialties in childrenswear design. The function of swimwear imposes a number of very rigid limitations within which the designer must work and still produce a new and fresh line year after year. First of all, swimsuits are most definitely active sportswear. Swimsuits must move with the child and be completely nonrestrictive, while at the same time hugging the body without irritating or binding in any way.

The fabrics used for swimsuits must meet very rigid specifications. Colors must be impervious to sun, salt, and chlorine. Children's swimsuits are not only used for swimming, but they must take constant abuse from active play in the sand as well as on the playground. When the suit is taken off, it usually goes into the washer and the dryer so that it will be clean and ready for another round of water, sand, and sun on the next day.

Certain colors and weaves cannot take this sort of endless harsh wear. The designer must limit her choices to the fabrics that can. Nylon, with its great strength, stretchability, and quick-drying property is an excellent choice, and stretch-knit nylon has become a classic for swimsuits. Woven cottons that are completely colorfast are somewhat less expensive to use. Most swimsuits need linings; when they are used, they must be carefully chosen so that they work well with the outer fabric. Nylon tricot is usually used inside a 100 percent stretch nylon suit, whereas cotton batiste may be used to line a cotton suit.

When designing a bathing suit, the designer must work within a very small garment. Working out the right proportions sometimes poses a special problem. Toddlers and preschool children tend to look appealing in most bathing suits, and sub-teens with their developing young bodies are not particularly difficult to design for. The 7–14 girl, however, is the real problem here. Her taste often demands a grown-up look, but her figure has not achieved the right curves as yet. Her tummy still protrudes more than her chest, and it is difficult to make her look as curvacious as her older sister. At the same time, the 7–14 girl is usually an avid swimmer and needs suits that really function well in the water, suits that stay in place during all sorts of active swimming and diving. For this sort of activity, a tank suit with built-up shoulder straps always works well, and designers must try to do something new with the tank suit every season. But functional tank suits are not the complete answer to the 7–14 swimsuit problem. Most schoolgirls are very fashion-conscious and like to adopt the ideas that are popular for the sub-teen and junior market. Bikinis, swim dresses, rompers—if it is in for juniors, it has to be worked out proportionally so that it also looks well on the 7–14 girl.

Most designers create two kinds of swimsuits: those used primarily for actual swimming and those that function as a playsuit as well. Both are needed by most children who spend their summers at the shore or in the country. Even the average youngster, living in a suburban house with a plastic pool in the backyard, wears swimsuits all day long. When one suit is wet, a child will change into another one. The swimsuit that also doubles as a playsuit is usually made of cotton and is often trimmed.

All sorts of trimmings are suitable for swimsuits as long as they also meet all the necessary requirements of absolute colorfastness and general durability. Ruffles or permanent pleats are fine in matching or contrasting fabrics. A large variety of sturdy braids are also suitable trimmings. Appliqués can be used if the necessary machines are available in the factory. Colorfast embroideries are suitable as long as the stitching does not interfere with the stretch in the fabric. Buttons used on swimsuits must not rust and, therefore, most metal buttons or self-covered buttons with metal bases cannot be used.

In spite of all the qualifications that swimsuits for children have to meet, they will not sell if they are too expensive. The designer must carefully stay within a rather rigid price structure. This limits the choice of fabrics not only to those that give high-quality performance, but also to those that are relatively inexpensive. Labor costs must be kept to a minimum without sacrificing a perfectly clean finish and construction that holds up under the most rugged wearing conditions. Trimmings, when used, must be sturdy but not costly.

The manufacturers who have become successful in the children's swimwear business have achieved this position by consistently turning out a reliable product at a saleable price. A certain trust is established between the manufacturer and the retailer, so that often the buyer will rely more than is usual on the advice of the manufacturer and the designer when making selections from the line. Needless to say, the designer in this position must be a real professional, one who not only has a good sense of design, but one who also, with experience, has learned to understand production and merchandising problems.

13
Loungewear and Sleepwear

There is perhaps no other area of childrenswear design that offers as much opportunity for free expression as creating pajamas, nightgowns, and robes. For "at home" wear, clothing can be imaginative and fanciful as long as it is also comfortable and washable. Little girls can look feminine and fragile in long, ruffled gowns, or they may romp through the house in tomboy pajamas with a sportswear look. Robes, usually designed to match sleepwear, also can be either softly feminine or tailored.

Current fashion finds its own expression in sleepwear and loungewear. For example, when the peasant look is popular, peasant prints and bright colors will appear in special fabrics for pajamas and nightgowns. These are then styled with their own peasant-inspired flair. In other seasons, the inspiration might be derived from Victoriana or jogging suits.

Designers create two major collections each year. The fall and winter collection includes sleepwear of brushed fabrics, and robes designed for warmth. For winter holiday selling, additional items especially designed for gift purchasing are usually added to the line. Novel accessories, such as quilts that zip into sleeping bags, booties, pajama bags, and dolls or other soft toys, are designed to match coordinated groups of pajamas, nightgowns, and robes.

The other major collection is for spring and summer selling. Fabrics are cool and airy. Pajamas may have bloomer panties or shorts instead of long legs. Nightgowns or pajama tops may be sleeveless or have short sleeves replacing the long sleeves that are required for winter warmth. Robes for spring and summer either serve as cover-ups for scantily cut nightgowns and pajamas or are designed in terrycloth for bath and beachwear.

■ Sleepwear

A federal standard for the flammability of fabrics used in children's sleepwear sizes 0–6x, has been in effect since 1975. In 1982, children's sleepwear in sizes 7–14 was also covered by this standard. As shown in the *Federal Register*, Vol. 40, No. 250, December 30, 1975, the general requirements of the standard are as follows:

A. *Summary of Test Method*

   Five conditioned specimens, 8.9 × 25.4 cm. (3.5 × 10 inches) are suspended one at a time vertically in holders in a prescribed cabinet and subjected to a standard flame along their bottom edge for a specific time under controlled conditions. The char length and residual flame time are measured.

B. *Test Criteria*
   1. Average Char Length—The average length of 5 specimens shall not exceed 17.8 cm (7.0 inches).
   2. Full Specimen Burn—No individual specimen shall have a char length of 25.4 cm (10 inches).
   3. Residual Flame Time—No individual specimen shall have a residual flame time greater than 10 minutes.

In its entirety, the standard describes the test method in detail and the proper labeling of all items, including care instructions so that flame-resistant properties are maintained after laundering. It is recommended that all flame-resistant garments be laundered with detergents, since soap leaves a fatty residue which is flammable.

In compliance with this standard, virtually all children's sleepwear sold in the United States after 1972 was made of textiles that were chemically treated for flame retardance. One of these chemicals was Tris. In April 1977, the United States Consumer Product Safety Commission banned the use of Tris because it was found to cause cancer in laboratory animals. Since then, sleepwear for children usually has been made from 100 percent polyester. Nylon and nylon tricot have a smaller share of the market, and some modacrylics are also used. None of these fabrics are treated with flame-retardant chemicals. They owe their flame-resistance to the inherent properties of the fiber. It is important to note that in addition to the fabric, all trimmings used on children's sleepwear must also meet the requirements of the Flammability Standard.

Although some sleepwear manufacturers specialize in garments that are made in either knitted or woven fabrics, most firms handle both woven and knitted goods.

Manufacturers of knit pajamas use warm brushed acrylic knit fabrics for winter wear and lighter weights for spring. One-piece knitted pajamas with front closure and attached feet are popular for infants and toddlers. These garments are comfortable and keep the child warm on chilly nights when covers might be kicked off. The attached feet usually have a non-slip plastic sole covering for safety.

Table VI gives the garment measurements for infants and toddler's one piece pajamas.

Table VI—Infants' and Toddlers' One-Piece Pajamas

SIZE		12 MO.	18 MO.	2	3	4
Width of Garment	(H–I)	10	11	11	12	12
Total Length:	(A–B)					
To heel of garment (with feet)		26	28	30	32½	35
Cuff (without feet)		25	27	29	31	33½
Sleeve Length	(C–D)	9	10	11	12	13
Armhole Length	(E–C)	5½	5½	6	6	6½
Neck Opening		11	11	12	13	13
Front Crotch to Shoulder	(F–A)	17¾	18½	19¼	20	20¾
Back Crotch to Shoulder	(F–A)	18¾	19½	20¼	21	21¾
Width Across Seat	(J–K)	12½	13½	13½	14½	14½
Width of Thigh	(F–L)	5½	6	6	6½	6½
Width of Ankle	(M–N)	3¾	4	4	4½	4½
Length of Foot	(O–P)	6	6	6½	7	7½

Method of Measuring

- Width of garment—Measured across the garment 1 inch below the bottom of the armhole.
- Total length [with feet]—Measured from the point where the shoulder joins the collarette or neck opening to the heel of the garment with the heel extended as the foot is folded back over the ankle of the garment.
- Total length [cuff, without feet]—Measured from the point where the shoulder joins the collarette or neck opening to the bottom edge of the leg.
- Sleeve length—Measured in a straight line from the point under the arm where the sleeve is seamed to the garment to the lower outside edge of the sleeve, or sleeve cuff, if a cuff is used.
- Armhole length—Measured from the point where the sleeve is attached to the shoulder to the lowest point under the arm.
- Neck opening—Measured by taking the circumference of the neck at the seam, from the center of the collarette button to the outside end of the buttonhole.
- Front, crotch to shoulder—Measured from the bottom of the crotch, across the front, to the point where the shoulder joins the collarette or neck opening.
- Back, crotch to shoulder—Measured from the bottom of the crotch, across the back, to the point where the shoulder joins the collarette or the neck opening.
- Width across seat—Measured across the back of the garment at the widest point.

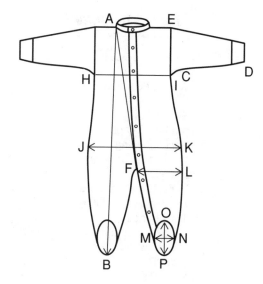

- Width of thigh—Measured across the leg at the bottom of the crotch.
- Width of ankle—Measured across the leg where the foot is joined to the leg.
- Length of foot—Measured from toe to heel of the bottom of the foot, with the foot laid out flat.

Some parents prefer two-piece pajamas because diapers and pants can be changed as needed without completely undressing the child. Also it is easier for the toddler to learn to dress and undress with separate pants and tops. Two-piece pajamas that button at the waist with double sets of snaps stay neat and provide extra room for growth. For the older child, the top of the sleeper is shaped like a pullover, and the trouser waistline is elasticised all around.

For the spring and summer collections, fabrics are light, airy and absorbent knits of cotton and polyester. The cut of the sleeper remains the same as for winter except that the foot coverings are eliminated and sleeves are short.

These basic functional garments have been used for children for many years, but each season, designers add that little something to make them appealing and just a little different. Appliqués and embroideries can be used for trimming. Color combinations can vary. New prints are used as well as solid colors. It is surprising what is done every season with an item that has not been changed in basic cut for more than two generations.

Tables VII and VIII give the garment measurements for Infants', Children's, and Girls' knit pajamas as recommended by the United States Department of Commerce.

Table VII—Infants' and Toddlers' Two-Piece Pajamas

SIZE		12 MO.	18 MO.	2	3	4
Top:						
Width of Garment	(H–J)	10	11	11	12	12
Length	(A–B)	11	12	13	14	15
Sleeve Length	(J–G)	9	10	11	12	13
Armhole Length	(F–N)	5½	5½	6	6	6½
Neck Opening		11	11	12	13	13
Waistband Location	(E–K)	9	9½	10	10½	11
Pants:						
Waist Circumference		20	21	22	22½	23
Front Waistband length		10½	11	11½	12	12½
Total Length:	(A–B)					
To heel of garment (with feet)		17	18½	20	22	24
Cuff (without feet)		16	17½	19	20½	22½
From Rise	(D–G)	8¾	9	9¼	9½	9¾
Back Rise	(D–H)	9¾	10	10¼	10½	10¾
Width Across Seat	(K–J)	12½	13½	13½	14½	14½
Width of Thigh	(D–P)	5½	6	6	6½	6½
Width of Ankle	(R–S)	3¾	4	4	4¼	4½
Length of Foot	(L–N)	6	6	6½	7	7½
Suit Buttoned:						
Trunk		36½	38	39½	41	42½
Total Length		26	28	30	32½	35

Method of Measuring

Top

- Width of garment—Measured across the garment 1 inch below the bottom of the armhole.
- Length—Measured from the point where the shoulder joins the collarette or neck opening to the bottom edge of the top.
- Sleeve length—Measured in a straight line from the point under the arm where the sleeve is seamed to the garment to the lower outside edge of the sleeve, or sleeve cuff, if a cuff is used.
- Armhole length—Measured from the point where the sleeve is attached to the shoulder to the lowest point under the arm.
- Neck opening—Measured by taking the circumference of the neck at the seam, from the center of the collarette button to the outside end of the buttonhole.
- Location of waistband—Measured from the neck seam at the shoulder to the upper edge of the trouser when buttoned.

Pants

- Waist circumference—Measured as twice the distance between the outside edges of the waistband, elastic relaxed and smooth.

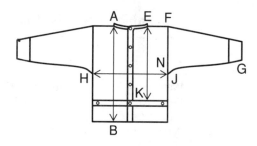

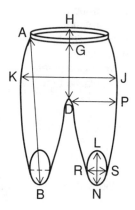

- Front waistband length—Measured from end to end of the front waistband.
- Total length [with feet]—Measured from the outside top edge of the waistband to the heel of the garment with the heel extended as the foot is folded back over the ankle of the garment.
- Total length [cuff, without feet]—Measured from the outside top edge of the waistband to the bottom edge of the leg.
- Front rise—Measured from the bottom of the crotch to the top edge of the waistband at center front.
- Back rise—Measured from the bottom of the crotch to the top edge of the waistband at center back.
- Width across seat—Measured across the back of the garment at a point halfway between the bottom of the crotch and the top edge of the waistband at center back.
- Width of thigh—Measured across the leg at the bottom of the crotch.
- Width of ankle—Measured across the leg where the foot is joined to the leg.
- Length of foot—Measured from toe to heel of the bottom of the foot, with the foot laid flat.

Suit Buttoned

- Trunk—Measured as twice the distance from the point where the shoulder joins the collarette to the bottom of the crotch.

Table VIII—Children's and Girl's Knit Pajamas

SIZE		2	4	6	7	8	10	12	14
Blouse:									
Width	(H–J)	11	12	13	14	14	15	16	17
Length	(A–B)	14½	16	17½	19	20	21½	23	24
Sleeve Length	(N–G)	11	13	15	16½	17½	19	20	21
Armhole Length	(F–N)	6	6½	7	7½	7½	8	8½	9
Neck Opening:									
Ribbed Knit Flat		12	12½	13	13½	13½	14	14½	15
Stretched		20	20½	21	21½	21½	22	22½	23
Border Rib Length	(C–D)	3	3	3	3	3	3	3	3
Trousers:									
Waist Circumference									
(All-elastic Web)	(A–C)	17	17¾	18½	19	19½	20	20¾	21½
Total Length	(A–B)								
Rib Bottom		20	23½	27½	31	32½	35½	37	38½
Hem Bottom		19	22½	26½	30	31½	35½	36	37½
Front Rise	(D–G)	9	10	10¾	11½	12¼	13	13¾	14½
Back Rise	(D–H)	11	12	12¾	13	14¼	15	15¾	16½
Width Across Seat	(K–L)	13	14	15	16	17	18	19	20
Width of Thigh	(D–N)	8	8½	9	9½	10	10½	11	11½
Leg-cuff Length	(E–B)	4	4	4	4	4	4	4	4

Method of Measuring

Blouse

- Width of garment—Measured across the garment 1 inch below the bottom of the armhole.
- Length—Measured from the point where the shoulder joins the collarette to the bottom edge of the blouse.
- Sleeve length—Measured in a straight line from the point under the arm where the sleeve is joined to the garment to the lower outside edge of the sleeve, or the sleeve cuff, if a cuff is used.
- Armhole length—Measured from the point where the sleeve is attached to the shoulder to the lowest point under the arm.
- Neck opening, flat—Measured by taking the circumference of the neck at the top edge with the fabric relaxed and smooth.
- Neck opening, stretched—Measured by taking the circumference of the neck at the seam with the fabric stretched.
- Border rib length—Measured from the middle of the seam attaching the rib to the edge of the blouse to the bottom edge of the border rib.

Trousers

- Waist circumference—Measured as twice the distance between the outside edges of the waistband, elastic relaxed and smooth.

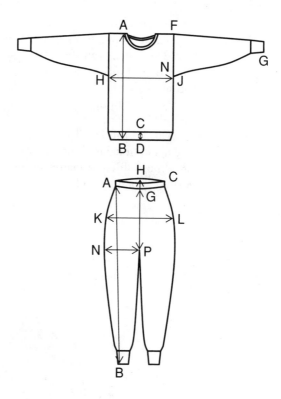

- Total length—Measured from the outside top edge of the waistband to the bottom edge of the leg.
- Front rise—Measured from the bottom of the crotch to the top edge of the waistband at center front.
- Back rise—Measured from the bottom of the crotch to the top edge of the waistband at center back.
- Width across seat—Measured across the back of the garment at a point halfway between the bottom of the crotch and the top edge of the waistband at center back.
- Width of thigh—Measured across the leg at the bottom of the crotch.
- Leg-cuff length—Measured from the middle of the seam attaching the cuff to the leg to the lower outside edge of the cuff.

Manufacturers in the other major area of sleepwear work primarily with woven fabrics: flannels for fall and winter, and batistes for spring and summer. Some firms also use tricot knits. These can be brushed for soft warmth for winter wear. In general, nighties or pajamas of tricot combine excellent washability with a grown-up look. They are especially popular in 7–14 and Sub-teen sizes.

Robes are designed in the same fabrics as sleepwear to form ensembles that can be merchandised together. Quilting is used to add extra body and warmth to winter robes. It is in this part of the industry that most of the exciting styling takes place. High fashion, fairy tales, sportswear, and the old and quaint all show their influence.

Since most manufacturers must produce good-looking, practical sleepwear at moderate prices, production has become extremely mechanized. Factories are equipped with the latest machinery, and in this area it is particularly important that the designer makes herself familiar with exactly what can be produced with the machinery at hand, and what could be done if additional investments were made in automated facilities. At present, almost all large manufacturers can do machine-smocking, quilting, tucking, appliqué, and small embroideries in their own plants.

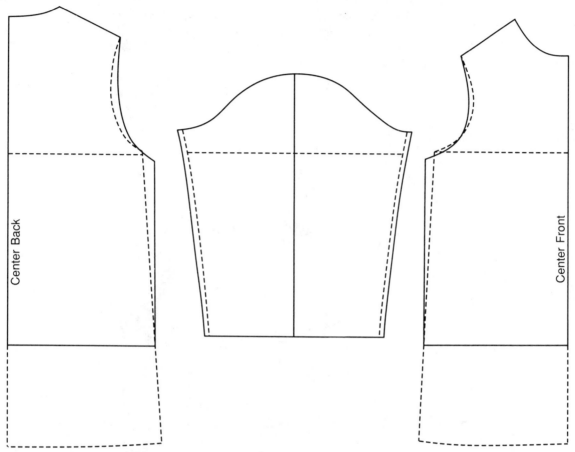

Adjustment of Basic Shift Pattern for Pajama Top or Nightgown

Nightgowns and pajamas must be cut so that they fit easily and comfortably with plenty of room for movement. Elastic, if used, must be soft, and buttons should be flat so that no discomfort can interfere with sleep.

To adjust the basic pattern for a pajama top or nightgown:
1. Drop the armhole ¼ inch.
2. Extend the side seam ½ inch.
3. Straighten out the armhole as illustrated.
4. Mark off the length of the pajama top on the foundation pattern. The center-back length for a standard pajama top, size 4, is 15¼ inches; for size 10, it is 19½ inches.
5. Adjust the sleeve pattern by flattening the cap 1 inch (see shirtwaist sleeve, page 134). Add ¼ inch at the underarm seam as illustrated.

To adjust the basic slacks pattern for pajama trousers:

1. Check crotch level. There should be a minimum of ¼ inch ease.

2. Add ½ inch to the width at each side seam of both front and back (a total addition of 2 inches to the hip circumference).

3. Align front and back so that the lower sections of the side seam meet. Since the waistline is elasticised, the side seams and darts are eliminated.

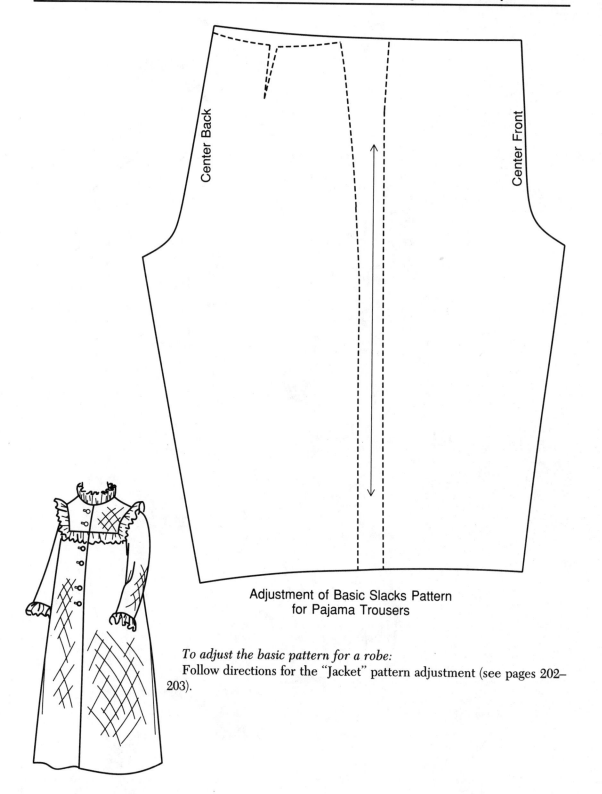

Center Back

Center Front

Adjustment of Basic Slacks Pattern
for Pajama Trousers

To adjust the basic pattern for a robe:
Follow directions for the "Jacket" pattern adjustment (see pages 202–203).

14 Underwear

Designing little girls' underwear can be very pleasant for a designer. This is especially true if she likes ruffles and lace and has a delicate touch. There are two kinds of children's underwear: the strictly functional white cotton-knit vest or shirt with panties, and the feminine, often delicately trimmed, slips and panties designed for gift-giving and impulse-buying.

Both types may be made by the same manufacturer, but, more often, the basic shirts and panties are produced by the people who make cotton-knit underwear for both boys and girls in all size ranges, while the more highly designed type of girls' lingerie is made by the manufacturers who also produce sleepwear and loungewear. In most cases, different designers work for each of the various divisions within a firm, and separate factories are maintained for each specialty.

Basic vests and panties for girls are usually made from 1×1 ribbed or flat-knit cotton. The fabric is highly absorbent and comfortable in all sorts of climates. To aid in shape retention, special finishes are added or polyester is blended with the cotton. White is the basic color and is very practical for washing. But here lies a challenge for the designer. Perhaps the time is right for some color and excitement in this area. In any case, for the designers who want to try their hand at it, Tables IX and X give the garment measurements for Girls' vests and panties as recommended by the United States Department of Commerce.

Table IX—Girls' Vests

SIZE		2	4	6	7	8	10	12	14
Width of Garment	(C–D)	7½	8¼	9	9½	10	10½	11¼	12
Total Length	(A–B)	16	18	20	21½	23	24½	26	27½
Armhole Length	(E–F)	6½	7	8	8	8½	9	9½	10
Neck Opening		22	23½	25	26	27	28	29	30

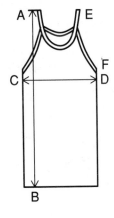

Method of Measuring

- Width of garment—Measured across the garment 1 inch below the bottom of the armholes.
- Total length—Measured from the top edge of the shoulder strap to the bottom edge of the vest.
- Armhole length—Measured from the top point of the armhole at the shoulder along the outer edge of the armhole to the lowest point under the arm (half the length of the armhole band).
- Neck opening—Measured by taking the circumference of the neck at the top edge with the fabric relaxed and smooth.

Table X—Girls' Panties

SIZE		2	4	6	7	8	10	12	14
Waist (circumference)									
Elastic Around	(A–C)	16	16¾	17½	17½	18¼	19	19¾	20½
Side Length	(A–B)	6½	7¼	8	8½	9	9½	10	10½
Front Rise	(D–G)	8¾	9¾	10½	11¼	12	12½	13	13½
Back Rise	(D–H)	9¾	10¾	11½	12¼	13	13½	14	14½
Width Across	(K–L)								
Seat:									
ribbed (1 × 1)			10½	11¼	12	12¾	13½	14½	15½	16½
flat knit			11½	12¼	13	13¾	14½	15½	16½	17½
Leg Opening,									
Ribbed-cuff Style			9	10	11	12	13	14	15	16
Width Across Crotch	(F–J)	3½	3¾	4	4¼	4½	4¾	5	5

Method of Measuring

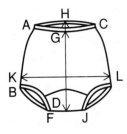

- Waist (circumference)—Measured as twice the distance between the outside edges of the waistband, elastic relaxed and smooth.
- Side length—Measured from the top outside edge of the waistband to the bottom edge of the leg opening at the side.
- Front rise—Measured from the bottom of the crotch to the top edge of the waistband at center front.
- Back rise—Measured from the bottom of the crotch to the top edge of the waistband at center back.

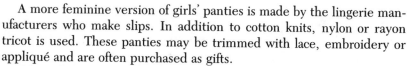

- Width across seat—Measured across the back of the garment at the widest part.
- Leg opening—Circumference, measured at the bottom edge.
- Width across crotch—Measured between the outside edges at the bottom of the crotch.

A more feminine version of girls' panties is made by the lingerie manufacturers who make slips. In addition to cotton knits, nylon or rayon tricot is used. These panties may be trimmed with lace, embroidery or appliqué and are often purchased as gifts.

When slips are not purchased as gifts, they are usually bought to go with a particular dress or skirt. Therefore, they must be designed to harmonize with the current fashion silhouette for girls. When full skirts are in fashion, crisp, ruffled slips or petticoats will make them stand out and look even fuller. When straight shifts are in, the soft nylon slip will underline the dress without adding any unnecessary bulk. A gentle A-line skirt needs a gentle A-line slip with perhaps just a ruffle at the lower edge to make the hem stand out.

Slips for girls may be full-length slips or half-slips. For toddlers and preschool children, the half-slip tends to slide down, so full slips are recommended. Schoolgirls and sub-teens prefer half-slips or petticoats. To them they represent a more grown-up look, especially when the vest has given way to a "training bra."

All slips are designed with some sort of trimming. A little narrow Val lace to finish the neckline and the armholes may be all that is necessary for a toddler slip. To keep the outer edges of slips as light and delicate as possible, narrow laces applied with a zigzag stitch are used instead of hems or bindings. Delicate embroideries and appliquéd lace are also widely used as trimming. Ribbons laced through eyelet beading often add a touch of color. For added interest and variety, stitching and tucking may be used. It is important to remember that trimming on underwear should always be flat so that there will not be any unwanted bulky areas under the dress. All ribbon bows are pressed flat. Ruffles are only used on slips when they are deliberately placed to add width to the skirt of the outer garment. Pleated flounces are sometimes used when extra fabric is desired for movement, but the silhouette must be kept straight and smooth.

Fabrics for slips should be soft and comfortable, as well as washable without the need for ironing. Cotton and polyester batiste is used for all size ranges. For older girls, the grown-up look of nylon tricot is popular. When crisper fabrics are needed, woven nylon or nylon net may be used for ruffles. With these crisp fabrics, care must be taken so that they do not rub or irritate the child's skin.

Slips and half-slips or petticoats can be cut in the same way that dresses and skirts are cut. Princess seaming is often used. It permits an infinite variety of shapes, since as much or as little flare can be added as desired. Waistlines can be placed at any level: raised, normal, or lowered, depending on the silhouette that is wanted. For Infants' and Toddler sizes, slips are cut with built-up shoulder straps because narrow straps tend to slip down from small shoulders. For 3–6x and 7–14 sizes, shoulder straps can be adjustable ribbons, the same as are used in adult lingerie.

Slips may be worn over a vest, but in many cases are worn just with panties for a pretty lingerie look. They should be cut to softly hug the upper part of the body so that there is no unnecessary bulk under dresses or blouses. Many slips are designed with an elasticised panel at the side seam for flexible fit. A slip should fit fairly close to the body and should be cut low enough at the underarm so that it will not show when the child wears a sleeveless dress.

To adjust the basic shift pattern for slip:

1. Drop the armhole ¼ inch.
2. Reduce width at the side seam and armhole ½ inch.
3. Draw in the built-up shoulder straps as illustrated.
4. When ribbon straps are used, they must be placed no farther apart than the center of the shoulder; otherwise, they tend to slip off the shoulders of the child.
5. Shorten basic pattern at least 1 inch.

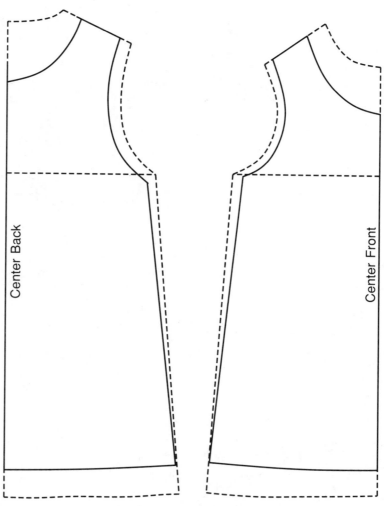

Draft for a Basic Slip Pattern

15 Outerwear

Designers of children's outerwear create dress coats, sport coats, and waterproof raincoats. They design jackets of various lengths and weights, as well as snowsuits and ski suits.

With the development of man-made fiber fabrics, outdoor clothing for children has undergone some revolutionary changes. Acrylic pile linings and polyester fiberfill insulation have made outerwear of virtually weightless fabrics entirely practical. Heavy, cumbersome garments have been replaced by washable, comfortably warm, protective clothing. Whereas the warm wool overcoat was once a necessity for daily winter wear, it is now used only for special occasions. Many children never own one. They stay dry and comfortable in all sorts of weather with lightweight but warmly insulated coats or jackets.

Outerwear manufacturers fall into two general categories. The traditional coat manufacturers make coats for boys or girls that are mostly cut from wool fabrics. Coats of acrylic pile or other novelty fabrics are included in most collections, but, by and large, these manufacturers make conventional coats, warmly interlined for winter and in lighter weights for spring.

Other outerwear manufacturers, those that originally may have started out as snowsuit producers, are now making a comprehensive line for both boys and girls. These manufacturers may make garments in all size ranges: for babies, there are buntings and pram bags; for toddlers and preschool youngsters, snowsuits, raincoats, and jackets; and for the older child, there are duffle coats, trench coats, and other kinds of sportscoats and raincoats, in addition to ski suits and all sorts of odd jackets.

Outerwear manufacturers present two lines each year. The winter line must be ready in March and is shown until August. The spring line opens in September and is shown until February. During such a long selling season, it must be expected that new numbers will be added here and there to meet the immediate selling needs of the retailer. On the other hand, mail-order catalogues are planned so far in advance that the designer may be called upon to design special numbers for catalogues far in advance of the regular collection.

Sample sizes for outerwear differ somewhat from the other areas of children's apparel. For the Toddler size range, 2T–4T, the sample size is 4T. If the sample looks well in a size 4, the manufacturer may run the number from size 2 to 6x, spanning two size ranges. This is particularly practical for snowsuits and raincoats since styling for the younger and older preschool child does not vary much in these areas. Samples of styles that are to be run only in the 3–6x size range are usually made in size 5. The sample size for 7–14 is size 10.

The designer working for a traditional coat house often only submits sketches. She selects fabrics and trimmings, but an expert patternmaker takes over to cut the first sample, and skilled tailors take care of the construction. For the comprehensive outerwear house, on the other hand, the designer often cuts the first sample and works with a samplemaker as in other childrenswear areas. To save time, occasionally only the fronts of coats and jackets may be made in the sample room. This is especially true for snowsuits and ski suits. The jackets are completed and matching pants are added in the factory. Aside from enabling the sample room to turn out more samples, this practice results in samples that are finished exactly like stock garments, an effect that is difficult to achieve when special machinery is not available in the sample room.

■ Coats

The tailored dress coat requires a very special kind of styling. In a way, this is the area of childrenswear that is closest to designing for adults. To begin with, there are the classics. These are the basic, practical coats that develop gradually and recur periodically whenever they seem right in adult fashion. Among these styles are polo or boy coats, trench coats, and princess coats.

The princess coat for children has been a perennial favorite. Shaped at the waist and with a moderately flared skirt, it creates a flattering silhouette for most little girls. Many stores have traditionally imported these coats from England, where fine tailoring is a specialty. Made from good,

durable tweeds and plaid wools, these coats are made to last, and have been handed down from child to child in many families.

Besides the classics, every coat line must also include many more highly styled models. Winter coats are sometimes trimmed with fur. Leather and velveteen are also used as trimming. Many dress coats for children have hats designed to match. For the little sizes, matching leggings may be sold with the coat. The spring coat, often referred to in the trade as the "Easter coat," is usually designed in pastels or light, bright colors.

Many children's dress houses compete with coat manufacturers for the spring-coat business by designing ensembles of matching coats and dresses. Dress manufacturers, however, do not have the skilled labor available to produce a tailored coat, and the ensemble is usually designed without the interlinings and tailoring details of the conventional coat.

All coats must be designed with collars of some sort. Either a built-up neckline or a collar is needed to cover the neckline of dresses or blouses. When the necklines of these garments are exposed, they should match the coat, or the general effect is spoiled. Since most children are not likely to wear coordinated coats and dresses, it is best to always include a collar and have the coat button right up to the neckline.

Another feature essential in designing coats is pockets. Most children do not carry handbags, and pockets are needed for handkerchiefs, occasional change, and other little necessities. Therefore, pockets should not only be worked into every coat, but they should also be large enough to hold quite a few items.

The basic pattern must be enlarged for a coat foundation pattern. Coats should fit easily over normal indoor clothing, and patterns must be large enough to compensate for the bulk of heavy coating fabric. The measurements, below, may be varied according to the type of fabric used and the bulk of the lining or interlining. For example, the bulk of a quilted lining is usually greater than the bulk of acrylic pile, and both are bulkier than a conventional wool interlining.

To cut a coat it is best to begin with a shift sloper. To make an average adjustment of the shift pattern for a coat (See page 232):
1. Lower the neckline ⅛ inch all around.
2. Raise the shoulder ¼ inch at the armhole.
3. Extend the shoulder ¾ inch at the armhole.
4. Lower the armhole 1 inch.
5. Extend the side seam 1 inch.
6. Slash the sleeve as illustrated. Spread ¼ inch at the center vertical slash, ⅜ inch at the other vertical slashes, and ½ inch at the horizontal slashes.

When designing outerwear for the manufacturer who produces a comprehensive line, the designer must be especially aware of the possibilities inherent in new fabrics and the needs of active children. The coats made

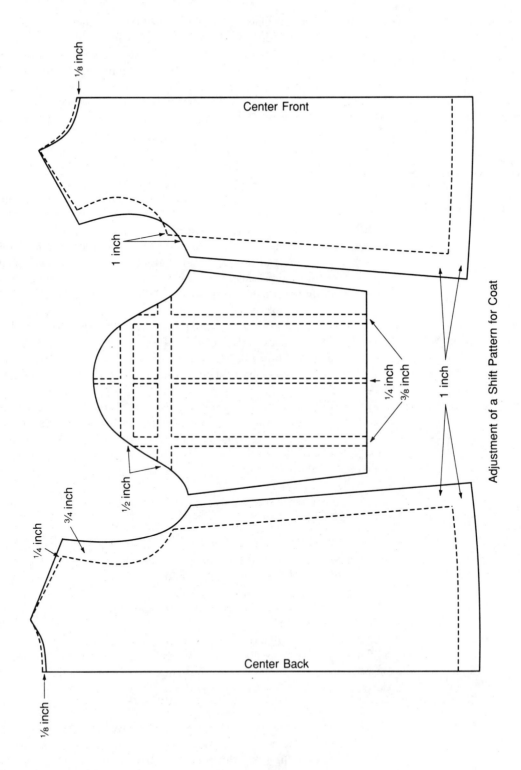

1/8 inch

Center Front

1 inch

1/4 inch
3/8 inch

1 inch

Adjustment of a Shift Pattern for Coat

3/4 inch
1/4 inch

1/2 inch

Center Back

1/8 inch

by these manufacturers are generally called "sport coats" and are designed for play and daily wear. Usually included in this category are duffle coats, peacoats, trench coats and other kinds of raincoats. The fabrics used may be closely woven cotton and polyester blends, or nylon. Other fabrics may be coated with polyurethane film to provide a waterproof finish.

Acrylic pile fabrics may be used for the lining or the shell of coats, and made to resemble fur of any kind.

The general styling of these coats is usually inspired by the current fashion in adult sportswear. The most important points for the designer to consider are: Is it rugged? Is it comfortable? Does it have the look of today?

■ Snowsuits and Ski Jackets

Snowsuits and ski jackets are the other major items of outerwear for children. For the small child, the dress coat is a luxury, and raincoats are hardly necessary. Most toddlers manage very well with only a snowsuit in their winter wardrobes. Snowsuits for boys and girls must be washable and water repellent. Colors range from pastels to navy, with clear, bright hues in between. Quilted nylon or plain nylon shells with acrylic pile linings are most popular. Acrylic pile jackets are often teamed with harmonizing nylon snowpants. Although most snowsuits consist of a jacket and pants, one-piece snowsuits are preferred by some parents. They find it easier and faster to dress small children when there is just one garment to handle.

Contrasting colors, embroidery, stitching, or braid are used as trimmings. Generally, snowsuits have zipper closings, and these may also be handled in a decorative manner. Many snowsuits are designed with hoods attached to the jacket. Hoods should have a drawstring or tab that fastens securely under the chin. Nothing is as annoying as a hood that will not stay in place. When there is no hood attached to the jacket, the snowsuit is usually sold with a matching hat. Girls' hats tie securely under the chin, and boys' caps are designed with a visor and ear flaps as well as a chin strap that is closed with snaps.

For the 7–14 group, the snow suit has evolved into the ski parka that is sold with separate ski pants. Parkas are often worn with all sorts of school and play clothes and in many cases never see a ski slope. The styling, however, is patterned strictly on adult ski wear. Quilted nylon, both printed and plain, acrylic pile, vinyl coated fabrics, and vinyls that resemble leather are all used. Ski pants for this age group are patterned after their adult counterparts.

For snowsuits and ski suits, certain design features are essential. Openings should be windproof and close snugly. Necklines have attached hoods or well-fitted collars. Sometimes, turtleneck dickeys and scarfs are included in the design. Wrist openings have rib-knit cuffs or are equipped with an inside cuff for a windproof finish. Some parkas have sleeves that are elasticised at the wrist. Ski pants have straps that fit under the instep or have ribbing at the ankle, so that the pants stay securely inside the boots. For Toddler and 3–6x sizes, ski pants must be suspended from the shoulders. Pants are often built up, but when simple suspenders are used, the waistline is elasticised.

To cut a snowsuit jacket or ski parka, the same basic adjustment as for the coat pattern may be used (see page 231). For a quilted jacket, additional ease must be added:

1. Extend the shoulder an additional ¼ inch.
2. Lower the armhole an additional ¼ inch.
3. Extend the side seam an additional ½ inch.
4. For a size 4, mark length of jacket 18 inches at center back.
5. Shape side seam very slightly as illustrated.
6. Slash the coat sleeve pattern vertically, as illustrated, and spread ¼ inch on each side.

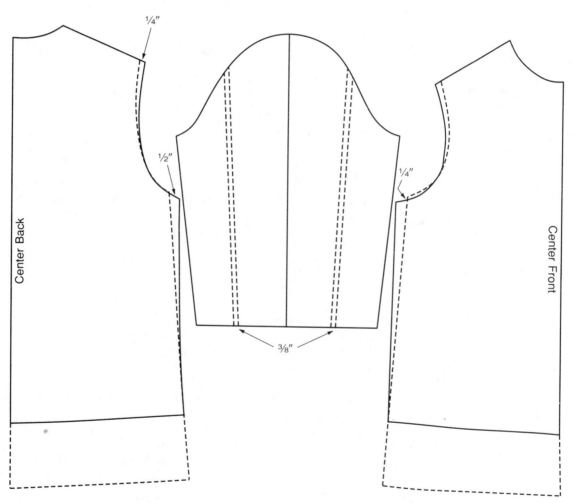

Adjustment of Coat Pattern for a Quilted Snowsuit Jacket

■ Hoods

To cut a basic pattern for a hood the measurements shown in Table XI are necessary. Once a basic hood pattern has been developed, variations may be achieved by adding style lines or extra fullness as desired.

Table XI—Measurements for Hoods

SIZE	1	2	3	4	5	6	8	10
Head Length	6½	6¾	7	7⅛	7¼	7⅜	7½	7⅝
Head Width	4⅞	5	5¼	5⅜	5½	5⅝	5¾	5⅞
Head & Neck Height	6¼	6⅝	7	7¼	7½	7¾	8¼	8½

Measuring for Hood

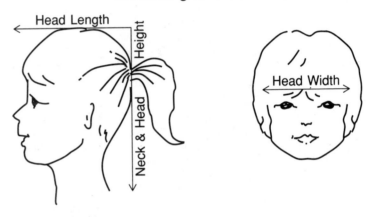

To cut a basic pattern for a hood:

1. Fold paper in half with fold at top edge.
2. Square a line down from fold for front edge of hood. This line measures the total of head and neck height, and head width.
3. On fold, mark distance of head length.
4. Square a second line down at this point equal in length to the first line.
5. On second line, place a mark equal to one-half the head width from the fold.
6. Extend a perpendicular line at this point that also equals one-half the head width.
7. Connect this extension to the base of the hood with a shallow curve.
8. Add ½ inch to the top of the hood cut-out, and finish with curved lines as illustrated.
9. Add ¾ inch at the front edge for chin extension, and finish neckline with a curve.
10. Neckline of hood should equal the neckline of the garment. Adjust if necessary. Place crossmark to match shoulder seam.

Hood Pattern

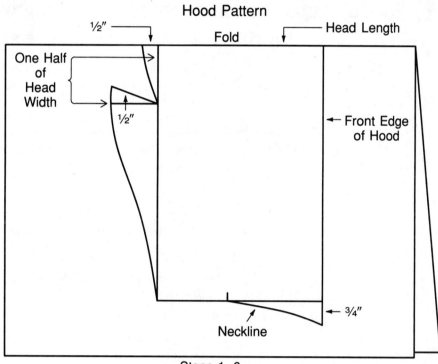

½″

One Half
of
Head
Width

½″

Fold

Head Length

Front Edge
of Hood

Neckline

¾″

Steps 1–9

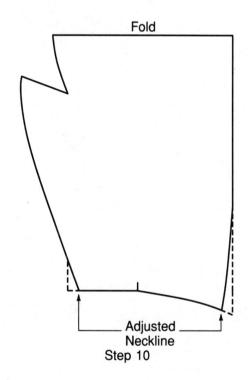

Fold

Adjusted
Neckline
Step 10

■ Special Patternmaking Features for Outerwear

Although for most areas of childrenswear patternmaking is relatively simple, jackets, coats and parkas require some more complex features for a functional well-constructed garment. Garments must be interfaced and lined in order to hang well and provide the necessary warmth. Collars should be properly tailored so that they will roll nicely. The "tailoring" referred to here is not the strict tailoring that we think of in men's wear or in women's tailored garments. It is a more modified approach that lends itself to volume production, and still gives us good-looking children's outerwear items.

Collar Patterns

Initial collar patterns for the upper collar are developed using the methods described in Chapter 10.

The tailored under collar is cut with a center back seam on the bias grain. The under collar is usually cut ⅛ inch smaller at the outer edges than the upper collar. The difference in size between the upper and under

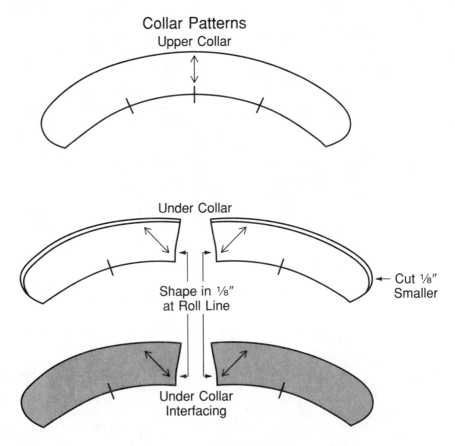

Collar Patterns
Upper Collar

Under Collar

Shape in ⅛"
at Roll Line

← Cut ⅛"
Smaller

Under Collar
Interfacing

collar may vary according to the thickness of the fabric used in the garment. The thicker the fabric, the greater the difference.

The collar will roll smoothly if the center back seam of the under collar is shaped-in ⅛ inch at the point where the collar rolls over.

Interfacings

Collars, shoulder areas, necklines and armholes should be interfaced. Cut interfacings for front and back as illustrated. Collar interfacings should match the under collar in grain and outline.

Interfacings

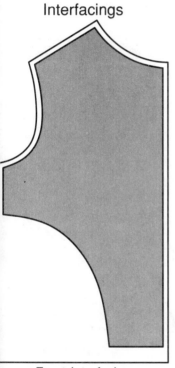

Front Interfacing

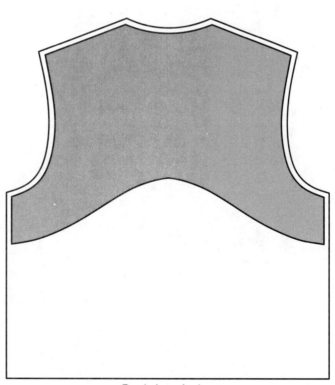

Back Interfacing

Facings and Linings

Facings are used on garments that button. Zipper jackets and parkas have only linings.

For buttoned jackets or coats:

1. When the basic pattern for the garment has been completed, fold up the hem allowance; trace the outline of the pattern to serve as the foundation for the facing and lining.

2. Establish the width of the facing at the shoulder (Approximately one third of the shoulder seam). Draw a slightly curved line to the hem of the jacket or coat as illustrated. Facings for double-breasted garments should be wide enough so that all buttons can be sewn to the facing.

Facings and Linings

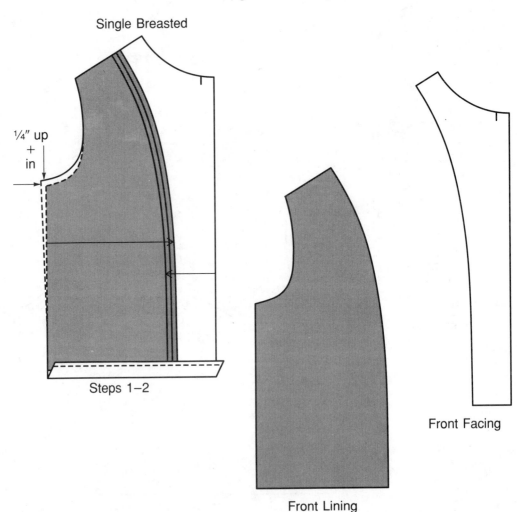

Single Breasted

¼" up
+
in

Steps 1–2

Front Lining

Front Facing

3. If the jacket or coat has a lapel, the facing must be cut ⅛ inch larger than the jacket at the lapel's outer edge. This slight extension disappears at the point where the lapel rolls over.

4. The remainder of the jacket pattern beyond the facing seams becomes the pattern for the lining. Both facing and lining length are cut to the level of the up-turned hem of the jacket.

5. When the lining of a coat or jacket is either quilted or pile fabric, the lining is cut ¼ inch higher at the lower third of the armhole and ¼ inch narrower at the upper part of the side seam, tapering to nothing at the hem.

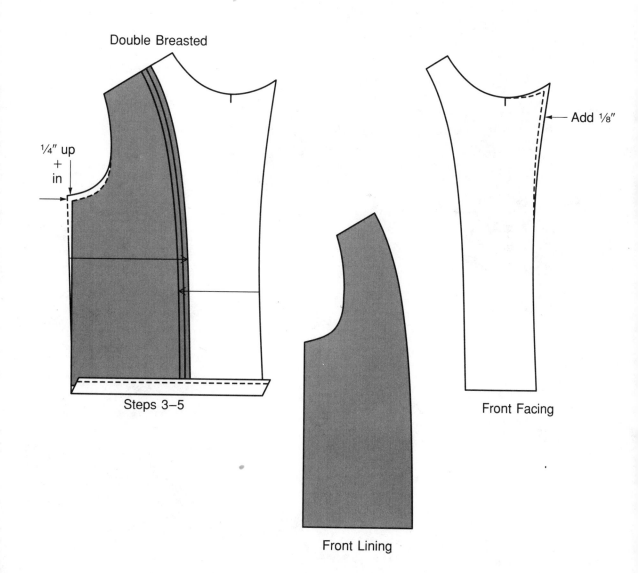

Double Breasted

¼″ up
+
in

Add ⅛″

Steps 3–5

Front Lining

Front Facing

6. The back lining is cut the same length as the front lining with the rest of the lining pattern following the outline of the garment pattern. If adjustments for quilted or pile linings were made in the front, they must be repeated for the back.

7. Sleeve linings follow the outline of the garment sleeve pattern except for the adjustment at the hem of the sleeve. The sleeve lining is shortened following the same procedure as for the front and back lining pattern.

8. If a jacket has a band at the waist or a cuff at the wrist, the lining pattern is cut the same length as the jacket pattern.

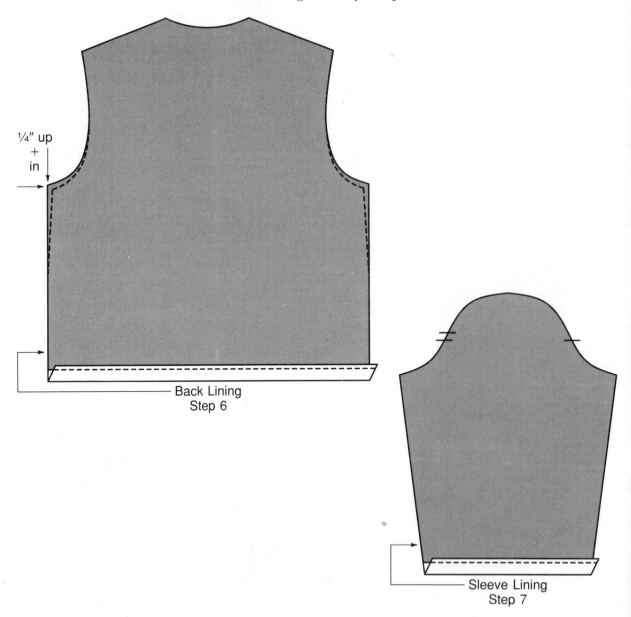

¼" up
+
in

Back Lining
Step 6

Sleeve Lining
Step 7

Pockets

Tailored pockets finished with welts or flaps are a much used functional and decorative design feature in children's outerwear. The patterns for these pockets must be precisely drafted so that all pieces fit together in the construction.

Inside Welt Pocket

   A. Draft:
      1. Draw the finished welt on the jacket or coat front pattern.
      2. Trace the welt in order to get the accurate dimensions.
      3. Below the traced welt, add the outline of the inside pocket lining.
      4. On the pocket lining, draw a line indicating the facing that will be sewn on the back pocket lining.

Inside Welt Pocket Draft

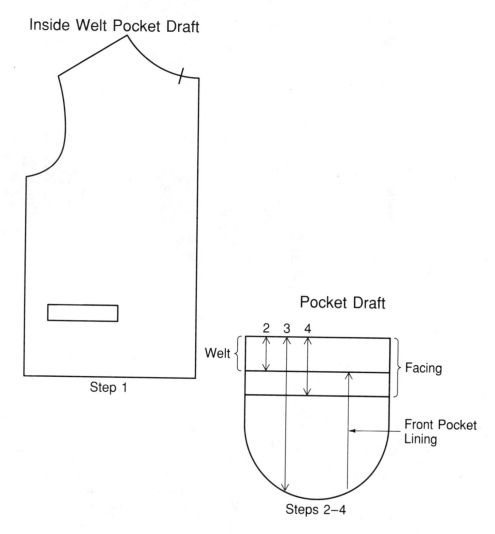

Step 1

Pocket Draft

Steps 2–4

B. Pattern:
1. Using the draft, develop pattern for welt with upper edge on fold.
2. Develop pattern for facing from the upper edge of the welt to the indicated facing line.

3. Develop pattern for the back pocket lining from the upper edge of the welt to the bottom of the pocket.
4. Develop pattern for the front pocket lining from the lower edge of the welt to the bottom of the pocket.

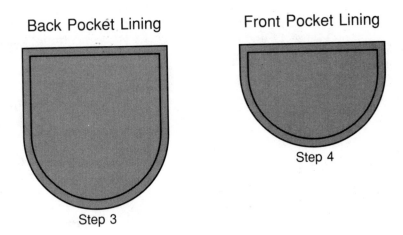

Outside Welt Pocket

A. Draft:
1. Draw the finished welt on the jacket or coat front pattern.
2. Trace the welt in order to get the accurate dimensions.
3. Below the traced welt, add the outline of the inside pocket lining.
4. Draw a line ½ inch above the lower edge of the welt.

Outside Welt Pocket Draft

Pocket Draft

2   3

4

Front Pocket Lining

Steps 2–4

Step 1

B. Pattern:
1. Develop pattern for welt by tracing the outline. Two pieces will be needed unless the upper edge of the welt is cut on the fold.
2. Develop pattern for back pocket lining by tracing the line ½ inch above the lower edge of the welt and the outline of the rest of the pocket lining.
3. Develop pattern for front pocket lining by tracing the lower edge of the welt and the rest of the pocket lining.

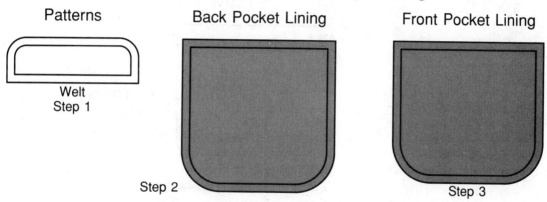

Patterns

Welt
Step 1

Back Pocket Lining

Step 2

Front Pocket Lining

Step 3

Inside Welt Pocket With Flap

A. Draft:
　　1. Draw the finished flap on the jacket or coat front pattern.

Inside Welt Pocket with a Flap
Draft

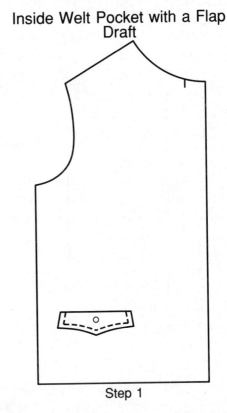

Step 1

　　2. Trace the flap in order to get accurate dimensions.
　　3. Draw a line ½ inch below the upper edge of the flap for the inside welt.
　　4. Draw the outline of the pocket lining.

Pocket Draft

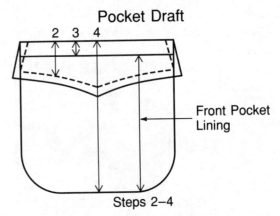

Front Pocket
Lining

Steps 2–4

B. Pattern:

    1. Trace the pocket flap. Cut two unless lower edge of the flap is cut on the fold.

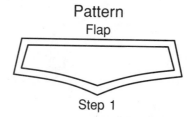

Pattern
Flap

Step 1

    2. Trace the inside welt with the upper edge on the fold.

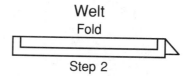

Welt
Fold

Step 2

    3. Trace the back pocket lining outline from the top of the flap to the lower edge of the pocket lining.

    4. Trace the front pocket lining outline from the lower edge of the welt to the lower edge of the pocket lining.

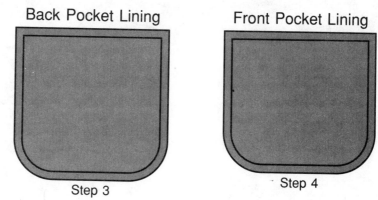

Back Pocket Lining   Front Pocket Lining

Step 3   Step 4

16 Boys' Wear

Infants

During the first year of a child's life, there is very little difference between boys' and girls' clothing. Shirts, nighties, diapers, and plastic pants are styled identically for both sexes. At this stage, from booties to buntings, often the only difference between boys' and girls' wear is in the color, traditionally pink for girls and blue for boys.

Although the basic cut of the garment is usually the same, there is sometimes a difference in the use of the trimmings. Ruffles and bows are reserved for girls, while more tailored touches are used for boys' clothing. Collars are squared off rather than rounded for boys' wear. Sleeves are tailored and never puffed. Trimmings are flat and neat. Embroidery and appliqués can be cute and whimsical, but never flowery.

Toddler Sizes

When a boy reaches the toddler stage, his clothing has developed some more distinct features. Most obviously, on dress-up occasions, boys now

249

wear pants and most girls wear skirts. Although girls and women also wear slacks as well as skirts, boys and men traditionally wear trousers for all occasions. There are other distinctions. The generally tailored look of boys' wear requires fabrics with more body and firmer weave. The piece-goods houses develop special fabrics for the boys' wear market. To complete their wardrobes, boys need shirts in woven as well as knitted fabrics. They need jackets designed in various weights for winter, transitional, and summer weather.

In the Toddler sizes, jackets are often designed to match pants. For spring and fall, these outfits are cut in corduroy or cotton twill with flannel linings for lightweight warmth. Winter jackets are lined with acrylic pile or quilted linings. For special occasions, little boys may wear shorts-and-shirt outfits in dressy fabrics; for example, velveteen shorts with a linen shirt, or matching shorts and shirt out of fine cotton broadcloth in pastel colors. One-piece jumpsuits are also becoming increasingly popular for little boys.

Colors are generally light and bright for toddler clothing. Embroideries and appliqués are used freely for trimmings. Edgings, when used for boys, are somewhat restrained, and it is better not to use any frilly effects. Contrasting cording, piping, or stitching usually work well to underline and emphasize any design features.

Firms manufacturing Toddler sizes often make both boys' and girls' wear. Sometimes, matching outfits are sold for brother and sister. Overalls for boys and jumpers for girls are cut out of the same fabric and teamed with matching shirts and blouses. Dresses and suits designed to harmonize lend themselves to attractive displays and advertising.

■ Children's Sizes

Most manufacturers producing boys' clothing in the 3–7 size range are specialists in boys' wear. For this size range, much of the toddler cuteness is replaced by a more tailored look. Trimmings and embroideries are almost completely eliminated. Overalls suspended from the shoulders or slacks with elasticised waistbands are paired with knitted shirts for daily wear.

The preschool boy is very active and needs rugged clothing for indoor and outdoor play. Corduroy, denim, or sturdy weaves of polyester and cotton are used for trousers. Combined with a knitted or woven shirt, this is a comfortable and protective outfit for active play. If well constructed, this sort of clothing is easily laundered and wears well.

For spring and fall, jackets and sweaters are needed.

Outerwear manufacturers provide the snowsuits, warmly lined jackets, or duffle coats needed for winter. Raincoats are also a necessary item, and these are made of plastic-coated cotton or other waterproof material. The Eton suit with its collarless jacket and short pants is popular for parties and other special occasions. By the time a boy is six or seven years old,

however, he will prefer a sport jacket or blazer with long trousers, just like his older brother.

We shall limit our discussion here to boys' wear in the 2–4 and the 3–7 size ranges. Creating boys' wear in the 8–20 range requires the same methods of tailoring and design as men's wear and is beyond the scope of this volume.

■ Trousers

Toddler Trousers

Trousers for toddler boys are constructed very simply. Sample size is usually size 2. Since the child has no waist development, trousers are usually suspended from the shoulders or attached to the shirt.

To cut toddler trousers and shorts (see page 252):
1. Draft slacks (see pages 122–123). Allow 1 inch ease in the crotch and ¾ inch ease at the hip. There will be no need for darts or shaping at the waistline. When the legs are not tapered, the side seam may be eliminated as in infants' wear.
2. For shorts, measure to the crotch level at the side seam and 1 inch down at the inseam. Connect guide markings as illustrated.
3. When shorts button to the shirt, allow a deep hem or facing at the waistline to provide backing for buttonholes. A placket is constructed at the side seam, and overlapping buttonholes from the front and back button to the shirt at the side seam.

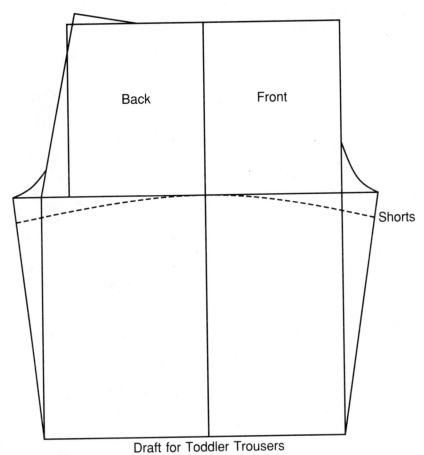

Back   Front

Shorts

Draft for Toddler Trousers

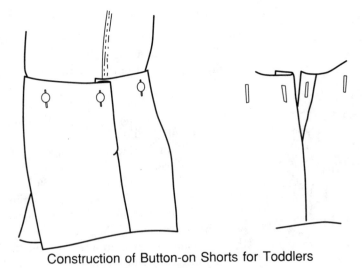

Construction of Button-on Shorts for Toddlers

Jumpsuits and Overalls

All-in-one jumpsuits and overalls may be designed for both boys and girls in all size ranges. Instructions for patternmaking are included here because these garments are staples for toddler boys clothing. Never-the-less, these instructions are applicable for all childrenswear.

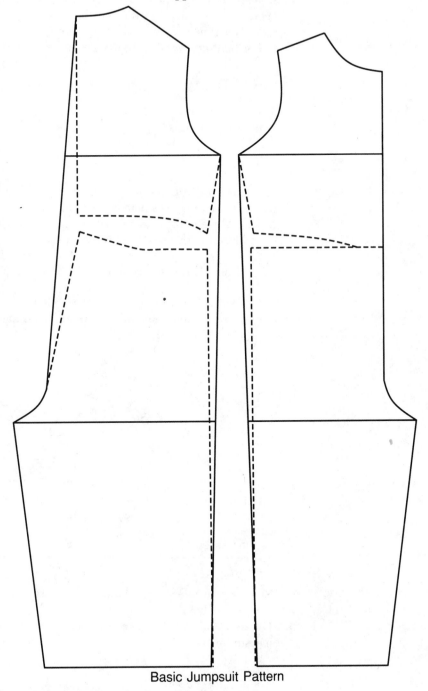

Basic Jumpsuit Pattern

To cut a jumpsuit or overalls:
1. Separate trouser pattern at the side seam.
2. Place the front and back waist slopers so that the waistline of the front sloper meets the waistline of the trousers at center front. Align back waist to front waist at the underarm.
3. Blend in side seam and center-back seam as illustrated on page 253. There will be a space in the waistline area at the side seam and center-back. This is necessary for fit in a jumpsuit.
4. For built-up overalls, draw style lines on the basic jumpsuit pattern.

Boys' Trousers with Front Placket

By the time the boy is three or four years old, his trousers are cut, more or less, like mens'. Typical features are the front placket opening and pockets. Legs may be straight, tapered, or flared, according to the current style.

To cut boys trousers in size 4 with a simplified front placket opening:
1. Use the basic slacks pattern (see pages 122–123).
2. Plan pockets. Mark off pocket opening on the front pattern.
3. Indicate the shape of the inside pocket.
4. Add a placket extension, 1¾ inches wide and 6 inches long, at the center front. This will accommodate a 6-inch zipper.

The following table gives the garment measurements for Boys' size trousers as recommended by the United States Department of Commerce for sizes 4, 5, 6, and 7.

Table XII—Boys' Trousers

SIZE		4	5	6	7
Waist	(A–B)	22½	22½	23	23½
Seat	(C–D)	28½	29½	30½	31½
Front Rise[1]	(E–F)	9¼	9½	9¾	10
Back Rise [1]	(E–G)	12½	12¾	13	13¼
Outseam[2]	(A–H)	23	25¼	27	28¾
Inseam finished	(E–J)	15	17	18½	20

[1]Rise measurements are based on trousers extending ¾ inch above waistline of boy.
[2]Difference in inches between outseam and inseam is true rise or crotch measurement.

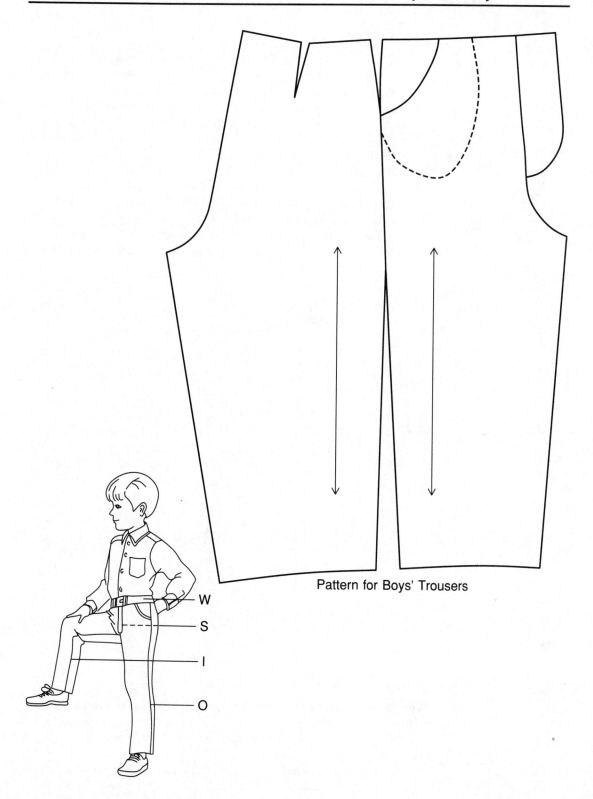

Pattern for Boys' Trousers

W

S

I

O

Method of Measuring

- Waist—(A–B) Twice the distance across the waist of the trousers with the waistband smooth and flat. (If elastic waistbands are used, then the waist should be measured reasonably taut.)
- Seat—(C–D) About 2 inches above the crotch, measure the distance straight across the trousers, with the back seat fully pulled out.
- Front rise—(E–F) Measured from the crotch up along the edge of the fly to the top of the waistband.
- Back rise—(E–G) Measured from the crotch up the back seam of the trousers to the top of the waistband.
- Outseam—(A–H) Measured from the top of the waistband along the side seam to the bottom of the cuff.
- Inseam—(E–J) With one leg thrown back over the upper part of the trousers, measure from the crotch seam to the bottom edge of the cuff.

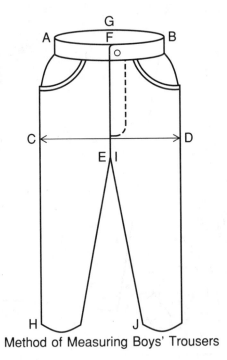

Method of Measuring Boys' Trousers

■ Shirts

Boys' Dress Shirts

The dress shirt, cut from woven fabrics, complements the Eton suit or other tailored jackets but may also be worn on its own with all sorts of shorts or overalls. Sometimes, dress shorts of velveteen, linen, or fine cotton are designed to button onto the shirt. The collar may be rolled or flat. Sleeves may be long or short, and the shirt closing may be plain or finished with a band. A patch pocket is sometimes applied to the left front of the shirt. Sleeve caps are flattened. The armhole is straightened out and somewhat enlarged to create a roomy, comfortable garment which can be easily sewn with double-needle construction.

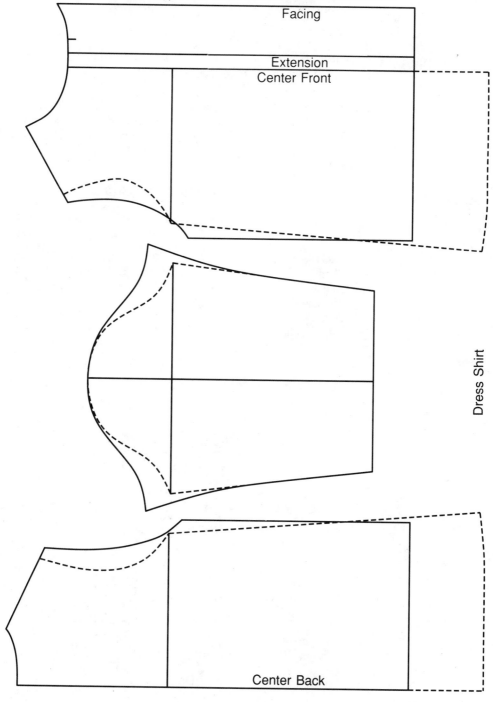

To cut a size 4 boys' shirt from a shift sloper:

1. Mark the length of the shirt at the center back at 16½ inches.
2. Extend the shoulder ½ inch at the armhole; drop the armhole ½ inch at the underarm; add ½ inch to the width of the shirt at the side seam.
3. Add extension for buttons at the center front.
4. Plan band if desired.
5. Add facings at center front.
6. Flatten the cap of the sleeve sloper an additional 1 inch. Ease in the sleeve cap should not exceed ½ inch.

The following table gives the garment measurements for boys' size sport and dress shirts as recommended by the United States Department of Commerce for size 4, 6, and 8. Measurements for size 2 were not available in this category and were extrapolated for sport shirts.

Table XIII Boys' Shirts

SIZE	SPORTS SHIRT				DRESS SHIRT		
	2	4	6	8	4	6	8
(N) Neckline	11	11½	12	12½	11	11½	12
(C) Chest	25	27	29	31	27	29	31
(L) Length	15½	17	18½	20	19	21	22½
(A) Armhole Girth	11	12	13	14	12	13	14
(Y) Yoke Width	10¾	11½	12¼	13	11½	12¼	13
(S) Sleeve Length	17½	19	21½	23½	19	21½	23½

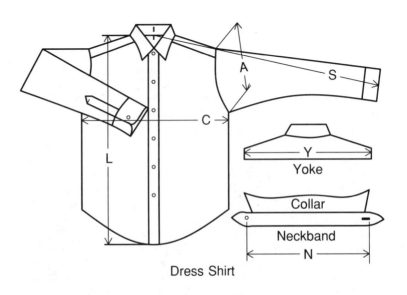

Dress Shirt

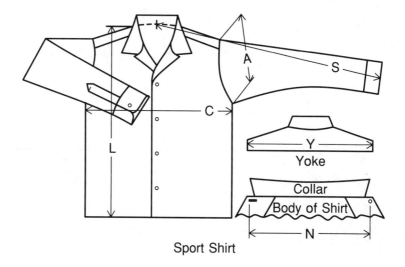

Sport Shirt

Method of Measuring

- Neckline—(N) Measured from the center of the button parallel to the neckline to the far end of the buttonhole.
- Chest—(C) Twice the distance across the buttoned-up shirt measured to its outer limits, 1 inch below the bottom of the armhole.
- Length—(L) Measured from the highest point of the yoke to the bottom of the shirt when the front and back lengths are even at the bottom.
- Armhole girth—(A) Twice the distance across the sleeve at the armhole, measured in a straight line from the top to the bottom of the armhole.
- Yoke width—(Y) Measured across the body of the yoke where it joins the body of the garment.
- Sleeve length—(S) Measured from the center of the yoke to the bottom of the cuff.

Knit Polo Shirts and T-Shirts

Knit shirts are popular with everyone because they are comfortable and simple to care for. Even before the days of permanent press, cotton knit shirts could be laundered and worn without having to use an iron. Most boys like these shirts for their free and easy fit and comfortable, soft texture.

To cut a size 4 knit shirt from a shift sloper:
1. Mark the length of the shirt at the center back at 15½ inches.
2. Reduce the width of the sloper at the underarm by ¾ inch.
3. Drop the armhole ½ inch and straighten the armhole as illustrated on page 260.

4. Flatten the cap of the sleeve 1½ inches, and reduce the width of the sleeve so that there is no more than ½ inch ease in the sleeve cap. Smooth out some of the shaping in the sleeve cap as illustrated.

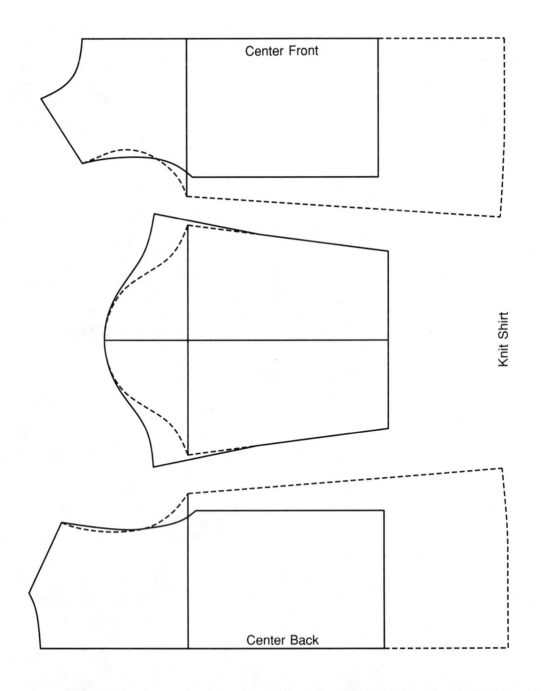

Center Front

Knit Shirt

Center Back

The following table gives the garment measurements for Boys' knit shirts as recommended by the United States Department of Commerce for sizes, 2, 4, 6, and 8. Sizes 3 and 5 are extrapolated.

Table XIV—Boys' Knit Shirts

SIZE	2	3	4	5	6	8
Width of Garment (H–J)	10½	11	11½	12	12½	13¼
Total Length (A–B)	14½	15¼	16	16¾	17½	19
Sleeve Length: (N–G)						
Short, underarm	3½	3½	4	4	4	4½
Long, underarm	10½	11½	12½	13½	14½	16
Armhole Length (F–N)	5	5¼	5½	5¾	6	6½
Collar Length for Polo Shirt	11½	11¾	12	12¼	12½	13
Ribbed-knit Neckline for T-Shirt	12	12¼	12½	12¾	13	13½
Stretched	20	20¼	20½	20¾	21	21½

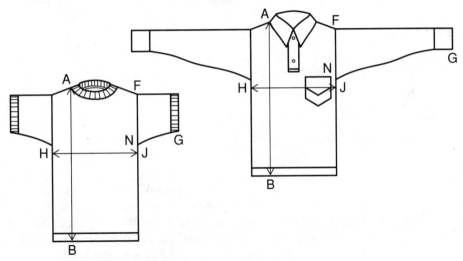

Method of Measuring

- Width of garment—Measured across the garment 1 inch below the bottom of the armholes.
- Total length—Measured from the point where the shoulder joins the collar to the bottom edge of the shirt.
- Sleeve length—Measured from the point under the arm where the sleeve is seamed to the garment to the lower edge of the sleeve cuff, if a cuff is used.
- Armhole length—Measured from the point where the sleeve is attached to the shoulder to the lowest point under the arm.
- Collar length—Measured from the center of the collar button around the neckband to the outside end of the buttonhole.
- Ribbed-knit neckline—Measured by taking the circumference of the neck with the fabric relaxed and smooth.

17 Professional Samplemaking

The manufacturing process in childrenswear requires a more simplified method of construction than that of women's wear. Regardless of price, all children's garments must be mass produced in order to be competitive with the rest of the market. In this chapter we will describe various simplified construction methods unique to sewing sample garments for the childrenswear industry. This is not meant to be a comprehensive sewing chapter. We assume that the designer using this book already has a rudimentary knowledge of sewing.

■ Seams and Seam Finishes

The safety overlock stitch machine is widely used in children's garments to provide a strong and clean seam finish. Although this is essential in sportswear and necessary in knits, overlocked seams are used in all types of childrenswear from the infant's layette to rugged outerwear.

For added detail in sportswear, flat-felled seams might be appropriately used. These seams require two stitching operations when done in the sample room, but in production they are completed in one operation on a machine designed for this purpose.

Occasionally, a designer using fine, delicate fabrics on dresses or infant's wear might use french seams. Only when garments are manufactured in parts of the world where labor is cheap and plentiful, can this type of seam be used on mass-produced garments. In virtually all other cases french seams will be replaced in stock by either overlocked seams or mock french seams. Mock french seams are achieved by passing two layers of fabric through a narrow hemming attachment.

■ Assembling a Lined Jacket

In childrenswear, the professionally finished jacket or parka is put together without any hand sewing. The following sequence of assembly results in a neatly finished and sturdy garment.

1. Stitch interfacing to undercollar on seam line and in a zig-zag pattern (Both undercollar and interfacing should be cut on the bias); stitch upper collar to undercollar; layer seam allowances and clip curve in a V form as illustrated.

Assembling a Lined Jacket

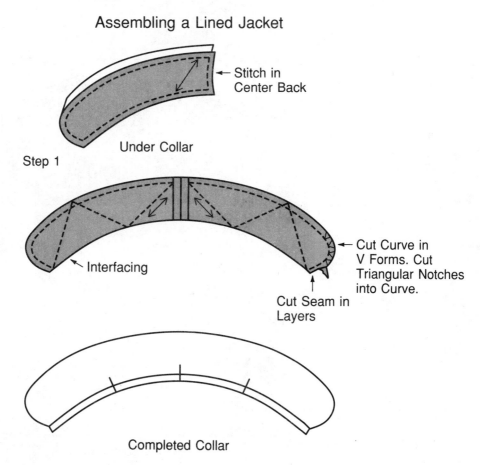

Step 1

Stitch in Center Back

Under Collar

Interfacing

Cut Curve in V Forms. Cut Triangular Notches into Curve.

Cut Seam in Layers

Completed Collar

2. Stitch interfacing to front and back panels.

Step 2

3. Stitch front facing to front lining sections.

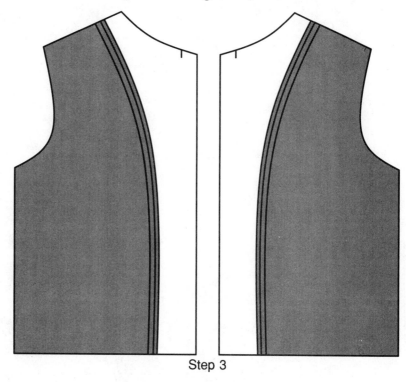

Step 3

4. Sew shoulder seams together and insert sleeves into armholes with the side seams open.

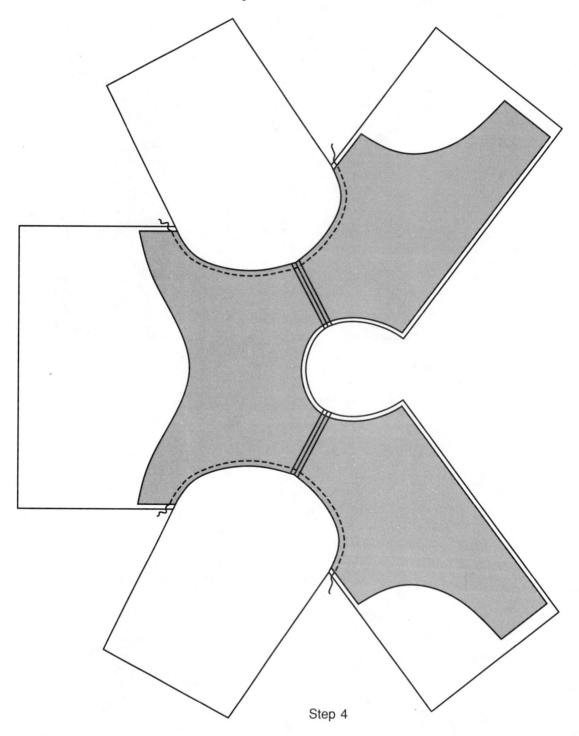

Step 4

5. Repeat step 4 for the lining, but first sew front lining and front facing together.

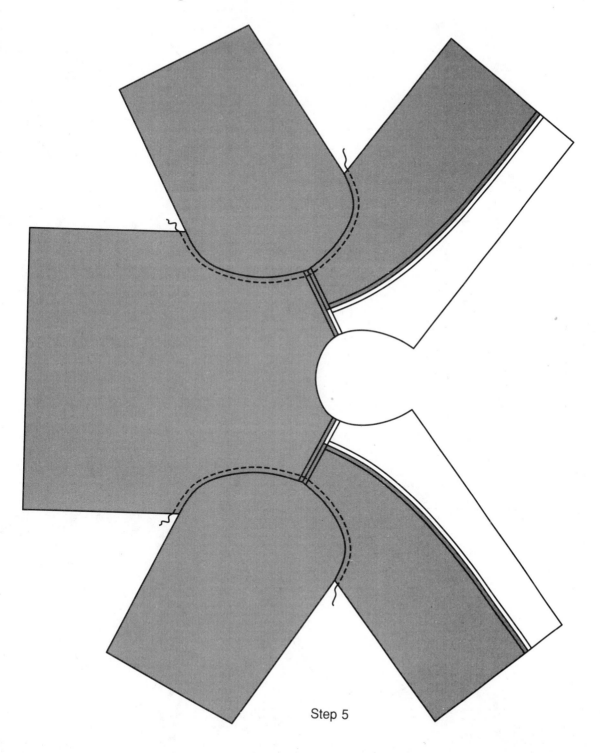

Step 5

6. Sew completed collar to jacket neckline.

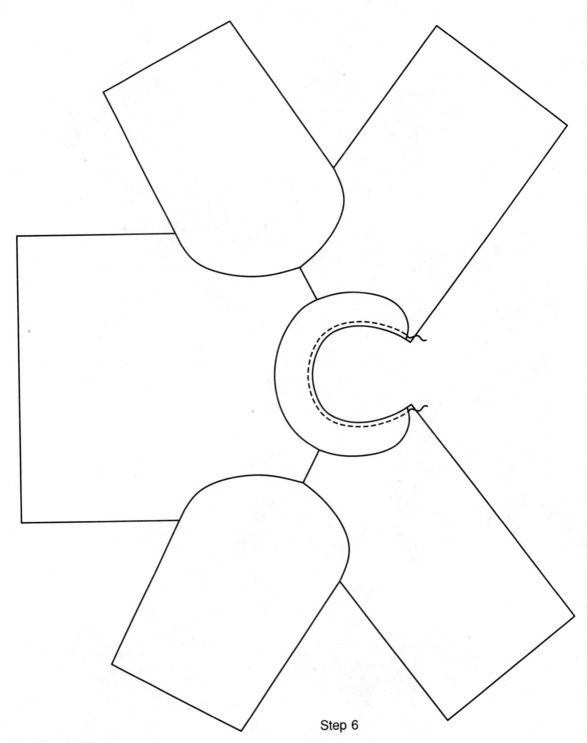

Step 6

7. a. For a buttoned jacket, place jacket and lining right sides together and beginning at center front, 2 inches up from the hem edge, sew lining and jacket together; continue stitching along the neckline; and down the other side of the center front leaving the last 2 inches open.

    b. For jackets with a front zipper, stitch jacket and lining together at neckline only, leaving entire center front open.

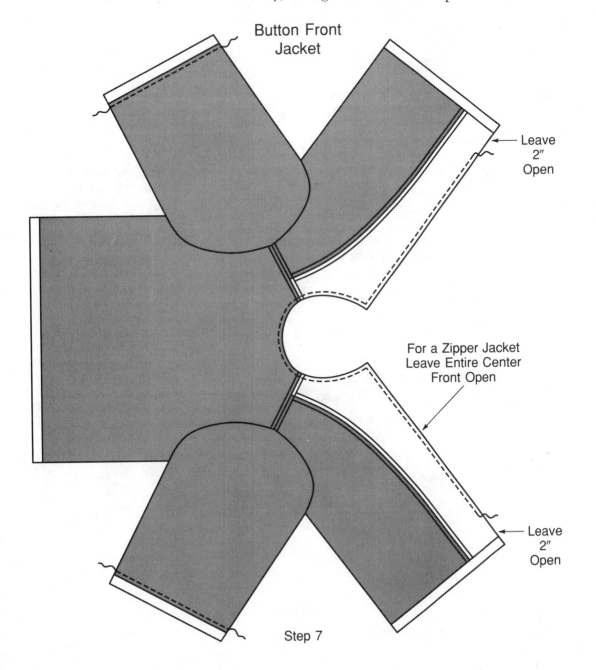

Button Front
Jacket

Leave
2″
Open

For a Zipper Jacket
Leave Entire Center
Front Open

Leave
2″
Open

Step 7

8. Stitch jacket and lining together at wrist edge of sleeves. If knit cuffs are used, they can be inserted between the lining and the jacket.

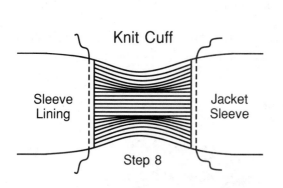

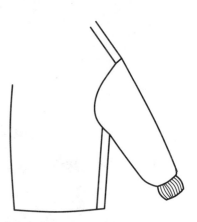

9. Lift lining very carefully and begin to sew front and back lining together at the lower end of the side seams; continue sewing into the underarm seams of both lining and jacket sleeves and end these continuous seams at the lower end of the jacket side seams. (After this step is completed, lining and jacket sleeves are connected at the wrist and form a circle, as illustrated.)

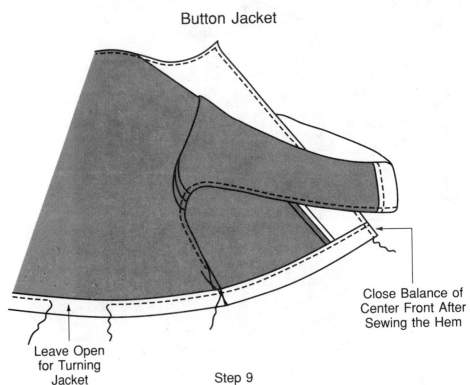

Button Jacket

Close Balance of
Center Front After
Sewing the Hem

Leave Open
for Turning
Jacket

Step 9

10. a. For a buttoned jacket, sew lining and jacket together at hem edge leaving an opening in the back for turning the jacket inside out. Let jacket hem turn up and close the opening at the lower front edge.

b. For jackets with a front zipper, sew lining and jacket together completely at hem edge. Jacket is turned inside out through front openings. When jacket and lining are completed and turned, a separating zipper is inserted between jacket and lining.

Zipper Front Jacket

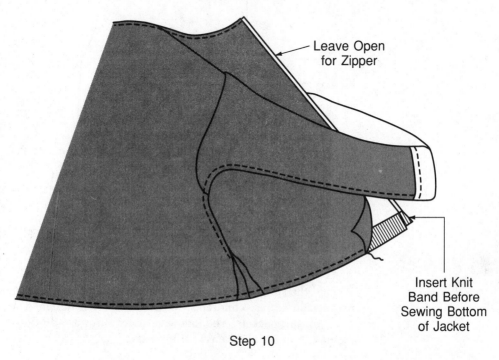

Leave Open for Zipper

Insert Knit Band Before Sewing Bottom of Jacket

Step 10

NOTE—For a jacket with a knitted band at the waist, the knitted band is inserted between the lining and the jacket before the lower edge is sewn together.

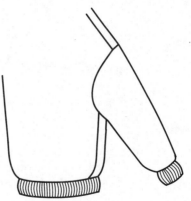

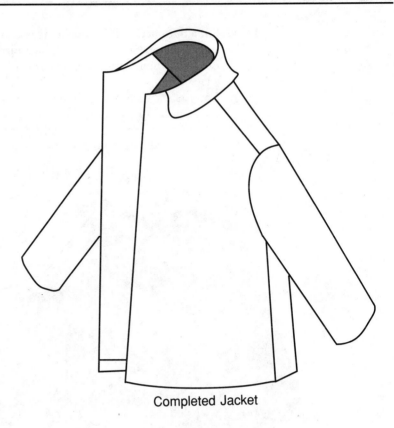

Completed Jacket

■ Pockets

Beyond the simple and familiar patch pockets and those pockets that are inserted in seams, children's outerwear is often designed with various types of welt pockets. The following procedures are those used by samplemakers in the childrenswear industry.

Inside Welt Pocket

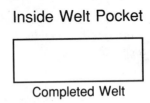

Completed Welt

The Inside Welt Pocket

1. On the face of the garment, mark off the exact placement and dimensions of the welt pocket with four dots.
2. Prepare the welt by folding it in half. Interface it if necessary. The finished size of the welt must be exactly the same as the dimensions indicated on the garment. Pin and stitch welt to the face of the garment making sure that the stitching starts and ends at the indicated dots.

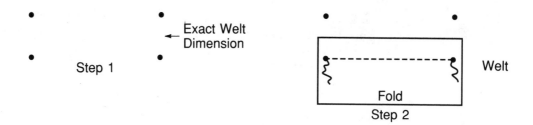

Step 1

← Exact Welt Dimension

Welt

Fold

Step 2

3. Stitch facing to the upper part of the pocket lining and stitch both parts of the lining over the welt, stitching from dot to dot as illustrated. Bar tack at beginning and end of pocket stitching.

4. Cut the pocket opening from the wrong side of the garment as illustrated.

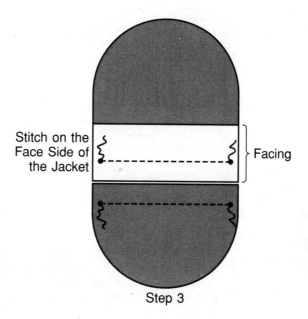

Stitch on the Face Side of the Jacket

Facing

Step 3

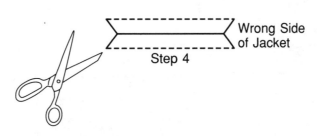

Wrong Side of Jacket

Step 4

5. Push welt pocket through the opening to the wrong side of the garment and stitch the triangular corners to the welt and pocket lining as illustrated.

6. Complete the pocket by stitching the two pocket lining pieces together.

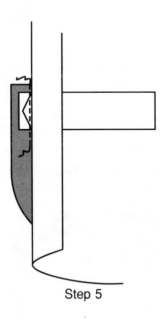

Step 5

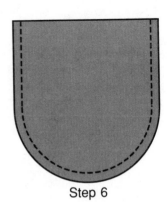

Step 6

Outside Welt Pocket

Outside Welt Pocket

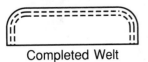

Completed Welt

1. Complete welt leaving ½ inch seam allowance at the lower end. On the face of the garment, mark the exact placement and length of the finished welt with two dots; place an additional dot ½ inch up and ¼ inch in from the dots at each side.

2. Stitch facing over back pocket lining and place the finished welt over the lower dots on the garment and stitch from dot to dot, bar tacking at both ends.

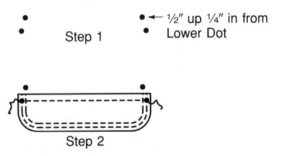

Step 1

½" up ¼" in from Lower Dot

Step 2

3. Place pocket lining pieces above and below the welt, as illustrated, and stitch both pieces from dot to dot, bar tacking at both ends.

4. On the wrong side of the garment, cut through the fabric of the garment between the stitching lines stopping ½ inch from the end of the welt and cutting triangularly to the corners, as illustrated.

5. Push pocket lining pieces through the opening, and let both sections of the pocket lining fall down. The welt turns up on the right side of the garment.

6. Lift garment at end of welt and stitch triangular corners to the pocket lining pieces on both sides.

7. Complete stitching the inside of pocket, as illustrated.

8. Tack sides of welt to the garment.

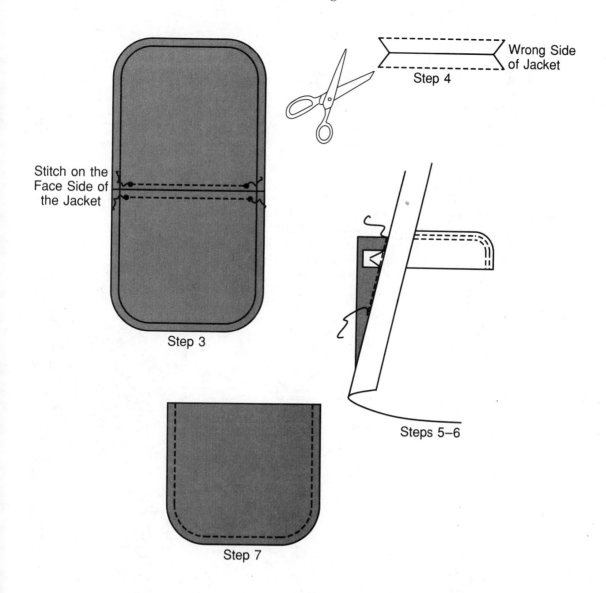

Wrong Side of Jacket

Step 4

Stitch on the Face Side of the Jacket

Step 3

Steps 5–6

Step 7

Inside Welt Pocket With Flap

1. Complete flap with desired details. On the face of the garment, mark the exact placement and length of the finished flap with two dots. Place an additional dot ½ inch down and ¼ inch in from the dot at each side.
2. Place flap over upper dots on the face of the garment; stitch from dot to dot bar tacking at both ends.
3. For the welt, cut a 1 inch strip of fabric 1 inch longer than the finished flap and fold in half so that the welt is exactly ½ inch wide.

Inside Welt Pocket with a Flap

← Welt

Step 1

•
•

Step 2

•
•← ½" down ¼" in
from top dot

Fold

Step 3

4. Place the welt over the lower dots on the face of the garment, with raw edges overlapping the seam allowance of the flap. Stitch from dot to dot, bar tacking at both ends.
5. Place pocket lining pieces over flap and welt and stitch from dot to dot, bar tacking at both ends.

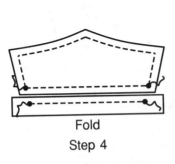

Fold

Step 4

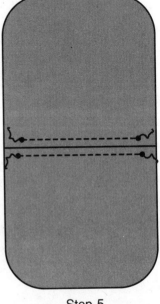

Step 5

6. On the wrong side of the garment, cut through the center of the fabric between the stitching lines, stopping ½ inch before each end, and cutting triangularly to the corners, as illustrated.

7. Push pocket lining pieces through opening and let both sections of the pocket lining fall down. The welt will stand up finishing the lower section of the pocket opening. Ends of welt should be pushed through to the wrong side of the garment. The flap will fall down covering the pocket opening.

8. Turn up garment at the end of the flap and stitch triangular corners to the welt at both ends of the pocket.

9. Complete pocket by stitching the pocket lining pieces together.

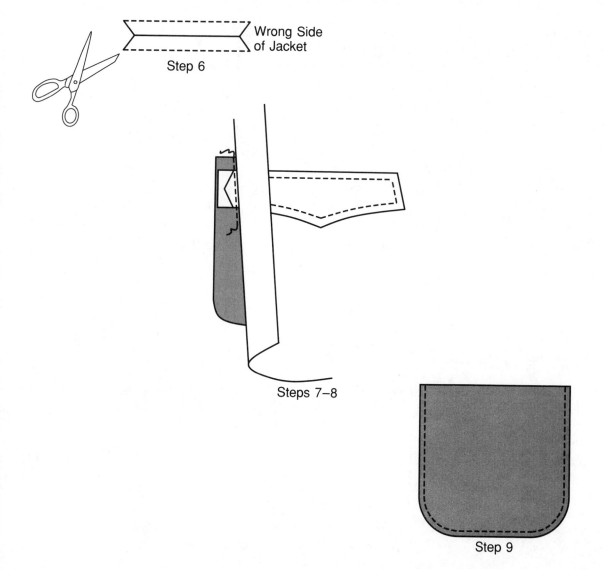

Wrong Side of Jacket

Step 6

Steps 7–8

Step 9

■ Simplified Front Placket Opening for Boys' Slacks

The following simple method for constructing a front zipper placket opening may be used for childrenswear. Although there are no separate facings and extensions to handle, the resulting placket is neat and professional.

1. Add a placket extension, 1¾ inches wide and 6 inches long at the center front of the slacks. This will accommodate a 6-inch zipper.
2. Overedge the seam allowance of the extensions.

Placket Opening for Boys' Slacks

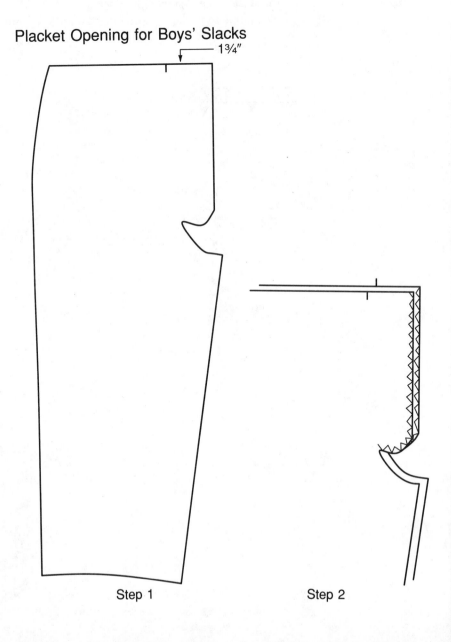

Step 1   Step 2

3. Place zipper, face up, on left side front so that the right edge of the zipper tape is ¼ inch away from the extension. Stitch left zipper tape to the extension.

4. Enclose left zipper tape by folding the extension over the edge of the tape, forming a pleat. Topstitch into place.

5. Place the right front over the left front so that center front notches match. Crotch seam should also match. Making sure that the left extension is folded back so that it will not get caught in the stitching, stitch zipper to the right extension along the edge of the right zipper tape. Stitch crotch seam.

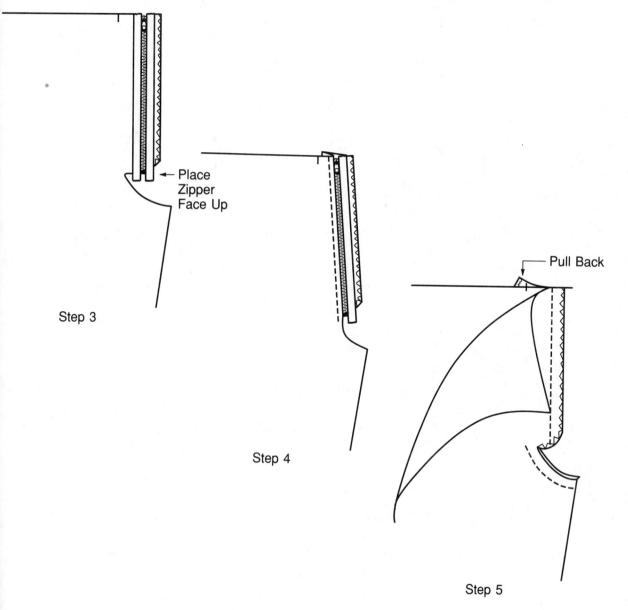

← Place Zipper Face Up

Step 3

Step 4

Pull Back

Step 5

6. Turn to the right side. Straigthen out fold of placket on the right extension, and stitch the placket about 1¼ inches from the center front, curving the lower end. Tack lower end of the placket at the center front, and topstitch the entire front crotch seam making sure that the left extension is not caught in the stitching.

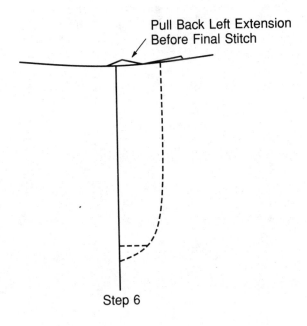

Pull Back Left Extension
Before Final Stitch

Step 6

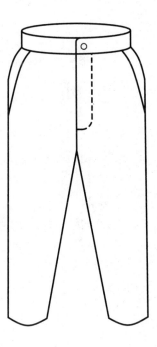

Appendix

■ Measurement Charts for Childrenswear

The following tables of size designations and body measurements were developed from data published by the United States Department of Commerce. These data were based on original research conducted by the United States Department of Agriculture in the 1930's. The measurements published here also take into consideration children's growth patterns as reflected in the 1980 charts for the National Center for Health Statistics and the 1977 Anthropometric Study of U.S. Infants and Children conducted by the University of Michigan. The tables of Infants' Body Measurements, Childrens' Body Measurements, and Girls' Body Measurements were influenced by the work of the Childrenswear task group working within the subcommittee on Apparel Sizing under the aegis of the Textile Committee of the American Society for Testing and Materials (ASTM).

All sudden shifts of proportion have been eliminated so as to reflect the gradual growth and development of the child from birth to adolescence. Infant's, Toddler's, Children's and Girl's size ranges flow into each other in a continuous growth curve. The measurements for the Sub-Teen size range reflect the changes in proportion as girls mature. They are the transition to adult sizes.

All the measurements in the following tables represent "body measurements" taken over light underwear, such as a vest and panties. To convert them to "nude" measurements, the following amounts may be subtracted:

- Chest—¾ inch for all sizes
- Waist—½ inch for all sizes
- Hip—¾ inch for all sizes
- Vertical trunk girth—1 inch for all sizes
- Total crotch length—½ inch for all sizes

These body measurements serve as a guide for the manufacture of model forms and for the sizing and grading of garment patterns. "Garment measurements" are arrived at after the necessary ease has been added. For example:

- Size 4 chest body measurement—22 inches
- Size 4 chest dress measurement—24 inches
- Size 4 chest coat measurement—28 inches

281

Stretchable knitted garments may measure less than body girth. For example, the chest measurement of a size 4 rib-knit polo shirt equals 21 inches.

Garment lengths depend on the proportions desired by the designer. Dress lengths vary depending on the effect desired. Coats should cover dresses completely and, therefore, should be 1 to 2 inches longer than dresses. It is highly desirable that designers work with a full-length model form or use live models to establish the correct length of each garment.

Definitions of Body Landmarks

Definitions of the more important body landmarks illustrated are as follows:

- Crown—Top of head.
- Cervicale—The prominent point on the seventh or lowest cervicale vertibra at the back of the neck, which becomes more prominent when the head is bent forward. (Cervicale height measurements are taken, however, only when the head is in an erect position.)
- Waist—The lower edge of the lower floating rib, located at the side of the body in a line directly below the center of the armpit.
- Hip—The outer bony prominence of the upper end of the thigh bone (the femur).
- Knee—the inner bony prominence of the upper end of the tibia, the larger of the two long bones of the leg extending from the knee to the ankle.
- Ankle—The inner bony prominence of the lower end of the tibia.

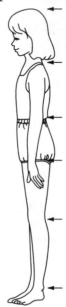

Definitions of Body Landmarks

Methods of Measuring

- Stature—Measure from the crown to the soles of the feet.
- Chest—Measure horizontally around the body under the arms and across the nipples so as to include the lower portion of the shoulder blades, Figure 1,A.
- Waist—Measure horizontally around the body at waist height, Figure 1,B.
- Hip/Seat—Measure horizontally around the body at hip height, Figure 1,C.
- Vertical Trunk—Measure from a point on the shoulder, midway between the neck and the normal armhole line, around the bottom of the crotch and back to original shoulder point, Figure 2,D to E.
- Neck Base—Measure around the neck touching the cervicale at the back and the upper borders of the collar bone at the front, Figure 3,H.
- Armscye—Measure from a point at the armhole edge of the shoulder, midway between the arcromion and the highest prominence at the outer edge of the collar bone, through the mid-point of the underarm, and back to the point of origin, Figure 3,I.
- Upper Arm—Measure the circumference of the arm midway between the outer edge of the shoulder and the elbow, Figure 2,F.
- Elbow—Measure the circumference of the elbow while the arm is straight, Figure 2,F.
- Thigh—Measure around the upper part of the leg, close to the crotch, Figure 2,G.
- Shoulder Length—Measure from the widest point of the neck-base measurement at the shoulder to the armscye point of the shoulder, Figure 4,K.
- Across Shoulder—Measure across the back from the widest point of one shoulder to the widest point of the other shoulder.

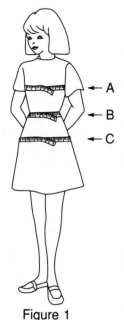

Figure 1

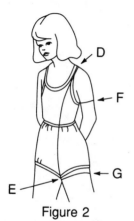

Figure 2

Figure 3

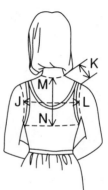

Figure 4

Figure 5

Figure 6

- Total Crotch Length—Measure the distance from the waist level at the center front through the crotch to the waist level at the center back, Figure 5,O.
- Arm Length—With the arm bent at the elbow, measure from the top of the shoulder along the outside (posterior surface) of the arm to the prominent wrist bone at the back of the hand, Figure 6, P to R.
- Cervicale to Wrist—With the elbow bent, measure from the cervicale by way of the top of the shoulder and along the outside surface of the arm, around the elbow to the prominent wrist bone at the back of the hand.
- Head and Neck Length—With the head erect, measure the distance from the crown to the cervicale.
- Cervicale Height—Measure the distance from the cervicale to the soles of the feet.
- Cervicale to Knee—Measure the distance from the cervicale to the knee.
- Scye Depth—Measure along the spine from the cervicale to an imaginary line connecting the mid-underarm points, Figure 4, M to N.
- Cervicale to Back Waist—Measure along the spine from the cervicale to the waist.
- Neck to Front Waist—Measure from the front of the neck base to the front of the waist.
- Waist Height—Measure the distance from the waist to the soles of the feet.
- Waist to Knee—Measure the distance from the waist to the knee.
- Hip Height—Measure the distance from the hip to the soles of the feet.
- Crotch Height—Measure the distance from the midpoint of the crotch to the soles of the feet.
- Knee Height—Measure the distance from the knee to the soles of the feet.
- Ankle Height—Measure the distance from the ankle to the soles of the feet.

Table I—Infants' Body Measurements
(Composite of Boys' and Girls' Measurements)

SIZE	0–3 MONTH	3–6 MONTHS	6–12 MONTHS	12–18 MONTHS
Stature (inches)	up to 23½	24–26½	27–29½	30–32½
Weight (pounds)	0–12	13–16	17–20	21–24
Chest	16½	17½	18½	19½
Waist	18	18½	19	19½
Seat	17	18	19	20
*Vertical Trunk	28	30	32	34
Neck Base	8½	8⅞	9¼	9⅝
Armscye	6	6⅝	7¼	7⅞
Upper Arm	5⅛	5⅜	5⅝	5⅞
Elbow	5¾	6	6¼	6½
Thigh	9¼	9⅞	10½	11⅛
Shoulder Length	2⁹⁄₁₆	2⅝	2¹¹⁄₁₆	2¾
Across Shoulder	8¼	8½	8¾	9
Crotch Length Total	11⅛	12¼	13⅜	14½
Arm Length	6⅝	7⅞	9⅛	10⅜
Cervicale to Wrist	10¾	12⅛	13½	14⅞
Head & Neck Length	5¾	6	6¼	6½
Cervicale Height	17¼	20	22¾	25½
Cervicale to Knee	12¼	14	15¾	17½
Scye Depth Along Spine	3½	3¾	4	4¼
Cervicale to Back Waist	6	6½	7	7½
Neck to Front Waist	4½	5	5½	6
Waist Height	11¼	13½	15¾	18
Waist to Knee	6¼	7½	8¾	10
Hip Height	8¾	10¾	12¾	14¾
Crotch Height	6½	8¼	10	11¾
Knee Height	5	6	7	8

*Measurement includes diaper

Table II—Standard Size Range for Certain Infants' Garments

GARMENT	3 MO.	6 MO.	12 MO.	18 MO.
Layette Items	x	x		
Shirts	x	x	x	x
Pants, plastic	x	x	x	x
Pants, training			x	x
Sweaters	x	x	x	x
Stretch Coveralls	x	x	x	x
Crawlers		x	x	x
Dresses		x	x	x
Sun Suits		x	x	x

*An "X" in any column indicates that the garment is to be made in that size.

Table III—Childrens' Body Measurements
(Composite of Boys' and Girls' Measurement)

SIZE	2	3	4	5	6	6x/7
Stature (inches)	33–35½	36–38½	39–41½	42–44½	45–47½	48–50
Weight (pounds)	25–28	29–32	33–36	37–40	41–46	47–53
Chest	20	21	22	23	24	25
Waist	20	20½	21	21½	22	22½
Seat	21	22	23	24	25	26½
Vertical Trunk w/o diaper	33	35½	38	40½	43	45½
Vertical Trunk with diaper	36	38½	41	–	–	–
Neck Base	10	10⅜	10¾	11⅛	11½	11⅞
Armscye	8½	9⅛	9¾	10⅜	11	11⅝
Upper Arm	6⅛	6⅜	6⅝	6⅞	7⅛	7⅜
Elbow	6¾	7	7¼	7½	7¾	8
Thigh	11¾	12⅜	13	13⅝	14¼	15⅛
Shoulder Length	2⅞	3	3⅛	3¼	3⅜	3½
Across Shoulder	9⅜	9¾	10⅛	10½	10⅞	11¼
Crotch Length Total	15⅝	16¾	17⅞	19	20⅛	21¼
Arm Length	11⅝	12¾	13⅞	15	16⅛	17¼
Cervicale to Wrist	16¹⁵⁄₁₆	17⅝	18¹⁵⁄₁₆	20¼	21⁹⁄₁₆	22⅞
Head & Neck Length	6¾	7	7¼	7½	7¾	8
Cervicale Height	28¼	31	33¾	36½	39¼	42
Cervicale to Knee	19¼	21¼	23¼	25¼	27¼	29¼
Scye Depth Along Spine	4½	4¾	5	5¼	5½	5¾
Cervicale to Back Waist	8	8¾	9½	10¼	11	11¾
Neck to Front Waist	6½	7¼	8	8¾	9½	10¼
Waist Height	20⅜	22⅜	24⅜	26⅜	28⅜	30⅜
Waist to Knee	11⅜	12⅝	13⅞	15⅛	16⅜	17⅝
Hip Height	16¾	18⅜	20	21⅝	23¼	24⅞
Crotch Height	14¼	15¾	17¼	18¾	20¼	21¾
Knee Height	9	9¾	10½	11¼	12	12¾
Ankle Height	1⅞	2	2⅛	2⅛	2⅜	2⅜

*The body measurements for sizes 2, 3, and 4 are also used for the Toddler size range.

Table IV—Girls' Body Measurements

SIZE	6x/7	8	10	12	14	16
Stature (inches)	48–50	50½–52½	53–55	55½–57½	58–60	60½–62½
Weight (pounds)	47–53	54–63	64–74	75–84	85–94	95–104
Chest	25	26½	28	29½	31	32½
Waist	22½	23	24	25	26	27
Seat	26½	28	30	32	34	36
Vertical Trunk w/o diaper	45½	47¾	50	52¼	54½	56¾
Vertical Trunk with diaper	–	–	–	–	–	–
Neck Base	11⅞	12⅜	12⅞	13⅜	13⅞	14⅜
Armscye	11⅝	12⅜	13⅛	13⅞	14⅝	15⅜
Upper Arm	7⅜	7¾	8⅛	8½	8⅞	9¼
Elbow	8	8⅜	8¾	9⅛	9½	9⅞
Thigh	15⅛	16	17⅛	18¼	19⅜	20½
Shoulder Length	3½	3⅝	3¾	3⅞	4	4⅛
Across Shoulder	11¼	11¾	12¼	12¾	13¼	13¾
Crotch Length Total	21¼	22⅜	23½	24⅝	25¾	26⅞
Arm Length	17¼	18⅜	19½	20⅝	21¾	22⅞
Cervicale to Wrist	22⅞	24¼	25⅝	27	28⅜	29¾
Head & Neck Length	8	8¼	8½	8¾	9	9¼
Cervicale Height	42	44¼	46½	48¾	51	53¼
Cervicale to Knee	29¼	30¾	32¼	33¾	35¼	36¾
Scye Depth Along Spine	5¾	6	6¼	6½	6¾	7
Cervicale to Back Waist	11¾	12¼	12¾	13¼	13¾	14¼
Neck to Front Waist	10¼	10¾	11¼	11¾	12¼	12¾
Waist Height	30⅜	32⅜	34⅜	36⅜	38⅜	40⅜
Waist to Knee	17⅝	18⅞	20⅛	21⅜	22⅝	23⅞
Hip Height	24⅞	26½	28⅛	29¾	31⅜	33
Crotch Height	21¾	23¼	24¾	26¼	27¾	29¼
Knee Height	12¾	13½	14¼	15	15¾	16½
Ankle Height	2⅜	2½	2½	2⅝	2⅝	2¾

Table V—Sub-Teen Girls' Body Measurements

SIZE	8S	10S	12S	14S
Stature (in inches)	58½	59½	60½	61½
Weight	79	89	99	109
Bust	28½	30	31½	33
Waist	23½	24½	25½	26½
Hip	30	32	34	36
Vertical trunk	52	53½	55	56½
Thigh	16¾	18	19¼	20½
Neck base	12⅞	13¼	13⅝	14
Armscye	13	13½	14	14½
Upper Arm	8	8½	9	9½
Cross-back width	11¾	12⅛	12½	12⅞
Shoulder and arm length	25¼	25¾	26¼	26¾
Shoulder length	3⅞	4	4⅛	4¼
Total crotch length	25	25¾	26½	27¼
Head and neck length	8⅞	8⅞	8⅞	8⅞
Cervicale height	49⅝	50⅝	51⅝	52⅝
Cervicale to knee	33¼	34	34¾	35½
Cervicale to waist, including curve of spine	13¼	13⅝	14	14⅜
Waist height	37	37⅝	38¼	38⅞
Waist to knee	20⅝	21	21⅜	21¾
Waist to hip	6⅞	7	7⅛	7¼
Crotch height	27	27⅜	27¾	28⅛
Knee height	16⅜	16⅝	16⅞	17⅛

Metric Conversion Table (Inches to Centimeters)

INCHES		1/16	1/8	1/4	3/8	1/2	5/8	3/4	7/8
		0.16	0.32	0.64	0.95	1.27	1.59	1.91	2.22
1	2.54	2.70	2.86	3.18	3.49	3.81	4.13	4.45	4.76
2	5.08	5.24	5.40	5.72	6.03	6.35	6.67	6.99	7.30
3	7.62	7.78	7.94	8.26	8.57	8.89	9.21	9.53	9.84
4	10.16	10.32	10.48	10.80	11.11	11.43	11.75	12.07	12.38
5	12.70	12.86	13.02	13.34	13.65	13.97	14.29	14.61	14.92
6	15.24	15.40	15.56	15.88	16.19	16.51	16.83	17.15	17.46
7	17.78	17.94	18.10	18.42	18.73	19.05	19.37	19.69	20.00
8	20.32	20.48	20.64	20.96	21.27	21.59	21.91	22.23	22.54
9	22.86	23.02	23.18	23.50	23.81	24.13	24.45	24.77	25.08
10	25.40	25.56	25.72	26.04	26.35	26.67	26.99	27.31	27.62
11	27.94	28.10	28.26	28.58	28.89	29.21	29.53	29.85	30.16
12	30.48	30.64	30.80	31.12	31.43	31.75	32.02	32.39	32.70
13	33.02	33.18	33.34	33.66	33.97	34.29	34.61	34.93	35.24
14	35.56	35.72	35.88	36.20	36.51	36.83	37.15	37.47	37.78
15	38.10	38.26	38.42	38.74	39.05	39.37	36.69	40.01	40.32
16	40.64	40.80	40.96	41.28	41.59	41.91	42.23	42.55	42.86
17	43.18	43.34	43.50	43.82	44.13	44.45	44.77	45.09	45.40
18	45.72	45.88	46.04	46.36	46.67	46.99	47.31	47.63	47.94
19	48.26	48.42	48.58	48.90	49.21	49.53	49.85	50.17	50.48
20	50.80	50.96	51.12	51.44	51.75	52.07	52.39	52.71	53.02
21	53.34	53.50	53.66	53.98	54.29	54.61	54.93	55.25	55.56
22	55.88	56.04	56.20	56.52	56.83	57.15	57.47	57.79	58.10
23	58.42	58.58	58.74	59.06	59.37	59.69	60.01	60.33	60.64
24	60.96	61.12	61.28	61.60	61.91	62.23	62.55	62.87	63.18
25	63.50	63.66	63.82	64.14	64.45	64.77	65.09	65.41	65.72
26	66.04	66.20	66.36	66.68	66.99	67.31	67.63	67.95	68.26
27	68.58	68.74	68.90	69.22	69.53	69.85	70.17	70.49	70.80
28	71.12	71.28	71.44	71.76	72.07	72.39	72.71	73.03	73.34
29	73.66	73.82	73.98	74.30	74.61	74.93	75.25	75.57	75.88
30	76.20	76.36	76.52	76.84	77.15	77.47	77.79	78.11	78.42

Metric Conversion Table (Inches to Centimeters)

INCHES		1/16	1/8	1/4	3/8	1/2	5/8	3/4	7/8
31	78.74	78.90	79.06	79.38	79.69	80.01	80.33	80.65	80.96
32	81.28	81.44	81.60	81.92	82.23	82.55	82.87	83.19	83.50
33	83.82	83.98	84.14	84.46	84.77	85.09	85.41	85.73	86.04
34	86.36	86.52	86.68	87.00	87.31	87.63	87.95	88.27	88.58
35	88.90	89.06	89.22	89.54	89.85	90.17	90.49	90.81	91.12
36	91.44	91.60	91.76	92.08	92.39	92.71	93.03	93.35	93.66
37	93.98	94.14	94.30	94.62	94.93	95.25	95.57	95.89	96.20
38	96.52	96.68	96.84	97.16	97.47	97.79	98.11	98.43	98.74
39	99.06	99.22	99.38	99.70	100.01	100.33	100.65	100.97	101.28
40	101.60	101.76	101.92	102.24	102.55	102.87	103.19	103.51	103.82
41	104.14	104.30	104.46	104.78	105.09	105.41	105.73	106.05	106.36
42	106.68	106.84	107.00	107.32	107.63	107.95	108.27	108.59	108.90
43	109.22	109.38	109.54	109.86	110.17	110.49	110.81	111.13	111.44
44	111.76	111.92	112.08	112.40	112.71	113.03	113.35	113.67	113.98
45	114.30	114.46	114.62	114.94	115.25	115.57	115.89	116.21	116.52
46	116.84	117.00	117.16	117.48	117.79	118.11	118.43	118.75	119.06
47	119.38	119.54	119.70	120.02	120.33	120.65	120.97	121.29	121.60
48	121.92	122.08	122.24	122.56	122.87	123.19	123.51	123.83	124.14
49	124.46	124.62	124.78	125.10	125.41	125.73	126.05	126.37	126.68
50	127.00	127.16	127.32	127.64	127.95	128.27	128.59	128.91	129.22
51	129.54	129.70	129.86	130.18	130.49	130.81	131.13	131.45	131.76
52	132.08	132.24	132.40	132.72	133.03	133.35	133.67	133.99	134.30
53	134.62	134.78	134.98	135.26	135.57	135.89	136.21	136.53	136.84
54	137.16	137.32	137.48	137.80	138.11	138.43	138.75	139.07	139.38
55	139.70	139.86	140.02	140.34	140.65	140.97	141.29	141.61	141.92
56	142.24	142.40	142.56	142.88	143.19	143.51	143.83	144.15	144.46
57	144.78	144.94	145.10	145.42	145.73	146.05	146.37	146.69	147.00
58	147.32	147.48	147.64	147.96	148.27	148.59	148.91	149.23	149.54
59	149.86	150.02	150.18	150.50	150.81	151.13	151.45	151.77	152.08
60	152.40	152.56	152.72	153.04	153.35	153.67	153.99	154.31	154.62

■ Suggested Sources of Inspiration

Periodicals

Children's Fashion

BIMBI DI ELEGANTISSIMA (twice a year)—In Italian. Includes all ages through subteen.

EARNSHAW'S INFANTS, GIRLS AND BOYSWEAR REVIEW (monthly)—Edited for retailers and manufacturers of infants' and children's clothing and accessories.

KIDS FASHIONS (monthly)—Merchandising of childrenswear.

MODA BIMBI (3 times a year)—In Italian. Fashions for children and a few examples of teen apparel.

TEENS AND BOYS (monthly)—For apparel retailers, boys' wear ages four through nineteen. Forecasts style trends.

VOGUE BAMBINI (4 times a year)—In Italian. An exceptionally fine example of children's fashion publishing.

YOUNG FASHIONS (monthly)—Fashion magazine for youthwear.

General Fashion Interest

ELLE (monthly)—Aimed at young women. The American edition of the French weekly.

GLAMOUR (monthly)—Aimed at young women. Contains many features on food, health, etc., with an emphasis on current fashions available at popular prices.

HARPER'S BAZAAR (monthly)—One of the leading high fashion magazines in the United States.

SEVENTEEN (monthly)—Directed at teen girls. Departments on fashion, beauty, entertainment, home furnishings, food.

VOGUE (monthly)—Widely regarded as the leading American magazine devoted to high fashion in clothing and all fashion related subjects.

WOMEN'S WEAR DAILY (5 times a week)—Trade paper for the entire industry. Regular reports on trends in fashion, activities of designers, arrival of buyers in New York, business developments, and gossip.

Museum Fashion Collections

Fashion Institute of Technology, New York, N.Y.
Metropolitan Museum of Art, New York, N.Y.
Smithsonian Institute, Washington, D.C.
Arizona Costume Institute, Phoenix, Ariz.
Chicago Historical Society, Chicago, Ill.
Dallas Museum of Fashion, Dallas, Texas
Kansas City Museum of History and Science, Kansas City, Mo.
Los Angeles County Museum of Art, Los Angeles, Calif.

Bibliography

Borgenicht, Louis, as told to Harold Friedman. *The Happiest Man*. New York: G. P. Putnam and Sons, 1942.

Boucher, François. *20,000 Years of Fashion*. New York: Harry N. Abrams, Inc., 1967.

Contini, Mila. *Fashion: From Ancient Egypt to the Present Day*. New York: The Odyssey Press, 1965

1897 Sears Roebuck Catalogue. New York: Chelsea House Publishers, 1968.

Ewing, Elizabeth. *History of Children's Costume*. New York: Charles Scribner's Sons, 1977

Felger, Donna H. *Boy's Fashions, 1885 to 1905*. Cumberland, Md.: Hobby House Press, 1984.

Garlen, Hyla B. *Children's Clothing: An Indicator of Social Change in the Concept of Childhood*. Thesis (P.H.D.) Walden University, 1986.

Guppy, Alice. *Children's Clothes 1939–1970, The Advent of Fashion*. Poole: Blandford Press for the Pasold Research Fund, 1978.

Gesell, Arnold. *The First Five Years of Life—A Guide to the Study of Preschool Child*. New York: Harper & Row, Publishers, 1940.

Gesell, Arnold, Frances Ilk, and Louise Bates Ames. *The Years from Ten to Sixteen*. New York: Harper & Row Publishers, 1956.

Hill, Margot H. and Peter Bucknell. *The Evolution of Fashion*. New York: Reinhold, 1968.

Horn, Marilyn J. *The Second Skin: An Interdisciplinary Study of Clothing*. 3rd ed., Boston: Houghton Mifflin, 1981.

Ireland, Patric John. *Drawing and Designing Children's and Teenage Fashions*. New York: John Wiley and Sons, 1979.

Joseph, Marjory L. *Introductory to Textile Science*. New York: Holt, Rinehart & Winston, Inc., 1966.

Josselyn, Irene M. *The Adolescent and His World*. New York: Family Service Associates of America, 1952.

Kismaric, Susan. *American Children: Photographs from the Collection*. New York: Museum of Modern Art, 1980.

Laver, James. *Children's Fashions in the 19th Century*. London: B.T. Batsford, Ltd. 1951.

Linton, George E. *The Modern Textile Dictionary*. New York: Duell, Sloan & Pearce, 1963.

Man-made Fiber Fact Book. New York: Man-made Fiber Producers Association, Inc., 1967

Martin, Linda. *The Way We Wore: Fashion Illustrations of Children's Wear, 1870–1970*. New York: Charles Scribner's Sons, 1978.

Moore, Doris. *The Child in Fashion*. London: B.T. Batsford, Ltd. 1953.

Mussen, Paul Henry, John Janeway Conger, and Jerome Kagan. *Child Development and Personality*. New York: Harper & Row, Publishers, 1963.

Rosen, Selma. *Children's Clothing*. New York: Fairchild Publications, 1983.

Ryan, Mary Shaw. *Clothing, A Study in Human Behavior*. New York: Holt, Rinehart & Winston, 1966.

Schneider, Coleman. *Machine Made Embroidery*. Hackensack, N. J.: Schneider International Corp., 1968.

Schorsch, Anita. *Images of Childhood: An Illustrated Social History*. Pittstown, N.J.: Main Street Press, 1985.

Sichel, Marion. *History of Children's Costume*. London: Batsford Academic and Educational Ltd., 1983.

Smart, Mollie S. and Russel C. Smart. *Children, Developments and Relationships*. New York: The Macmillan Co., 1967.

Tate. Mildred Thurow and Oris Glissen. *Family Clothing*. New York: John Wiley and Sons, 1961.

Textile Fibers and Their Properties. Greensboro, N.C.: Prepared by Burlington Industries, Inc., 1970.

Walker, Herbert. *Children's Wear Merchandiser*. New York: New York Merchandising Division, National Retail Merchants Association, 1967.

Wilcox, Ruth Turner. *The Mode in Costume*. New York: Charles Scribner's Sons, 1958.

Wingate, Isabel B. *Fairchild's Dictionary of Textiles*. New York: Fairchild Publications, 1967.

———*Textile Fabrics and Their Selection*. Englewood Cliffs, N.J.: Prentice-Hall, Inc., 1970.

Worrell, Estelle Ansley. *Children's Costume in America, 1607–1910*. New York: Charles Scribner's Sons, 1980.

Index

ABOUT THE AUTHORS

Hilde Jaffe

Before she began her career in academia, Prof. Hilde Jaffe was a designer of children's dresses and separates for well over a decade. This experience brought her to the Fashion Institute of Technology where she developed the Childrenswear Specialization curriculum.

During her tenure at F.I.T. she has served as chairperson of the Fashion Design Department and as Dean of the Art and Design Division. Currently, she has returned to teaching and is active in research regarding sizing for childrenswear.

Rosa Rosa

Prof. Rosa Rosa has spent more than twenty years designing for major childrenswear manufacturers, concentrating in dresses, boys' and girls' sportswear, outerwear, sleepwear, ranging in sizes from infants to pre-teens. She has also been very active in the childrenswear industry as a fashion consultant and judge in numerous events.

Prof. Rosa has been teaching at the Fashion Institute of Technology since 1965 and is presently an assistant professor in the fashion design department. She has been elected evening coordinator for the continuing education department.